T0053711

Praise for Shawn L...

THE CASTLE ON SUNSET

"So wild that even Hollywood's best screenwriters couldn't make this stuff up." —*Fortune*

"Reading *The Castle on Sunset*, I felt like I was sneaking around the hallways of the Chateau after midnight and peering through keyholes in history. Shawn Levy pulls back the velvet curtains to reveal all the decadence, glamour, ghosts, and gossip of a fabled and dreamy Hollywood."
—Joe Hagan, author of *Sticky Fingers*

"Very fun and informative . . . Levy chronicles one of Hollywood's most famous addresses." —*Milwaukee Journal Sentinel*

"A genuinely fascinating look at how Hollywood supports its stars." —*Booklist*

"Alongside an endless supply of famous guests, Levy has managed to make the hotel itself a living, breathing, and wonderfully endearing character. *The Castle on Sunset* is thoughtfully researched and gorgeously executed."
—Jacob Tomsky, author of *Heads in Beds*

"The great chronicler of films and pop culture has done it again. . . . As elegant and naughty as the hotel's guests, *The Castle on Sunset* tells a secret history of American film, fame, and decadence."
—Peter Ames Carlin, author of *Bruce* and *Homeward Bound*

SHAWN LEVY
THE CASTLE ON SUNSET

Shawn Levy is the former film critic of *The Oregonian* and KGW-TV. His writing has appeared in *Sight and Sound*, *Film Comment*, *American Film*, *The New York Times*, the *Los Angeles Times*, *The Guardian*, *The Hollywood Reporter*, and *The Black Rock Beacon*. He is the bestselling author of *Rat Pack Confidential*, *Paul Newman: A Life*, and *Dolce Vita Confidential*. He jumps and claps and sings for victory in Portland, Oregon.

www.shawnlevy.com

ALSO BY SHAWN LEVY

THE CASTLE ON SUNSET

LIFE, DEATH, LOVE, ART, *and* SCANDAL
at Hollywood's CHATEAU MARMONT

SHAWN LEVY

ANCHOR BOOKS
A Division of Penguin Random House LLC
New York

The Library of Congress has cataloged the Doubleday edition as follows:
Name: Levy, Shawn, author.
Title: The castle on Sunset : life, death, love, art, and scandal at Hollywood's Chateau
Marmont / Shawn Levy.
Description: First edition. | New York : Doubleday, a division of
Penguin Random House LLC, 2019 | Includes bibliographical references.
Identifiers: LCCN 2018023441
Subjects: LCSH: Chateau Marmont (Los Angeles, Calif.)—History. | Hollywood
(Los Angeles, Calif.)—History—20th century. | Motion picture actors and actresses—
Los Angeles—Biography. | Celebrities—California—Los Angeles—Biography. |
Hollywood (Los Angeles, Calif.)—Biography. | Hollywood (Los Angeles, Calif.)—
Social life and customs—20th century.
Classification: LCC TX941.M366 L48 2019 | DDC 647.95794/94—dc23
LC record available at https://lccn.loc.gov/2018023441

Anchor Books Trade Paperback ISBN: 978-0-525-43566-2
eBook ISBN: 978-0-385-54317-0

Author photograph © Vincent Levy
Book design by Maria Carella

www.anchorbooks.com

CONTENTS

THE CASTLE ON SUNSET

INTRODUCTION

THEY SAY THAT LOS ANGELES DOESN'T TREASURE ITS PAST. How, then, to explain Chateau Marmont?

For nearly ninety years, as a city and a world changed utterly around it, this unique building, perched above a famous road in West Hollywood, has stood steadily as an oasis of quiet, gentility, privacy, and bohemian charm, a clubhouse for people too rich and famous to belong to clubs, a bolt-hole, a trysting place, a recovery room, a hideaway, an opium den, an atelier, a last resort.

A snow-white fairy castle with slate-gray roofs, a dozen or so gables, and a dominating turret, it sits on a hill overlooking one of Southern California's busiest and most famous streets and has appeared, from the day it opened, as if it came from another world entirely. "The Chateau is a fluke, a marvelous fluke," according to the architecture critic Edgardo Contini. "In the midst of endless low-rise, it is a striking high-rise, like a cathedral in a medieval town." And its singular appearance houses an equally singular history.

From Greta Garbo to Howard Hughes, Bette Davis to Marilyn Monroe, Jim Morrison to Tony Randall, Johnny Depp to Lindsay Lohan, Chateau Marmont has drawn the most iconoclastic and outlandish personalities from the worlds of film, music, and other creative arts. It has been the site of wild parties and scandalous liaisons, of creative breakthroughs and marital breakdowns, of one-night stands and days-long parties, of famous triumphs and untimely deaths.

It was built with a mind toward luxury, status, permanence;

it became known for privacy, discretion, transience. It began as a dream of high living, settled into a steady hum of quiet gentility, then slipped into something more like practical value, gradually devolving into shabbiness, nearly becoming a dive, its arc mirroring the rise, plateau, and fall of the neighborhood in which it sat. But the Chateau never lost its place near the heart of the cultural story of the day, even as the tenor of that day changed again and again. And in the twenty-first century, when, by the arithmetic of Hollywood, it ought to have become anathema simply by virtue of its age, it turned out to be more robust than ever, chic and glamorous and glowing as never before, lifting its environs along with it into a prosperous new era.

People from all walks of life have found in Chateau Marmont a place to get their bearings while navigating the unfathomable depths of Los Angeles or, in particular, the shark-infested shallows of Hollywood. And people who know those waters well have relied on the Chateau as a patch of dry land—private, quiet, undemanding, even serene—where they could recuperate, revive, create, cavort, or otherwise behave in ways that they wouldn't necessarily at home.

Over the years, the Chateau has responded to this need for restorative isolation with tolerance and comfort, provided by a staff that could be relied upon to say nothing of what went on before their eyes or under their noses. "You can have a very, um, *elaborate* social life there, if you like," said the actress Geraldine Fitzgerald, "or you can live the nun's life, very monastic." Or, as another frequent visitor put it, "Just check in at the desk, and nobody ever need see you again. You could *die* here if you wanted, and they wouldn't always be bothering you, sticking notes under your door."

Hollywood has hotels that are more luxurious, handsome, exclusive, and prestigious, with bigger rooms and grounds, with finer restaurants, with shops and tennis courts and day spas and nightclubs and VIP services and other amenities. But it has only one Chateau Marmont, its castle on a hill, guarding secrets since before movies could talk or Sunset Boulevard was completely paved.

❊

The Chateau has spent nearly a century perched on the eastern edge of the Sunset Strip like the Rock of Gibraltar, a landmark defining a transition, a way station giving harbor to vagabonds, a milestone, a sentinel, a keep. For all that, the building long managed a kind of anonymity. Everyone has heard about it; everyone knows it on sight; everyone has trafficked rumors about it; and everyone who is anyone has at one time or another visited it. But until John Belushi's tabloid-feeding death-by-misadventure on the premises, more than fifty years after the hotel opened, relatively few Los Angeles residents outside the world of show business could say exactly where the Chateau was or precisely name the castle-like edifice on the hillside where Sunset Boulevard melts into the Sunset Strip. People who commuted past it daily for years recognized it and knew it was . . . a mansion, maybe, or a dormitory, or something to do with the movies or Scientology or some cult. It was an architectural curiosity even in a town where the vernacular building style was as coherent as a salad bar, seemingly parachuted into the most modern of streets from some other place and time. It barely announced its presence, sporting a minimal sign that passersby might even mistake as pointing to some other building. It didn't advertise. It simply *was.* All of which made it, to a certain way of viewing luxury, privacy, celebrity, and Hollywood . . . perfect: a place of secrets standing right out in the open, hidden in plain sight like Poe's purloined letter.

Perhaps that's why it has been such a magnet for legends, whispers, half-truths, gossip, suspicion. The stories that center on the Marmont—real and fictitious—span generations: Greta Garbo owned the place in secret (not true); Jean Harlow took lovers while resident with husband number three not long after the suicide of husband number *two* (pretty much true); Howard Hughes leased a suite simply to spy on the flesh available at poolside (true-true); F. Scott Fitzgerald suffered a heart attack there during a midday tryst (not true); Vivien Leigh mourned the end of her marriage to Laurence Olivier in a suite plastered with photos of him (true); Rock Hudson met his first live-in lover there, the nephew of the hotel manager (not true); James Dean met *Rebel Without a Cause* director Nicholas Ray by entering his bungalow via the window rather than the door (not quite); Anthony Perkins used the phone booth in the lobby because he didn't want the switchboard operator to listen in on his personal calls (sadly true); Jim Morrison climbed the ornate balconies and rooftops in drug-fueled antics (mostly, sorta); Led Zeppelin rode motorcycles through the lobby (nuh-uh); Scarlett Johansson and Benicio Del Toro hooked up *in the elevator* on Oscar night (Who can say?); Lindsay Lohan got the boot after racking up—and failing to pay—nearly $50,000 in charges in less than two months (all too true); and so on.

Over the decades, the chance to steep in the atmosphere that generated these stories, apocryphal or not, has drawn visitors as reliably as any advertising campaign ever could. Chateau Marmont is the ultimate Hollywood hotel because it is, like Hollywood itself, bigger than life even when it is obviously fake.

⁂

The story of Chateau Marmont parallels the story of Hollywood so thoroughly as to be inseparable from it: the silent era, the golden age of the studios, the rise of television, the influx of foreign cinema, the rebel heyday of the sixties and seventies, the blockbuster era, the indie movie upsurge, and the current mingling of film and digital media. At desks in various of its suites and bungalows, Hollywood screenwriters have produced scripts for films as diverse as *The Music Man, Butch Cassidy and the Sundance Kid, The Day of the Locust, The Color Purple,* and

Wild Palms. And at least one cinematic masterpiece and cultural landmark—Nicholas Ray's *Rebel Without a Cause*—might not have been made at all if its creators hadn't had the Chateau as a laboratory and workshop. Likewise, the chronology of the music business, from the era of the big bands and crooners to the many generations of rock and pop and hip-hop, has been tied to the hotel's history. Key figures from every era have slept, worked, and partied there, from Duke Ellington to Miles Davis to the Velvet Underground to Carly Simon to Rick James to Bono, and many of them have composed material at the hotel that they went on to record and release. So too painters, photographers, fashion designers, advertising executives: Sometimes they have created works of genius while in residence, sometimes flops. In some cases they've checked into the place to indulge in clandestine appetites, in some to escape persecution, in some because their homes were no longer open to them, in some because they needed a home away from home while they tried to get themselves—or their careers—back together, in some because great opportunities were spread out before them in the Southern California sun.

But the story of Chateau Marmont is even more than the story of a century of popular creativity. It is also the story of a very specific place, namely Hollywood and, even more precisely, the Sunset Strip. When the Chateau opened in 1929, the Strip was a dream, with only a few low-slung buildings dotting a rutted dirt road that connected the edges of Los Angeles and Beverly Hills. As the Strip added paving and showbiz agencies and swank nightspots, the Chateau became known as a reliably quiet and comfortable place for out-of-towners who didn't want to succumb to the glitz and tinsel of the movie colony, as Hollywood was called. After World War II, when the Strip became a haunt of rebels and teens and the fashionably countercultural, so did the Chateau, opening its doors to all—straight, gay, sober, addled, black, white, from all walks of life, at reasonable prices, making up with discretion and tolerance what it might have lacked in luxurious touches. When the Strip exploded in unrest in the sixties, and, soon after, when the action along it slowed, the Chateau entered a period of decline, finding rescue in an owner who fell in love with it and kept it alive when the idea of demolishing it altogether seemed tenable. And then a visionary came along, seeing in the Chateau and the surrounding Strip undervalued assets that, with patient restoration and a certain sense of style and, yes, some sizable investment, could bloom again into something glamorous, chic, and exclusive—more so, indeed, than at any time in their existence. Other Hollywood hotels have great claims to history: the Beverly Hills, the Beverly Wilshire, the Hollywood Roosevelt, the Beverly Hilton, and the Bel-Air, as well as such bygone icons as the Garden of Allah and the Ambassador. But among them all, Chateau Marmont has most perfectly mirrored its setting, and its setting has long been one of the shining mirrors of the culture of the entire world.

The tale of Chateau Marmont is a tale of investment and risk, bum luck, and great good fortune, visionaries and myopics, capitalists and laborers, celebrities and hangers-on, aspirants and has-beens, creators and sybarites, those who made and those who took—the gamut of a century's worth of American dreamers, schemers, and strivers within the parameters of a few acres. It's the story of the rise of Los Angeles and a roiling history of show business, a real estate saga and a string of simple human vignettes, a scrapbook of headlines and a junk heap of curiosities.

※

Everyone who has ever checked in to Chateau Marmont has had one thing in common: He or she has become part of the vital pulse of an inanimate object that hasn't aged—indeed, has gotten *more* vibrant—even as everyone attached to it has grown old or passed away. The lifeblood of a hotel is the people who have stayed in it, who have worked in it, who have used it as a base from which to satisfy private desires or to pursue great public acclaim. Actors and writers, musicians and deal makers, desk clerks and maids and parking valets and waiters, the stars and the investors and the people who've not been inside the walls but have always wished they could be: They live and they die as they pass through Chateau Marmont, and the Chateau gives them all what they need from it when their needs arise, a never-ending source of shelter, privacy, convenience, and stability for wanderers, speculators, and visionaries.

The Chateau has managed all this despite being small—only sixty-three rooms, including its (in)famous bungalows, at its current largest—and despite not providing, for most of its existence, some of the primary amenities expected of a swank hostelry: a restaurant, a bar, shops, salons, a spa, fitness facilities, a full-scale room service operation, even a swimming pool—they only dug one after World War II. To some, the lack of these tokens of luxury living made the Marmont seem déclassé and undesirable. But through another lens, these absences gave the place a special air: It seemed like a residence and not a way station, like an old European pensione and not some jazzed-up American megaresort. The lack of high-end amenities in what was otherwise a high-end hotel was a quirk—and a litmus test: If you needed to be surrounded by the trappings of wealth, you went elsewhere; if you were a little more self-contained, low-key, modest, Chateau Marmont suited you just fine. "The Chateau is the only cheap hotel here that one can stay in and people don't say, 'Poor guy, he's broke,' you know?" explained playwright Burt Shevelove, a regular guest of the place. "And because of this you meet friends, stage people from New York. There's a tendency to think that if an actor is staying here, he must be quite good."

The combination of high-profile location and modest appointments meant that the Marmont occupied a special place in Hollywood's geography. On the one hand, if you stayed there you were really in the middle of everything. On the other, you *had* to be near so much because your hotel offered (relative to its deluxe competitors) so little. For the pampered and status conscious, Chateau Marmont, however charming and central, was a no-go. Which, of course, made it perfect for other sorts. Among the hundreds of famous names that have been entered into the hotel's guest registry, many belonged to Europeans (especially Britons) who don't necessarily expect every hotel to be an all-inclusive resort. Many as well have belonged to creative artists lured to Hollywood to work but determined not to *go* Hollywood. For decades, the hotel's shabby-chic furnishings and creature *dis*-comforts gave them the sense of resisting the sirens' call . . . even as they cozied right up to the sirens' rocky outpost and made a nest for themselves. It was, ironically, an icon for iconoclasts, a comfortable hideaway that you stayed in to prove that you didn't care about comfort, a spot famous for being obscure, treasured for its scruff, sworn to by those allergic to allegiances.

⁂

A hotel can signal a getaway, a holiday, a spree, but it is also a vault of secrets, a haven, a port in a storm, a home away from home. People come and go from hotels all day every day for weeks, months, years. But a great hotel gives the impression of always being there, of having always been there, of being there forevermore. You can trust the Plaza, the Ritz, the Connaught, the Drake, the St. Francis, because their long histories include personages and episodes and scandals grander than anything the present day can serve up; they're almost natural phenomena, like canyons or waterfalls. Chateau Marmont, from the start, was intended to impart that sensation in its very structure, in the walls and floors and windowpanes. Its success in doing so for almost a century can be credited, in part, to ownership that did its utmost to cater to its clients' preferences and to stalwart employees who worked in the shadows, serving celebrities whose needs and privacy they respected as their own.

But in part, too, it can be credited to the very bones of the building. The Marmont offered advantages that few other hotels could match. The small scale means a more select clientele—and arguably one less likely to gawp at celebrities than folks might elsewhere. Because it was built as an apartment house and not as a hotel, there were aspects of the very layout that abetted anyone wishing to keep a low profile. It wasn't necessary to walk through the lobby to get to your room, for example; you could park in the basement garage and head right upstairs in an elevator. And if you stay in one of the famous bungalows on the property, you don't have to enter the hotel proper *at all;* you come and go through a back entrance as if you truly *live* there and aren't just a temporary guest, perhaps the best arrangement of all for someone—a movie actor, say—who needs to be in Southern California to work for a month or two but wants, in some portion of his or her brain, to deny it. For practitioners of the most public of businesses, living the most public of lives, it is ideal, at once well-known and anonymous, just like a movie star trying to pass for an ordinary civilian at a coffee shop.

❊

To tell the story of an institution—to write the biography of a *thing*—it's useful to speak of the humans whose lives have crossed it. In the case of Chateau Marmont, that means three sets of people. First, and most of all, there are the many thousands of guests whose passage through the halls and grounds has supported the hotel and given it life and purpose, in particular the ones who, through their connection to the popular or fine arts, have names—and creations attached to those names—that make us all curious about the details of their lives. Next come the employees, frequently anonymous but often crucial and even definitive of the place, whether they've been general managers who set the tone for guest relations, or switchboard operators who protect (or, sometimes, invade) privacy, or parking valets who inhabit a subterranean world where some of the hotel's most incredible secrets are bared. Finally, but perhaps most important, we have the owners, the men (and they have all been men) who built and transformed and expanded and restored and bought and sold and defined the place, the kings of this not-quite-a-castle, more royal within its confines than even the most exalted celebrities who have taken rooms in it.

Among this most select line, five stand out: the unlikely dreamer who envisioned and built the place; the venturesome businessman who turned it into a hotel; the canny investor who held it in an impersonal grip but fostered it and added to it and gave it some important aspects of its character; the gruff contractor who thought he'd found a tax write-off and fell in love with and rescued it; and the slick East Coast hotelier, a man who brought a never-before-known level of polish, sophistication, cachet, and allure to the place and, to date, has held it longer than any previous owner.

These five—plus perhaps half a dozen others whose hands the Chateau passed through as a financial asset, sometimes for long enough for them to do some ruinous harm to it out of indifference—have been guardians of a trust, wittingly or not, insurers of a kind of cultural continuity rare in Southern California. They have sometimes been tempted to liquidate, level, or abandon the hotel, but something in it has made them persist. And the result of their doggedness, their vision, their belief, is a legend now entering its tenth decade of existence with an energy more robust, a business model more lucrative, and a name more famous than it has ever enjoyed.

One of the great aspects of the Chateau today is that it connects people to the past, to simpler, grander, brighter, perhaps naughtier times. But that, like so much of what passes for reality in Hollywood, is illusory. Chateau Marmont is made of stone, steel, wood, glass, and iron, not "aura" or "mystique" or "je ne sais quoi." And to the extent it possesses any of those characteristics, it has accrued them through hard work, dodgy times, lucky breaks, quirks of history, and dashes of wildness, recklessness, determination, endurance, and happenstance.

This is the story of all that.

Part One
THE DREAM (1927–1932)

A classic postcard image. *Author's collection*

CHATEAU MARMONT
HOLLYWOOD

Before there was a Chateau Marmont, before there were limos to park, bags to schlep, parties to throw, secrets to keep, paparazzi to elude, and divorces, bacchanals, sunburns, and career missteps to recover from, before there was a Sunset Strip or even a Hollywood, there were onions and poinsettias and avocados growing on hillsides above a dirt road, and there were speculators and pioneers and dreamers imagining something great that no one else could see.

One of them, a well-connected attorney from Los Angeles, had the gumption, wherewithal, and perseverance to turn a vision of an Italianate castle on a rise in the Loire valley into an actual building on a corner of a town that had no name.

The history of California is the history of people reaching for the impossible and, often, actually stretching far enough to grasp it.

And Chateau Marmont was one of those unlikely fancies that emerged into the world, almost despite itself, just as the man who had first conceived it believed it would.

THE SUNSET STRIP: The very name hints of color, ease, spectacle, titillation, destiny, speed, a narrow specificity, a transition, an in-between, a climax, a rending, the end.

For more than eighty years, the phrase "Sunset Strip" has been a global shorthand for a certain blend of decadence, fashion, music, sex, secrecy, and freedom. The swank supper clubs of the thirties and forties; the coffeehouses and drive-ins of the fifties; the overheated discotheques of the sixties; the hedonistic VIP rooms of the eighties, nineties, and first two decades of the twenty-first century: Our popular ideals of courtship, indulgence, glamour, and cool have been informed, in no small part, by the way people have comported themselves in the hotels, nightspots, eateries, boutiques, and showbiz offices lining those famed not-quite-two sinuous miles of West Hollywood.

At times, the Strip has been the bull's-eye dead center of the pop world; at others, it's been a minor but unignorable element of the cultural conversation. And always, just when it seems to have fallen off the map altogether, when it has been declared dead and abandoned for newer, shinier locales, some novelty emerges—folk rock, or hair metal, or a hot restaurant, or a revitalized hotel, or a tabloid-fueling tragedy—and the Sunset Strip is back on everyone's radar.

But before it was the center of the world, it seemed more like the end of it.

⁂

You didn't always need a satellite to see the edges of Los Angeles. In the mid-twenties, you could get in a car downtown and within half an hour find yourself at a spot where the paved road ended and bridle trails began.

Such a place was the intersection of Sunset Boulevard and the road that led north into Laurel Canyon. At that corner, Los Angeles's bus and trolley lines made their last stops before turning back toward town. To the west, a cow path led through farmland— onion fields, poinsettia farms, and avocado groves—to the suburban city of Beverly Hills, some two miles farther along on the way to the sea.

At the time, L.A. was beginning the upsurge that would eventually make it a world-class metropolis. Between 1920 and 1930, the city would more than double in population; new houses were being built so rapidly that as many as seventy-five ships a day from Oregon and Washington arrived in port with loads of lumber for home building. But looking past where Sunset Boulevard ended, there was little sign of a land rush.

The road between Los Angeles and Beverly Hills was unimproved because it belonged to neither city. It lay in an unincorporated chunk of Los Angeles County known originally as Sherman or Shermantown, named for the railroad baron General Moses Sherman, who had helped create the Los Angeles trolley car system and built a massive rail yard outside the city limits. In the previous year, local business interests had christened their little patch "West Hollywood," hoping to accrue some of the stardust associated with the name of the Los Angeles neighborhood nearest to them, which had become world famous as the home of the movies.*

In the fall of 1926, Fred Horowitz, a downtown Los Angeles lawyer who had begun to speculate in property and construction, came to visit a hillside west of the Laurel Canyon road. Eastward lay the burgeoning movie town, Hollywood, where the twelve-

---

* Among the other potential names bandied about were Beverly Park, East Beverly, and Magnetic Springs.

story Roosevelt Hotel, still under construction, stood out boldly, and, beyond that, the skyline of downtown L.A., where a majestic new thirty-two-floor city hall was rising. To the west were Beverly Hills and Westwood, where a new campus for the University of California was being built, and beyond that the blue surge of the Pacific and, like dark clouds on its surface, the Channel Islands. To the south spread the chessboard of small communities that would eventually make up greater Los Angeles: Culver City, Venice, Inglewood, Crenshaw, Compton, dotted with cottages, businesses, and farms, crisscrossed by Wilshire, Olympic, Beverly, Pico, and Santa Monica Boulevards. It was, as Horowitz had hoped, a stupendous panorama.

And visible only to him was a castle, a French château of classic stature, elegance, and nobility, a monumental edifice designed to import some savor of the very old world into this very, very new one. He planned to build the most luxurious apartment house in all of Southern California on the spot where he stood: in a pitch of scrub alongside an unpaved road.

⁂

The Sunset Boulevard upon which Horowitz gazed wasn't *entirely* bare. There were a few farmhouses, not on the road, but visible from it, some of which had been occupied by the same families for nearly seventy years. Just below him stood a general store that sold groceries and gasoline and whatnot. A bit west, an enterprising family had recently opened a clutch of commercial buildings they were calling, with great optimism, Sunset Plaza; a pair of restaurants, the Russian Eagle and La Boheme, had opened there, and movie stars had started to pop in for meals. Another group of investors were building the Hacienda Arms, an imposing five-story apartment building with a Mediterranean facade. And there were—again, set back from the road—a handful of mansions built by members of the nouveau riche movie crowd, which had practically minted its own money in the past

few years and had splashed it on absurdly oversized and architecturally fanciful homes.

But none of those would remotely rival what Horowitz had
in mind. Horowitz was scouting locations for an audacious folly
he had conceived while traveling in the Loire valley of France.
There he came upon the Château d'Amboise, a Gothic castle that
had dominated the landscape in ever-grander form dating back
to when a stronghold was first built on the site in the eleventh
century. The massive building had significant claims to history:
Starting in the fifteenth century, it was one of the favored homes
of the kings of France, including Charles VIII, who died there
after hitting his head on a door lintel; Henry II, who, along with
his wife, Catherine de' Medici, raised his family on the grounds,
including his ward, Mary Stuart of Scotland; and Francis I, who
invited the great artists and architects of his time to live and
work there, including Leonardo da Vinci, who died during his
stay and was buried in a chapel on the château grounds.

Horowitz was less taken with the history of the château than
with the imposing spectacle of it: a formidable stone fortress
capped with conical towers perched on a bluff overlooking the
river Loire. He had a mind to build a fortress of his own, and
he envisioned it as inhabiting its own commanding vista, not of
the Loire and the great vineyards and orchards that lined it, but
of the burgeoning communities of Los Angeles. Like the Château d'Amboise, it would be built of pale stone, slate-gray gables,
balconies, Gothic archways, and turrets. It would be solid—
earthquake proof, even. And it would be not a castle but a luxury
apartment building, and—at seven stories high—the tallest and
most impressive edifice for miles and perhaps, given its elevated
setting, in the whole area.

Los Angeles in the mid- to late twenties was a kind of haven
for such audacious conceits. Not far from where Horowitz envisioned his demi-castle, other landmark apartment houses stood
or were being planned along French lines, such as the La Fontaine (built in 1928), the Granville Towers (1930), and the Vol-

taire (1930), or with Spanish-Mexican influences, such as the Andalusia (1926), the Villa Carlotta (1926), and the El Mirador (1929), or in the Italianate style, such as the Villa d'Este (1927). Just as Hollywood had made a specialty of imitating the whole world in its film studios, so the community around it seemed eager to imitate the whole world's architecture in its homes and offices, generally with no expense or gaucherie spared. The city was like a movie set and its architects and builders production designers.

But even in an environment where excess was a minimal standard, Horowitz's plan seemed, to put it politely, daft. A man who had been gaining a reputation as a fierce defense attorney and was said to have eyes on public office, he had never built or even managed an apartment house, much less a grand tower like the one he had in mind. What's more, he didn't have enough money for both the land *and* the construction project. And the site he had chosen was absurdly remote and desolate.

Actually, that latter might well have been a selling point. Land in undeveloped locations was generally cheaper than that in the heart of a bustling metropolis after all. Additionally, by crossing the line out of Los Angeles into West Hollywood, which hadn't yet been incorporated as a city, Horowitz was standing in a portion of Los Angeles County that wasn't subject to municipal taxes or building codes or other forms of regulation. If he were to build on the land that he was examining that day, he could legitimately claim his apartment house was within walking distance of the trolley line——not to mention a drive of approximately equal duration to downtown, the ocean, the San Fernando Valley, and the movie studios of Hollywood and the surrounding areas. "Fifteen minutes to everywhere," as he liked to say. It might have been along a stretch of dirt road and the edge of the city, but it was a spot that he believed would be the center of the region: a canny discovery.

✣

The parcel of land that Horowitz was scouting was part of a large tract owned by Florence E. Dean, a San Francisco heiress who would, if he proceeded, be a partner with him in the building, with the land providing her share of the stake. Horowitz had identified another investing angel, Inez Fredericks of San Francisco and New York, a socialite who was considering making a cash investment in the project. A third party to Horowitz's scheme, his law partner and former law school classmate Mabel Walker Willebrandt, was another matter: Of them all, she was the least convinced that Horowitz had the savvy to build and manage an apartment house as a viable business.

Willebrandt was a formidable and pioneering figure in regional and national legal circles. She had attended law school at the University of Southern California after working for several years as an elementary school teacher and principal. After serving without pay as the first public defender of women in Los Angeles, she was named assistant attorney general of the United States by President Warren Harding and given the responsibility of enforcing the Eighteenth Amendment, the law against the sale and consumption of alcohol—a task she undertook with such zeal and success that she became known, not with much fondness, as "Deborah of the Drys" and "Prohibition Portia." In the mid-twenties, she was the highest-ranking woman in the federal government, and it was said that during her nearly eight years in her post she argued more cases in front of the U.S. Supreme Court than any attorney except the solicitor general. After leaving government, she had considered a career in politics but was discouraged when, while campaigning for Herbert Hoover in the 1928 presidential race, her 1924 divorce became a talking point against her. When Horowitz approached her to consider investment in his apartment building project, Willebrandt was one of the best-known women in American life.

Horowitz didn't have Willebrandt's renown, but he must have shared some of her persuasive ability, because once he determined that the site on Sunset Boulevard was suited to the building he envisioned, he managed to get her, along with Dean and Fredericks, to sign contracts and fund the scheme. In total, he would have $350,000 as a construction budget.* In early 1927, armed with photos of the Château d'Amboise, which he hoped to imitate down to the fanciful masonry ornamentation, he enlisted another close ally, the architect Arnold A. Weitzman—who happened to be his brother-in-law—to draw up plans.

Weitzman dutifully gave shape to Horowitz's dream: an L-shaped edifice with a turreted tower rising at the point where its two wings met; steeply pitched slate roofs; as many balconies and outdoor terraces as possible so as to maximize the number of so-called penthouses and to take advantage of those remarkable vistas; diversity in the floor plan of each of the forty-three apartments; an underground garage with room for forty-six cars; an outdoor garden with a fountain; a modest lobby, lounge, and communal kitchen for tenants who wished to entertain guests in grander style than their apartments might accommodate. The building would have a modern ventilation system that would help diffuse smoke and odors from residents' kitchens; the bathrooms would feature high-grade tiling; the living rooms would be decorated with cornices and steel sashes; the decoration throughout, echoing the Gothic theme of the exterior, would feature wrought iron, mosaics, hand-painted murals, and stained glass. And the whole thing would be built of reinforced steel and concrete, meaning not only that it would be earthquake proof but that there would be excellent soundproofing between the units.

Best known for the elegant Beth Israel synagogue in downtown Los Angeles, Weitzman didn't have a lot of experience in tall buildings like the one Horowitz had in mind. While he was at work on the West Hollywood project, he was working on a twelve-story office tower, his first, the Trades Building, also downtown and also owned, in part, by Horowitz. After Weitzman had rendered some of his designs for the apartment building,

---

* About $4.957 million in 2019.

a second architect was called in: William Douglas Lee (sometimes known as W. Douglas Lee or W. D. Lee), who had built several high-rises of ten and more stories in the previous decade, including the impressive El Royale apartment building in Hancock Park. Lee would not only help perfect Weitzman's plans; he would personally design the concrete shell of the building, and he would supervise construction.* By February 1928, Horowitz was happy with the plans, and Los Angeles County issued all the requisite building permits the following month.† In April, ground was broken.

Horowitz might have appeared to be setting himself up for a new life as a builder of castles and towers, but he hadn't forsaken his legal career. He was on a path to becoming a federal prosecutor and a special assistant attorney general. And his interest in the building game seemed to focus at least as much on show as on substance. Witness his request for a very specific piece of ornamentation on the exterior of the building: On the southern side of the central tower, the side facing Sunset Boulevard, he had Weitzman add a large masonry shield bearing a gigantic letter *H* in a Gothic font. It had nothing to do with the name of the building; the *H* stood, unironically, for "Horowitz."

By January 1929, the building was mostly completed, and a name for it had been selected. Horowitz had always known that in honor of the castle that inspired it, his building would be called Chateau *Something*. But none of the ideas he initially entertained seemed to harmonize with that high-toned word. Chateau Holly-

---

* This division of labor would result in a lawsuit, when Horowitz withheld $27,314 ($396,000 in 2019) in payments to Lee because he deemed that the architect had broken his agreement by failing to stop by the building site at least once a day to supervise the work. In 1930, the Superior Court of Los Angeles County found for Lee, declaring that "an architect may supervise work through others employed for that purpose, and personal appearance on the job is not necessary."

† An account of those permits released by the Hollywood branch of the Los Angeles Realty Board cited the cost of construction as $150,000 ($2.174 million in 2019)—less than half of the overall budget for the project.

wood, one of the candidates, sounded oxymoronic; the town and its principal business were anything but noble after all. Another choice, Chateau Sunset, seemed to grant excessively lofty status to the unpaved thoroughfare below. Horowitz finally decided to name the building for the street on which, at least nominally, it stood, Marmont Lane.* It even sounded somewhat French: Chateau Marmont.

In truth, the curved uphill path that Horowitz had chosen as the site for his building had been named for an Englishman— Percy Marmont, one of the great stars of Hollywood silent cinema, a British stage actor who appeared as leading man in dozens of Hollywood films between 1916 and 1928, opposite the likes of Clara Bow and Ethel Barrymore, before returning to England and becoming a prominent presence on the stage and a favorite on-screen performer of the young director Alfred Hitchcock. For obscure reasons, the tiny dirt road that curled up from Sunset Boulevard into an onion field was christened for the star, providing an ironically suitable connection to the movies for the building that would put it on the map.[†]

⚜

In January 1929, Chateau Marmont was in its final stages of construction, and the maiden tenants hadn't yet moved in, when it hosted its first gala party. Surprisingly, it was Mabel Walker Willebrandt and not Fred Horowitz who served as host. On January 8, Willebrandt welcomed more than three hundred guests

* In fact, its initial address was designated as 8225 Marmont Lane, though it would be designated as 8221 West Sunset Boulevard before it opened and for the rest of its existence.

† During construction, it became necessary to pave Monteel Road, which ran behind the building site, parallel to Sunset Boulevard. The handful of local landowners along the road actually made a formal complaint about this upgrade, citing their fears of traffic and parking issues. Prescient, they were.

to a fete celebrating the achievement of May D. Lahey, who just a few weeks earlier was appointed a judge of the Municipal Court of Los Angeles, making her the second woman to sit on the county bench. "Never before in the history of women's public activities has a social affair of so much significance been given as the one today when a woman assistant United States Attorney General will give a function in honor of a woman municipal judge," said the *Los Angeles Times*. Among the guests Willebrandt entertained that afternoon were the wives of Louis B. Mayer and Arnold Weitzman, as well as, according to society columnist Alma Whitaker, "gentlemen judges and their wives, women lawyers galore, college nabobs, club women, et al." Throughout the course of the evening, Whitaker reported, "a stiff-backed flunky held the card tray at the door and looked like a frozen statue for four hours." Party guests were given tours of the not-quite-finished building, meaning that Whitaker would go down as the first person to describe in print the layout and atmosphere of Chateau Marmont: "I know it was designed by a male architect—it is so stingy with the closets. But otherwise it is a most imposing structure."

On February 1, three weeks after that party, Chateau Marmont opened to the public. Horowitz and his partners were on hand to greet visitors and point out the finer aspects of the grand new building. And it really was grand: the tallest structure for several miles, seeming even more so because of the perch on which it sat. With its imposing form and dominating location, it truly did appear to be a castle.

On the *outside*, anyhow.

Inside, though there were fine touches throughout, Chateau Marmont presented a somewhat less impressive face. For one thing, there was its eccentricity. By insisting that the layout of the apartments *not* be uniform, Horowitz had given his architects a task that might have been beyond them. True, there was charm to the singularity of each unit, but that charm came at the price of coherence. "The place had more doors than the fun house at Ocean Park pier," said an early resident, not necessarily intending praise. "There were rooms, cubbyholes, and little niches at almost every turn." Someday, the people for whom the Chateau's curious form seemed an asset and not a liability would embrace such quirks, but at first blush the queerness of the architecture turned away some potential renters.

And then there was the matter of the furnishings: Whatever sum Horowitz and his partners had poured into the construction, landscaping, and decoration of their fabulous new building, they operated on a very slender margin when it came to actually filling the units with furniture. No expense had been spared in the design, the moldings, the roof, the ornamentation, and so on. But the builders found themselves strapped when it came to beds, chairs, sofas, lamps, and such. They contracted with a wholesale furniture outfit in the Midwest and equipped their costly flats with inexpensive, serviceable, deflatingly drab pieces, the exceptions being the rugs that graced the floors of some of the more expensive apartments—which were actually taken from the homes of Horowitz and his co-investor Inez Fredericks.

The nondescript furniture made for a discordant note, especially considering the rental prices at Chateau Marmont. The largest penthouses—clocking in at as much as thirty-eight hundred square feet and with truly spectacular views—rented for $750 per month.* At that rate very few people at all could afford to live there, and fewer of those would want to live in a spot that combined such high rents with cheap furniture and an unimproved road outside the front door.

Seeking tenants, Horowitz and company put a discreet display ad in the *Los Angeles Times* announcing that the building was officially ready for habitation:

---

* Approximately $10,870 in 2019—more or less one-tenth, even when adjusted for inflation, of what the same units would fetch as hotel suites ninety years later.

That ad, or slight variations on it emphasizing the availability of the penthouses, would run for months. Chateau Marmont might have instantly become a physical landmark of Sunset Boulevard—the westernmost point of civilization before the bridle path to Beverly Hills began—but it would take some time for it to accrue cachet as an address.

Help came within a few weeks in the form of a puff piece in the popular newsweekly *Saturday Night,* which called it "Los Angeles's newest, finest, and most exclusive apartment house." Such an endorsement spurred word of mouth, which, coupled with the undeniable qualities of the building and its proximity to Hollywood and Beverly Hills, gave the building a little traction.

The first residents were largely people from Southern California high society—folks whose tea parties, bridge games, bon voyage suppers, and evenings dedicated to sharing tales of recent travels filled the spaces in newspapers dedicated to what was then considered women's news. It was a highfalutin, exclusive crowd, and for a while, even with some of the apartments having never been let, prospective tenants needed to provide references to be considered for leases. It was slow going, but Horowitz's unlikely scheme looked to be on a path toward profitability.

And then came October and the collapse of the stock market that had buoyed so many speculative projects just like Chateau Marmont. Horowitz and company had built and opened a luxury apartment house less than a year before the onset of the worst economic crisis in generations, and their investment looked utterly lost. Tenants whose fortunes had been gutted by the crash began to break their leases and move out; apartments that had yet to be leased at all seemed doomed to stay empty; and the shining success that looked possible in the summer appeared to fade and die as autumn turned to winter and the Great Depression took hold. The smell of fresh paint had barely left the corridors, and the very solvency of the building was legitimately in question.

⚜

Even before the crash, there were signs that Chateau Marmont was ill-omened. While many of those big, pricey penthouses Horowitz insisted on building were vacant, at least one was occupied right from the start, by Hollywood demi-royalty of the moment: director George W. Hill and his wife, famed journalist, novelist, screenwriter, and film director Frances Marion. The two had met in the late twenties, when he was married and she was a recent widow, her third husband, actor Fred Thomson, having died from an infection after sustaining a leg injury. Marion was immensely talented and respected—she would become the first person to win two Academy Awards for screenwriting—and had directed three films during the silent era, a truly rare achievement for a woman in the Hollywood of the time. Hill, for his part, was among the most accomplished and commercially successful directors of his age and was, unusually, associated with a particular visual style, favoring deep shadows and intricate details. The couple collaborated on several films, including the 1930 prison drama *The Big House* (which won Marion the first of her Oscars). They married at the end of 1929 and immediately took up residence in one of the upper-floor units at Chateau Marmont, where they continued their professional alliance with 1930's *Min and Bill*, a comic melodrama that won a Best Actress Oscar for its star, Marie Dressler.

It seemed a golden formula for both life and art, but it wasn't long-lived. After a short stay at Chateau Marmont, the couple moved to an oceanfront home in Venice, where Hill fell prey to a latent alcoholism that he had managed to keep hidden from Marion during their working partnership and romantic courtship. In 1931, she left him and filed for divorce. Soon after, he was severely injured in a car accident when he swerved to avoid hitting some kids who ran into the street. He tried to recover through work, but his progress was hampered by his drinking; he literally staggered into production meetings and was unable to contribute a thing, until his bosses at MGM simply pulled him out of action, scuttling an adaptation of Pearl Buck's *Good Earth* that he had gone to China to scout locations for. In August 1934, he attended funeral rites for Marie Dressler. It was his last public appearance. A week or so later, alone in that Venice Beach house, with neither work nor a wife to console him, he had a few drinks, got into bed with a pistol, fired a test shot into the ceiling, and then took his own life with a bullet to the brain.

❉

Mabel Willebrandt always thought that Fred Horowitz was reaching beyond his grasp by building a luxury apartment tower on an unpaved road in an unincorporated community of Los Angeles County. But she had agreed to invest in the project that so captivated the imagination of her USC law classmate and legal partner and to support his ongoing effort to make a profit of the thing—up to a point.

After the calamitous crash of the stock market and the economic depression that subsequently gripped the nation, Willebrandt felt it was time to reckon with the financial drain that Chateau Marmont had become. In 1930, barely a year after the building had opened to tenants, she demanded that Horowitz face the reality of the situation and put the building up for sale. He was loath to give up so quickly, and the two negotiated a compromise: They would give the thing another year before declaring it a failure, and Horowitz would cede oversight of day-to-day operation of the building.

Luckily, the financial collapse had made some excellent candidates for such a role available. Ben Weingart was a land speculator and hotelier who had owned and operated more than a hundred properties under the umbrella of his Consolidated Hotels Inc., a business he had started soon after the end of World War I with a loan of $350.* He, too, was reeling from the effects of the stock market collapse, but he had found a way to turn the collective misfortune of the moment into an opportunity: He had converted his mid-range and low-rent hotels into rooming houses to create lodging for people who'd lost their homes or who had come to California to work when every chance to earn a nickel back home had dried up. That formula was proving moderately successful, and Weingart realized that his facility at running multi-unit buildings was the seed of a new revenue source: property management. Consolidated began to hire itself out as an operator of other people's buildings just at a time when Horowitz and his partners were looking for a seasoned hand to run Chateau Marmont. A deal was quickly struck.

Weingart introduced a few changes to the operation of the place. For one, he removed the original manager, Blanche Bryson, and replaced her with Emma Lovell, who, it soon became clear, was on hand for more than just her ability to help residents with any problems or questions they might have. Among other things, Weingart was a ladies' man, and when he would visit Chateau Marmont, as he was wont to do two or three times a week, he and

_____

* Approximately $5,200 in 2019.

Lovell would repair to her first-floor apartment for hours-long meetings that only ended around supper time, when he would head home to his wife and children, making him the first notable to use the Chateau as the sort of private playground it would become famous for being.

But even as he was able to juggle his personal dealings, Weingart could only do so much with the apartments that Horowitz was paying him to manage. He was known for having a meticulous eye and for being extremely careful with money, and he applied his skills fully to the task of running the building. For the better part of a year, he cut costs; staff was trimmed by about half, repairs were only performed when essential, and whole apartments were sealed off, the furnishings covered by bedsheets as if the occupants had gone away on extended vacations when, in fact, the units had never been rented at all.

After a year, though, he hadn't pulled off a miracle. Chateau Marmont was still only partly occupied, and Fred Horowitz's partners called in their markers: They wanted out of the apartment house business, and Horowitz had to either buy them out of their stakes or join them in selling the building. Reluctantly, a little more than two years after welcoming the first prospective tenants to the site, he agreed to put the place on the market. It gave rise to the inevitable question: Who was going to buy such an expensive item in such a dodgy economy? The obvious first choice would have been Ben Weingart, the property manager, but his finances had suffered just as badly as everyone else's in the crash, and he had neither the means nor, perhaps, the appetite to acquire a pricey property at such a parlous moment. But before long, a white knight stepped in.

Part Two

A SECOND BIRTH (1932–1942)

The Chateau and the Players, early forties. *Bison Archives*

Fred Horowitz had worked out nearly everything about his dream castle, down to the last table lamp and water glass. But, like almost everyone else, he hadn't seen the Great Depression coming, and he had to walk away from the building just as it was fulfilling his idea of what it would be like as a living thing.

Unluckily for him, the whole area around Chateau Marmont would soon come to life, with nightclubs, restaurants, shops, and a number of swank places to live popping up. Horowitz's vision was becoming a reality, but not exactly as he had predicted. His castle would thrive—not as an apartment house for the upper classes of Southern California, but as a hotel catering to the movie trade. And a man who helped create the movies in the first place would be the one who led the transition.

Even as the Great Depression beleaguered the nation, Chateau Marmont stood solid, a safe harbor not only for vacationers and business travelers but for refugees from the gathering political storms in Europe. And the people who made their homes of it, albeit temporarily, whether in its most sun-dappled penthouses or its darkest nooks and corners, were more and more frequently the people who helped lighten the hearts and fuel the imaginations of a world teetering between economic wreckage and the impending darkness of war.

I.

In October 1932, Los Angeles newspapers carried accounts of the sale of Chateau Marmont for $750,000 cash* to Albert E. Smith, one of the men who had built from scratch the business that would help define Southern California for the world.

Smith was born in England in 1875 and moved with his family to New York as a child. He had a yen to be a stage performer, and following that dream in his teens, he was exposed to the new technology of motion pictures being created by Thomas Edison and his team of technicians in New Jersey. Being mechanically minded himself, Smith was drawn toward the machinery of moviemaking, and along with a partner, J. Stuart Blackton, another English expat, he acquired an Edison projector in 1897. Later that year, having figured out how to turn the projector into a camera, Smith began shooting motion pictures of his own, partnering with Blackton in a company they called Vitagraph.

These were the wildcatting days of cinema, and Smith and Blackton filmed everything they could in the hopes of finding the most appealing and lucrative content for the fledgling medium. They shot prizefights; they went to South Africa to film images of the Second Boer War; they were on hand at San Juan Hill when Teddy Roosevelt and the Rough Riders made their famous charge up it; and they were in Buffalo when President William McKinley was assassinated (Smith claimed that they had captured footage of the murder itself but that the film was lost to chemical deterioration). They made what was believed to be the first-ever stop-motion animated film (*The Humpty Dumpty Cir-*

* Approximately $13.977 million in 2019.

cus, 1897) and some of the earliest-ever Westerns—shot, oddly enough, in rural areas of southern New York state.

Throughout all this activity, Vitagraph was under constant threat of legal action by Edison, who sought to impose strict copyright protection over his equipment and even over the very notion of filming moving pictures. In 1910, in part to avoid Edison's attempts to enforce his patents, Smith and Blackton moved their company to Southern California, which offered harbor from Edison's lawyers as well as abundant sunshine in an era when all movies—even those set indoors—were shot outside using natural light. They first set up their studio in Santa Monica, only to abandon it because of the morning fogs that rolled in off the Pacific; the studio was housed permanently in Hollywood by 1911.

In the coming decade-plus, Vitagraph was one of the most successful movie companies in the world, producing comedies, biblical epics, literary adaptations, Westerns (including the first fictional film shot in the Grand Canyon), and action movies (including the first aviation film, *The Military Air-Scout*). The company introduced one of the very first movie stars whose name was known by the public (Florence Turner, a.k.a. the Vitagraph Girl) and, arguably, the first animal star, Jean (a female collie known as the Vitagraph Dog). Vitagraph helped launch the screen careers of the likes of Helen Hayes, Norma Talmadge, Rudolph Valentino, and Moe Howard (later of the Three Stooges). It even made several features starring that redoubtable leading man Percy Marmont.

In 1925, still fighting for the right to shoot and distribute films without interference from Edison and fending off the feverish competition of an increasing number of rival studios, Smith and Blackton gave up, selling Vitagraph and its New York and Hollywood studios to Warner Bros. for approximately $735,000.* Smith set about creating a new life for himself, spending money

---

* Approximately $10.292 million in 2019.

on yachts and yacht racing and investing in land, apartment houses, and other properties around Southern California. Among other splurges, he bought a massive tract of land outside Rancho Santa Fe, north of San Diego, and he purchased and renovated a forty-eight-unit apartment building in Hollywood. On the heels of that success, he took a flier and bought Chateau Marmont.*

✼

Newspaper accounts of the transaction ranged from routine— "New Owners in Possession of Multiple Unit"—to gobsmacked: "Did anyone say 'Depression'?" It was reported that Smith's purchase included the parcel of land on which the building sat, partly accounting for a price that was more than double the construction budget for the building, which, after all, wasn't yet three years old and was being sold because the owners were having trouble filling it.

That sizable sum didn't include the improvements and alterations that Smith envisioned. For one thing, he was going to transition Chateau Marmont from a residential building into a hotel. Whereas Fred Horowitz had envisioned the property as a set of luxury apartments designed for people in Southern California society, including the burgeoning movie business, Smith had his eyes on a transient (but well-heeled) population of travelers to Los Angeles, some of whom, he anticipated, would want long-term but still-temporary housing as they made footfall in a place that he believed they would fall in love with and come to call home. In particular, he told the *Los Angeles Times* a few months after his purchase, he foresaw a swell in permanent migrants to

---

* Fred Horowitz, his dream castle no longer in his possession, would pursue an active legal career into the sixties, enjoying a spell in the limelight while defending a variety of Hollywood studio employees from the oppression of the anti-Communist witch hunts of the forties and fifties. In 1986, not long before his death at age ninety-one, he visited Chateau Marmont for the first time since selling it to Smith, honored at a dinner by the then owners.

the area after the 1932 Summer Olympics, which were to be held throughout the city.

> During the past weeks, I have had almost daily telephone calls and letters from people all over the United States and even from foreign countries about apartment rentals in Los Angeles. They infer that they are coming for the Olympic Games. I am satisfied that many, many of those people will remain in Southern California after their summer visit, and that means that Los Angeles apartment house properties will soon command premium prices.

Initially, little changed under Smith's management. It was still difficult to find renters—long or short term—for high-end housing in an economic depression, and the penthouse units proved particularly tough to fill: Throughout the first years Smith owned Chateau Marmont, the largest, highest-priced, and most opulent units in the building were still regularly announced as available in ads in Los Angeles newspapers. And the majority of tenants were still people from what might be called the Southern California Social Register class: old-money types from around the area who only occupied their apartments at the Chateau part-time, as pieds-à-terre between cruises, trips abroad, or long spells in their other, larger homes. Even though it had technically transformed into a hotel, Chateau Marmont wasn't drawing the movie-land crowd that patronized other hotels: the rowdy Garden of Allah, the luxurious Beverly Hills Hotel or Beverly Wilshire.* Chateau Marmont wasn't hurting, exactly; Smith was right in assuming that there would be an uptick in demand for quality housing as the Olympics helped lift some of the pall of the Depression in at least some parts of Southern California. But

---

* Management of the latter two had, ironically, decided that the best way to survive the Depression was to convert from hotels to long-term residential apartment buildings, exactly the opposite of Smith's strategy.

he hadn't yet found the key to making his newly transformed hotel a success.

�֎

Albert Smith knew that as a hotel Chateau Marmont would have need of a new sort of person to run it. Apartment management required one set of skills: maintenance, troubleshooting, keeping squabbles between tenants to a minimum, and, perhaps above all, making yourself invisible and *not* needed. Hotel management required most of those plus stores of diplomacy and discretion and, most important, the ability to fix a fresh and happy countenance on the property and on one's self every single day— since each day was, in effect, move-in day for *someone*. An apartment manager can have a sour moment or two; a hotel manager must always be sunny, hospitable, inviting. Smith didn't only need brains and eyes to run the place; he needed *a face.*

Fortunately for him, his connections in Hollywood meant that he had access to a number of likely candidates for the job, and he hit on a fine one. Ann Little was a leading lady of the silent screen who had left the movies some years before and was supporting herself by building and then renting and selling units in bungalow courts, a revenue model that had thrived in the twenties but dried up during the early years of the Depression when Los Angeles housing stock was greater than the number of people who could afford to pay for it. She had a skill set that was rare even in Hollywood: a knowledge of dealing with tenants, familiarity with movie people and the press, a gracious and hospitable manner, a physical vitality, and a philosophical intellect. According to at least one of the people who would soon call Chateau Marmont home and make it famous, the screenwriter and director Billy Wilder, Little "was why the hotel became what it became."

Little was born in 1891 in the Northern California mountain town of Sisson (later renamed Mount Shasta). She was raised on a ranch and was riding, shooting, swimming, and performing other feats of outdoorsmanship at an early age. Dazzled by the theatrical troupes that passed annually through town, she left home after high school and joined the ranks of the Ferris Hartman stock company, a musical comedy outfit that toured California, Washington, and Oregon. She quickly became one of the leading players, a position she held for nearly four years.

Among the traveling company were a few actresses who had good things to say about a new racket. "I heard the other girls talking about the 'movies' and how a person might make as high as ten dollars a day in them," Little told a reporter, "and I began to take notice." On tour in San Francisco, she was approached by Gilbert Anderson—the famous Broncho Billy of the big screen— who asked if she was any sort of horsewoman. When he learned what she could do, he told her of all the advantages of the movies, and she signed on, shooting a few short Westerns in the Bay Area starting in 1911. Soon after, she arrived in Hollywood proper.

Little had gifts as a dramatic emoter to go along with her physical abilities, and audiences and filmmakers liked her. In not quite eight years, she appeared in more than 125 short films, serial episodes, and full-length features for several different studios, almost always as the leading lady, almost always doing her own stunt work along with her more serious scenes, and frequently playing the part of a Native American.* The pictures she made were Westerns and thrillers—sneering villains, distressed (if sturdy) damsels, white-hatted heroes. And they were shot all over the still-undeveloped land surrounding what would become the site of Chateau Marmont. "I could find my way blindfolded over every inch of the Hollywood Hills and Cahuenga Pass," she told a reporter. "Villains held me in shacks all over what is now West Hollywood." In 1918, she graduated to slightly nobler fare when she signed a contract at Paramount and was cast opposite

* During one memorable shoot, she was said to have helped capture a horse thief near Santa Barbara.

one of the age's great romantic leading men, Wallace Reid, in a few straight dramas. Soon after, she played the Native American maiden Naturich in Cecil B. DeMille's 1918 version of *The Squaw Man* (which he had first made in 1914 and would make yet again in 1931), the biggest feature in which she had yet been cast, and in a major role at that.

She was on the verge of real stardom, making regular appearances in *Photoplay* and other movie fan magazines. But she wasn't doing work that she loved; she was, in effect, an action star who aspired to be a serious actress. "I enjoy feats of horsemanship," she told a newspaper. "But I like most intense dramatic action. I am very fond of the drama and I hope before long to do some dramatic work on the stage." In interview after interview she was posited as a serious young woman, a thinking person's heroine. And the longer she tried to reconcile her ambitions and interests with the work she was being paid to do, the more she became disenchanted, maybe even exhausted by the movies. In the early twenties, she left Hollywood, deciding to try her hand on the legitimate stage in New York, where she worked to little acclaim and with little advancement. She was soon back in Hollywood, no longer willing to do stunt work, accepting only roles in dramas, making but one film per year, or even none at all. By 1925, she was out of movies altogether, appearing onstage in various productions of the Henry Duffy Players at the Hollywood Playhouse.

Little had been married once, for about two years, to Allan Forrest, one of her leading men. They divorced in 1918, after which she remained single, refusing interviews about her days in the movie business and taking care of her ailing mother, who, like her daughter, was a practitioner of Christian Science, the religious movement that, in part, believed in eschewing modern medicine in favor of prayer as a method of healing. The pair lived modestly and, like so many, were hobbled by the stock market crash of 1929. When Albert Smith came calling to ask her if she wanted to manage his new property, Little seized at the lifeline.

But she had conditions. She wanted a suite for herself and her mother in the hotel, which was readily granted. More important, she insisted that the place undergo a face-lift. As impressive as the Chateau was architecturally, she explained to Smith, its tacky furniture and decoration undermined its pretensions to grandeur; in an apartment house, people could bring their own furniture and art into their units, but hotel guests were stuck with what was there, and they wanted to feel as though they were living someplace more luxurious than (or, in the case of wealthy guests, equal to) their homes. The stuff with which Fred Horowitz had filled Chateau Marmont had absolutely no aura of class or elegance about it. At the very least, she told Smith, the furniture needed a complete upgrade.

She made a persuasive case. Smith began to acquire furnishings from various great homes and estates throughout Southern California whose owners were selling off everything in the wake of their losses in the Depression. The result was a potpourri of one-of-a-kind items—dressers, sofas, lamps, rugs, and so on—that, unlike the cookie-cutter pieces that Horowitz had been forced to settle for, bore no resemblance to one another. Thus began Chateau Marmont's famed style of decor, in which no two rooms looked alike; this was absolutely charming—return guests could feel a sense of discovery as each new set of rooms revealed its contents. Over time, it could cause some problems: There were no standard pieces to swap in or out as maintenance or guests' needs and tastes required. But as a management decision, it was a masterstroke: The hotel now had *character.*

Having put her stamp on the Chateau's appearance, Little began to exert influence over its operation. Characteristically modest ("I do not like sentences beginning with 'I,'" she said), she claimed to enjoy the challenge of facing up to the demands of finicky guests. "The tough tenants are the most fun," she said. "I suppose it's the same principle as the one sinner among the ninety and nine.... The real thrill is to tackle the 'sinner' and wear him down with kindness." At the same time, she had stan-

dards of decorum and behavior that she would not relax. "Everyone was high class," she recalled of her reign. "Of course, they all
knew we wouldn't put up with nonsense. They didn't stay if they
caused trouble."

Little also instituted a food service of a sort. It wasn't exactly
a restaurant, and there was no formally designated dining room,
but Little persuaded Smith to upgrade Horowitz's bare-bones
kitchen so as to provide in-room catering to guests and to hire a
chef with European experience, to run it. Guests could phone the
desk in the morning, learn about the day's offerings, and put in
orders for dinner or lunch—$1.25 per plate. The chef would cus-
tomize menus for dieters and others with special needs, and he
made himself available to consult with guests who weren't com-
petent cooks but who wanted to prepare meals for themselves in
their kitchens. It wasn't proper room service; you couldn't ring
downstairs late at night for a hamburger. But it was an amenity
that made each suite at Chateau Marmont feel well-appointed.
And, if managed properly, which Little assuredly did, it created
some revenue.

Little was still relatively new to her job on the evening of
March 10, 1933, when a 6.4-magnitude earthquake struck just
south of Long Beach, wreaking havoc throughout Southern California, killing as many as 120 people and causing $40 million in
damage.* People fled into the streets from nearby buildings, but
Little, ever the fearless cowgirl, rode out the tumult inside the
impregnable Chateau Marmont as if nothing had happened. "I
had just come downstairs," she recalled,

> when I felt the building starting to sway.... Nothing was
> broken. Nothing had even moved. The swaying had been so
> gentle. The most frightening thing was seeing the trees out-
> side. They were shaking so wildly their leaves were falling
> like confetti. But inside we were just fine.

* Approximately $786 million in 2019.

Fred Horowitz's insistence that his castle be built to withstand any sort of tremor proved canny. The Chateau even took in a few new residents from among those who found their nerves rattled, along with their bookcases and dinnerware, in other nearby buildings.

In addition to her sangfroid in a natural disaster and her savvy in decorating, catering, and pleasing difficult personalities, Ann Little brought to the Chateau an energy and manner that everyone in the movie world—which would soon become the hotel's lifeblood—could recognize and take comfort in. "My picture experience established wonderful contacts," she explained, and time and again that proved to be the case. "What are you doing here?" asked one Hollywood notable when checking in at the front desk soon after Little was hired. "Oh, I'm just here!" she replied. She understood the mentality of creative artists, divas, and movie tycoons, and she found ways to accommodate them all. Years later, for instance, she shared a memory of the classical pianist and conductor José Iturbi, not yet the household name he would become, visiting in her early days as manager; he would stay up all night, she said, "fingering the keys so softly he would never disturb anyone. Then he would order breakfast. He always wanted his eggs cooked in olive oil." Such was her genius for hospitality that she never dreamed of interrupting him at his practice and she made serving him his preferred meals a matter of invisible ease.

❋

Not long after Ann Little started her reign at Chateau Marmont, the hotel received its first important visitor from the world of cinema—and it wasn't, in retrospect, one to brag about. Martin Freudenthal was an emissary of the German Foreign Office in Berlin, entrusted with the task of taking the temperature of ordinary Americans on a variety of social and political subjects. In particular, he was to learn about the American movie studio

system and, most precisely, to improve the images of Germany
and the German people in Hollywood films. He spent almost
an entire year in the United States, traveling, lecturing, taking
notes, writing reports, and chatting with strangers on trains and
in cafés and saloons. He made many visits to the executive suites
of movie studios—he was particularly chummy with the folks
who ran Universal Pictures—and he actually persuaded some of
them to alter the content of films with German themes or set-
tings to present a more positive impression of his homeland. (In
one case, he was able to get a studio to scrap outright the production of a film about the German sinking of the *Lusitania* during
World War I.)

Freudenthal sent regular reports back to Berlin detailing
his impressions and his interactions with Hollywood studios (he
was particularly vexed by the use of Erich von Stroheim—an
Austrian who spoke Yiddish more fluently than German—as
the archetypal German villain in so many films). He did all of
this from a base at Chateau Marmont, where he was recognized
as a gracious, charming, and welcome guest by members of the
upper-class community that was then frequenting the place.
When he left Los Angeles in late 1932, he threw a farewell tea
for his friends that was reported on in a society column in the
Los Angeles Times. Identifying Freudenthal as "that nice German counselor of legation," Alma Whitaker reported that

> the Blue Book flocked, lots of men, too. Saw several judges
> toting cups of tea around and balancing pretty sandwiches on
> saucers. The tall doctor [that is, Freudenthal] had an anxious
> time trying to be hostess and flitting from group to group—
> and remembering names. He said remembering names came
> easy to him. So I wouldn't dream of protesting when he
> introduced me as Mrs. Bayley all the afternoon. I discovered
> the real Mrs. Bayley later. Such a handsome woman! Maybe
> that man was pretty subtle after all.

This sort of dull drawing room comedy was hardly the sort of sinful movie-land gathering that had become a staple of gossip writers in the previous decade. And, truly, little going on at Chateau Marmont in these early days rose to the level of sensationalism. For that, one had to cross Sunset Boulevard to a place that earned its reputation for sin and bacchanalia when the Chateau was still a fancy in Fred Horowitz's mind.

2.

Havenhurst, the plush two-and-a-half-acre estate that sat on the south side of Sunset Boulevard just opposite Marmont Lane, was the home of the celebrated Russian actress Alla Nazimova. The great diva had purchased the property in 1919, the centerpiece being the twelve-room main house and the adjacent swimming pool, built in the shape of the Black Sea, the site of the actress's childhood in the Crimea. Curiously, not only the estate but the *house* straddled the line between the city of Los Angeles and unincorporated Los Angeles County; when property taxes were calculated, Nazimova moved her most valuable possessions—including a grand piano—into the county portion of the house, where the levies on such items were lower.

The mixture of opulence and cunning in that money-saving gesture was absolutely typical of Nazimova, who was a living embodiment of the spirit of artistic libertinism and abandonment. A celebrated interpreter of Chekhov, Ibsen, and Turgenev, she had been a marquee name in Europe and New York since the turn of the century and had come to Hollywood to chase the huge sums offered to Broadway stars willing to appear on-screen. A pioneer of self-empowerment, she was as out of the closet as it was possible for a lesbian to be at the time and still keep getting jobs, and she routinely hosted salons and other gatherings where gay women met and mingled without fear of censure or consequences. She produced her own plays and films, includ-

ing a 1922 movie of Oscar Wilde's *Salome* in which many queer
men and women were cast. She made fortune after fortune and
squandered each of them on unimaginably high living, much of
which involved her "lavender marriage" to actor Charles Bryant, who had even more extravagant tastes (and brought in far
less income) than his wife. Nazimova orchestrated the affairs—
professional and romantic—of many of her acolytes, the most
famous being Rudolph Valentino, for whom she chose not one but
two wives, first Jean Acker and then Natacha Rambova.* She was,
in form and deed, the very picture of the grande dame.

In the late twenties, when her free-spending ways threatened
her solvency, Nazimova entered into a business partnership that
resulted in her mansion becoming the centerpiece of a residential hotel. For an annual fee of $14,500†—plus 50 percent of all
profits—Nazimova leased her property for ninety-nine years to a
builder who dotted the estate with two dozen bungalows. A bar
and a darkroom were built on the grounds, and the various guest
units were furnished with frills that had once been Nazimova's:
that tax-evading piano, a purple commode, a black marble bath-
tub, and so on.

Named punningly for its famous owner, the development
would be known as the Garden of Allah, and it would be the
site of the Sunset Strip's first famous bacchanals. The Garden
of Allah offered an amazing blend of rusticity and exotica, fame
and privacy, gilded revelry and bleary-eyed mornings after. All
of the clichés attached to Chateau Marmont about celebrities
boozing, drugging, sexing, indulging, flaunting, and otherwise

---

* It has been said that neither marriage was ever consummated and that both
brides *and* the groom were of ambiguous sexuality. Regardless, Acker, even after
being supplanted by Rambova, always insisted on being known as Mrs. Rudolph
Valentino, even in film appearances. She frequently stayed at Chateau Marmont
in the decades after her ex-husband's death, and her guest card in the hotel files
identified her strictly by her former married name.

† Approximately $205,000 in 2019.

not giving a rip about propriety were true of the Garden of Allah before ground was even broken on the Chateau.

The Garden bore not only Nazimova's name but her spirit as well. From the very earliest days, it was among the most debauched hostelries in all of Southern California. Playboys, liberated women, visiting libertines, soon-to-be divorcées, confirmed singles, and an array of artists, bohemians, schemers, and drug and booze hounds were among its habitués, and the hotel's instant notoriety only drew more of their type to stay or drop in for a visit. The swimming pool alone—into which just about everybody in Hollywood who enjoyed his or her tipple would someday be said to have fallen or leaped—was legendary.

The early guests—a mix of out-of-towners and locals who were between living arrangements—constituted a pantheon of silent movie icons and titans: Greta Garbo, John Barrymore, Clara Bow, Buster Keaton, Marlene Dietrich, director Ernst Lubitsch, producers Jed Harris and Alexander Korda. Later, even with rival hotels offering more luxurious accommodations in Beverly Hills or elsewhere in Hollywood, the Garden became a popular spot for the incoming tide of actors, writers, and directors from Broadway and Europe who were lured west when movies began to talk. And it was absolutely *the* favored place for the famed Round Table of writers and performers who gathered at Manhattan's Algonquin Hotel. Writer and comic actor Robert Benchley was their ringleader, a famous thrower of spontaneous parties and introducer of various men and women to romantic partners and artistic collaborators. Over the years he was followed west by his friends and peers Dorothy Parker, Alexander Woollcott, George S. Kaufman, John O'Hara, and Marc Connelly among them, turning the Garden into a Hollywood annex of one of Manhattan's most elite and storied gathering spots.

Presently, other out-of-town intellectuals made their Southern California homes at the Garden of Allah, including S. J. Perelman, William Faulkner, and, most famously, F. Scott Fitzgerald, who was in residence long enough to have received a letter from Thomas Wolfe reading, in part, "I'll be damned if I'll believe anyone lives in a place called The Garden of Allah." Fitzgerald stayed at the Garden for less than a year, during the slow decline of his career and his health. But his legend attached to the place, as did those of a variety of other residents of short tenure but long redolence: Errol Flynn, W. C. Fields, Harpo Marx, Dashiell Hammett, and Humphrey Bogart, who lived there with his third wife, Mayo Methot, the pair known as the Battling Bogarts for their drunken, plate-flinging spats. In a letter to a New York acquaintance, Woollcott described that era at the Garden of Allah as a fantastical mélange: "Rachmaninoff has the next [suite] to mine and begins practice every morning at dawn. Beyond him are the Charles Laughtons. Beyond them, Robert Benchley. Beyond him is Dorothy Parker. It's the kind of village you might look for down the rabbit hole."

For all the famed debauchees who made the place home, though, it was Benchley, even more than Nazimova, who was the presiding genius of the Garden. He was resident for years while writing and appearing in Hollywood films, organizing impromptu revels and cocktail binges and late-night carouses, knocking on doors to round up companions for dinner parties at Sunset Strip restaurants, keeping the bellboys running off to the liquor store at all hours for more of the hair of the dog that always had its jaws firmly clamped on his leg. He might or might not have once or twice fallen into the famed swimming pool in full evening dress, but he was credited, after one such apocryphal mishap, with coining the immortal quip "I have to get out of these wet clothes and into a dry martini." (The line was actually uttered by his chum, actor Charles Butterworth, during some wild scene at which Benchley was, inevitably, present. Benchley dined out on the line—he even gave it to himself as dialogue in the hit comedy film *The Major and the Minor*—but he was an honest thief, and he always credited Butterworth for it.)

Also legendary—but in this case true—was Benchley's fear

not only of driving in or around Los Angeles but even of *walking* in it. When invited to meet friends at Chateau Marmont—literally just across Sunset Boulevard—he would call for a taxi, then have the driver take him on a winding ramble through some nearby roads, hoping to disguise the fact that he was merely crossing the street. Only after what seemed to him a decent interval would he ask to be dropped off at his actual destination. It was no good offering to help walk him across the road; he was terrified of the cars whizzing by. And rightly so: There was no traffic light at the intersection, and the sudden curve in Sunset just west of Marmont Lane meant that eastbound cars would come blindly upon any pedestrians attempting the crossing. More than one person known to Benchley was injured—even killed—trying to cross the busy boulevard at that juncture. And so for the many years he was resident at the one hotel, he would take cabs to the other and back again—a perfect emblem of the New York dude trying to cope with the wide-open West.

❊

By the time Robert Benchley figured out a way to deal with his fear of getting across the West Hollywood portion of Sunset Boulevard, there was plenty of good reason to wander up and down the street. It was earning an international reputation as a lawless stretch where the authorities were seemingly indifferent to gambling, prostitution, and, especially, the sale and consumption of alcohol, which had been illegal in the United States for more than a decade.

The notoriety of the Strip began in the late twenties, when the Russian Eagle and La Boheme, the jewels of the infant Sunset Plaza, had both been celebrated—albeit quietly—for their stores of illegal booze, the latter boasting an especially notable wine cellar. Farther west, near the Beverly Hills city limits, a less swank operation called Maxine's took few pains to hide the fact that it was a saloon. Other entrepreneurs, noting the laxity of law enforcement in the area, soon opened nightspots that fronted for casinos; brothels popped up in private homes not far off Sunset Boulevard; and a handful of cafés and clubs where men and women could consort with romantic partners of the same gender appeared. By the thirties, a pair of gambling joints—the Clover Club and the Colony—did business on Sunset Boulevard almost without bothering to hide what they were. Similarly, the famed madams Lee Francis and Brenda Allen managed strings of prostitutes so brazenly either on or very near the street that they became demi-celebrities in the Los Angeles media. And such establishments as the Café Gala were known by everyone who knew such things as safe places for gay men and women to meet one another or simply be themselves in public without fear of exposure, harassment, or arrest. The nondescript stretch of road, convenient to almost everywhere, had become a midway of vice.

This activity was abided by the L.A. County sheriff's office, which had nominal jurisdiction over the area and which raked in payoffs from casino operators, madams, and speakeasy owners in exchange for laissez-faire oversight. Now and again, a surprise raid would be staged or a period of clampdown would be imposed. But these were shows. The business of sex and booze and games of chance profited everyone—except, inevitably, the customers, who were being fleeced of their own free will. Nobody wanted it snuffed.

At the same time, another breed of entrepreneur also found a home on this stretch of Sunset Boulevard: talent agents in the business of representing movie stars. Situating their offices between the mansions of Beverly Hills and the studios of Hollywood, they made it convenient for their clients to stop in to talk shop during a day's commute. And they managed as well to avoid a steep tax levied on their profession in Los Angeles proper. For decades, talent agencies would be among the most common tenants of office space on the street (the kinship with speakeasies, casinos, or brothels a matter entirely of coincidence).

And there was one more novelty. A name had been coined for

the stretch of road between Laurel Canyon and Doheny Drive, between the Los Angeles and the Beverly Hills city limits: the Sunset Strip. The phrase harked back to the well-established tradition of southern and western towns designating blue-light districts where a certain amount of late-night indulgence in vice was tolerated: strips, as they were often known. Some of the area's more staid local landowners and businessmen balked at the name and its shady implications, and the *Hollywood Citizen-News* ran a contest for its readers to come up with a replacement. The winner was "the Sunset Eighties," having to do with the fact that the Strip began in, more or less, the 8000 block of Sunset and ran to, more or less, the 9000. "It tells people where we are," a representative of Chateau Marmont told the newspaper, "and it's catchy." But it caught on with nobody other than the contest judges, and Sunset Strip stuck.

And with its sleek, moderne tenor, the name seemed more and more apt all the time. At the dawn of the thirties, the whole of Sunset Boulevard was paved, finally completing the road connecting Los Angeles to Beverly Hills. (The project was undertaken to suit the needs of legitimate businesses and property owners, but the boon to the shadier operations wasn't entirely coincidental.) During the years-long paving project, a second high-rise apartment building rose over the street to rival Chateau Marmont, both architecturally and as a business: the Sunset Tower, a fifteen-story Art Deco confection designed by the architect Leland Bryant. It opened in 1931 and boasted the highest residential penthouse in the entire region.

The whole Strip was starting to ignite. In 1934, the attention of the world's consumers of popular entertainment began to turn regularly toward the low-slung building in Sunset Plaza that had originally housed the La Boheme restaurant. Billy Wilkerson, the rakish publisher of *The Hollywood Reporter,* one of the movie business's powerful trade publications, had leased and renovated the space and renamed it the Trocadero. His showbiz connections guaranteed that the new club would attract boldfaced names to its gala opening, and the deluxe atmosphere, floor shows, European-influenced menu, and choice wine cellar induced them back for many, many nights to come. The Troc, as its habitués knew it, was the first truly swank nightclub on the Sunset Strip, serving as a handily located VIP room for Hollywood's elite. The spot filled so regularly with high-wattage talent that management didn't have to allow civilians entry; it was like a private club, a nighttime version of the studio commissary, a place where movie stars could behave like ordinary people and not pretend to be supernatural creatures.

Wilkerson, who had previously operated a restaurant near his newspaper offices, was a gracious host, whether his patrons were show folk or not. "The Trocadero was probably the best nightclub in this city in the '30s," recalled George Montgomery, who, as the son of the man who built Sunset Plaza, was the landlord of the joint. "Billy Wilkerson would give you an honest drink. You'd have your own little bottle so you knew you weren't getting slop." The success of the Troc encouraged others to open competing establishments, drawing their own share of celebrity clientele, and as news and photos of stars cavorting in one or another spot traveled the world, the Strip became synonymous with luxurious and sinful nightlife at such spots as Club Ballyhoo, the Centaur Club, Club Seville, and Club Madrid.

�֎

The Troc was a mere four blocks from Chateau Marmont, and proximity to its luster was no doubt a bonus for guests who wanted to party with, be seen among, or simply ogle Hollywood royalty. But a more useful novelty had popped up just across the street from the hotel not long before the Troc was christened, and its history would be closely knit with the Chateau's for decades.

Schwab's Pharmacy, a drugstore, luncheonette, soda fountain, and newsstand, opened in 1932, one of a string of such establishments owned and operated by the four Schwab brothers of East L.A. From the start, Schwab's became an essential piece not only of Hollywood day-to-day living but of Hollywood lore. Open from early in the morning until past midnight, the place was a clubhouse, a headquarters, and a hearth for up-and-comers, never-quite-ever-beens, rubberneckers, and strivers and schemers trying to pry a way into (sometimes *back* into) the movie business. No matter whether it was breakfast or last call, a quick nosh or an all-day vigil, actors, agents, screenwriters, and other Hollywood types crowded the place, nursing cups of coffee or ice cream sodas, thumbing through the trade papers, waiting for phone calls that could herald life-changing opportunities. Such was the crush of idled movie people dawdling in the booths and at the lunch counter that Schwab's installed dedicated telephone lines that took only incoming calls, presumably from agents and producers. But lest folks get too comfy, a minimum charge was imposed on diners, a practice unheard of in ordinary luncheonettes, and customers had to pay for magazines—and get them stamped to prove it—before taking them to their tables.

Schwab's wasn't only home to idlers and wannabes. Because of its location and hours, and because Chateau Marmont and the Garden of Allah were right on top of it, the clientele included real Hollywood royalty: Charlie Chaplin (who was fond of hopping behind the counter to make his own fountain treats), F. Scott Fitzgerald, the Marx Brothers, Clark Gable, Greta Garbo— everyone, truly. It was especially popular with displaced New Yorkers, who haunted similar places back home, and with screenwriters, many of whom were New Yorkers who had come west from Broadway.

Schwab's drew a crowd that was the envy of the area's restaurateurs and nightclub operators, and the golden circle of famous names who patronized it attracted lesser knowns with the passion of pilgrims. It was like a frat house that, for decades, served up coffee or a meal or simply gave people who were otherwise holed up in their hotel rooms working or waiting for phone calls a chance and a place to see other people. Even overrun as it often was by tourists keen to spy on movie stars in the flesh and blood, even as the vibes and trends of the Sunset Strip changed, Schwab's would maintain a central role in the daily life of Hollywood for more than fifty years. "It was like a duty to go there, just to show people that you were still around," recalled one regular customer. "It was open late, so there was more movie business done at Schwab's than at any other place in Hollywood."

Over the decades, Schwab's would become famous, inaccurately, as the spot where Lana Turner was discovered sipping a soda on a stool, a thing that actually happened but at another lunch counter farther east on Sunset near Hollywood High School, where she was a student. And it would be celebrated as a kind of Shangri-La-with-bagels by gossip columnists, especially Sidney Skolsky, who kept an office upstairs and trumpeted the doings at Schwab's in print and on radio; and by filmmakers, especially Billy Wilder, who set several crucial scenes of his classic film *Sunset Boulevard* at Schwab's.*

Wilder got to know Schwab's when he was living at Chateau Marmont, it being the nearest thing in his new home to the coffeehouses of his hometown, Vienna. For anyone living at the Garden of Allah or Chateau Marmont, Schwab's was like the restaurant/liquor store/gift shop/infirmary that neither hotel actually provided. Schwab's allowed guests of the neighboring hotels to run tabs during the duration of their stays, whether for meals consumed on the premises or for deliveries of sandwiches, groceries, booze, medicine, notions, and more to their rooms. Delivery boys, including the future monster movie star Billy Phipps, would zip orders to the Chateau on motorbikes, even though the store was only two hundred yards or so from the hotel. "I'd take over mostly sandwiches and whiskey," Phipps remembered.

---

* The exterior of the real Schwab's is seen in the film and identified as "headquarters" by the narrator; the interior was a relatively faithful replica built on a soundstage at Paramount.

"Sometimes they'd call for a couple of aspirins only. Or a single Baby Ruth candy bar."

Schwab's offered hotel guests other small but necessary services. A doctor whose shingle hung upstairs from the pharmacy was renowned for his hangover cures and his treatments for social diseases. A night watchman would dole out bandages or over-the-counter medications after hours if asked nicely. And certain celebrities were extended the courtesy of being allowed inside for a snack after closing, or of having their names kept *out* of Sidney Skolsky's column.

⚜

Elsewhere, the Strip continued to produce new places for movie people to recreate in one another's company. Not long after opening the Trocadero, Billy Wilkerson sold it, leaving it to stagger along under a variety of unsuccessful owners for a couple of years before it succumbed to bankruptcy. But he was only off the scene for about eighteen months before opening another club, Ciro's, two blocks closer to Chateau Marmont and the newest claimant to the title of the hottest spot for Hollywood stars to party. Ciro's was a performance venue, and it was especially noted for the high quality of entertainers it booked: Cab Calloway, Duke Ellington, Benny Goodman, Al Jolson, and many others of similar stature. And Wilkerson followed *that* success with La Rue, the area's most elegant French restaurant. While he was busily debuting novelties, others opened another topflight nightclub, Mocambo, a little farther west than its competitors but no less attractive to Hollywood's elite. It was a boom time.

This flowering of hot spots provided great spectacle for the popular culture. The names of various Sunset Strip haunts were printed in newspapers all over the country, and the clubs themselves appeared in movies about Hollywood crime and nightlife. It got so that comic strips and Warner Bros. cartoons could lampoon the mere names Trocadero or Mocambo or Schwab's or Garden of Allah and everyone in the country would get the joke.

But only the cognoscenti had by then ever heard of Chateau Marmont. Hidden in plain sight on a hill that caught folks' eyes only once they'd driven past it, with neither a lobby nor a bar nor a restaurant in which to ogle famous faces, it seemed destined to be a secret, a sanctum for the knowledgeable few. And then, not long after Ann Little got control of the place, the sunshine of celebrity gossip began to shine on it.

3.

Despite being owned by the former head of a movie studio, despite having a former silent film star as its manager and public face, Chateau Marmont didn't get nearly the attention from Hollywood as did other Los Angeles–area hotels. The Beverly Hills Hotel, the Beverly Wilshire, the Ambassador, and the Roosevelt all enjoyed more prominent names—not to mention offering more deluxe accommodations and amenities. And the Garden of Allah, just across the street, was far more famous as the site of Hollywood shenanigans and sinning.

At the start of Albert Smith's reign, the Chateau was still chiefly a haven for Southern California aristocracy. Even the gossip coming out of the place had less to do with film people than with blue bloods. And that was largely because of one resident in particular, Nellita Choate Thomsen, wife of Carl H. Thomsen, a wealthy jeweler, architect, and amateur travel film director.

The Thomsens had taken an apartment at the Chateau as soon as it opened, and their dinner parties were among the earliest noteworthy social events held in the building. Nellita was particularly well liked, gracious, lively, and, at just over thirty years old when she moved in, relatively youthful. She was, acquaintances noted, a particularly keen conversationalist and a great listener, qualities that helped her achieve a bit of renown as the Chateau's unofficial greeter and omnipresent gadabout.

There was nothing apparently unusual about her sociability or the fact that she was, in effect, a stay-at-home upper-class wife. She had been born to privilege as the daughter of a prominent Virginia family that could trace its roots to the Choates who landed in Massachusetts in 1642, a line that included, among other notables, Revolutionary War officers, U.S. senators, federal judges, and the founder of the famed Choate school. Nellita had been educated at Stanford, where she'd earned Phi Beta Kappa status and was active in a sorority, in student theatrics, and, especially, in student publications, where she advocated fearlessly for women's issues.

It was that last bit of her schooling that might have alerted residents and staff of Chateau Marmont to a secret that lay behind Nellita's gregarious and amiable manner. She wasn't only making friends and rolling out the welcome mat for new arrivals: She was working. As a reporter. A *gossip* reporter.

Before she married, Nellita Choate worked at the *Los Angeles Herald* (later the *Herald-Express*), writing about sensational local criminal trials and light feature subjects. After her marriage, under the pseudonym Pauline Payne, she had an even more prominent byline, producing a regular column, "The Merry-Go-Round," in which small bits of social news and Hollywood scuttlebutt would regularly appear, much of it originating in the hallways, suites, and public spaces of Chateau Marmont. Pauline Payne's work was lively enough and, crucially, *mild* enough to circulate throughout the many newspapers of the Hearst syndicate, giving its author a potential audience in the millions.

Pauline Payne was not a Hollywood gossip columnist in the vein of, say, Hedda Hopper, Louella Parsons, Rona Barrett, or Liz Smith. She had no public image, she didn't have enemies or favorites in the business, and the pseudonymous woman who wrote her columns didn't seek to use her voice and platform as a means to elevate her status in the media world. For her, movie people were simply among the interesting people one could meet, and from her station in the Chateau she had occasion to meet a fair share of them, always with an eye for quirks, never with a sharp word or a strong opinion about their work or careers.

Payne popped any number of notes about Hollywood people into her column, none especially barbed. She was fond of women in distress. There was Jean Acker, the onetime silent film star who was better known as the first wife of Rudolph Valentino. There was Katharine Hepburn, who showed up in early 1932 to make her maiden film, *A Bill of Divorcement*, for RKO. She had planned to put up at the Chateau for a week while seeking more comfortable accommodations, and, as Pauline Payne noted, she arrived at the front desk with her luggage filled with men's clothes and sporting an eye patch to cover an injury she sustained on the train ride west. There was Mary Astor, a more established Hollywood star, who was delivered to the hotel by ambulance from a film set in Lake Tahoe, where she'd been struck with pneumonia. In the midst of a marital crisis that would end in a sensational divorce trial, she checked into the hotel under duress and only briefly as she waited for her husband to vacate their home so that she could convalesce there. And there was Raquel Torres, a Mexican starlet whose short and spotty career as a movie sexpot ended with her marriage to a Wall Street tycoon.

It wasn't all soap opera. Payne wrote about the Ritz brothers—Harry, Al, and Jimmy—a popular vaudeville act of comical-musical zanies, a bit like the Marx Brothers but without the fantastical personae. They came to Hollywood several times in the thirties to make movies and often stayed at the Chateau, behaving with perfect civility, per "The Merry-Go-Round," save for their animated comings and goings through the lobby, when they seemed always to be excitedly concocting a new bit of business for their act.

Even more regularly than she shared stories about movie folk in her column, though, Payne wrote about people of wealth and social station whose names meant little to the public. She shared the story of Clara Clemens, the daughter of Mark Twain, who moved into the Chateau after the death of her concert pianist husband. She wrote about the wealthy eccentrics who occupied much of the second floor of the hotel, keeping rooms for their personal staff of maids, cook, and butler and setting aside an entire suite for their menagerie of pets, which included exotic birds and a long-haired monkey.

These sorts of tidbits—diverting little yarns that would be categorized as slice-of-life features rather than gossip—were Payne's specialty. For all her affability and energy, Nellita Thomsen was a bit of a wallflower when it came to her own personal fame. She left Chateau Marmont under a cloud; in 1938, her husband abruptly announced that he wanted a divorce so that he could marry his secretary, and the shock resulted in Nellita being put under psychiatric care and giving up her column. But she never fully distanced herself from her happy days gadding about the place. In 1977, when management decided to mark the fiftieth anniversary of the breaking of ground for the hotel's construction, she was one of the guests invited to recollect the early days. She shared some stories of the celebrities she'd known and, ever the reporter, deflected attention away from herself: When someone inquired if she was herself an actress, she laughed and said, "Oh heavens no!," and when she was asked about her married life in the Chateau, she replied, again with a grin, "My husband was a businessman. But we've been divorced for ages, so please don't mention him."

❊

The first *truly* famous celebrity to call Chateau Marmont home packed so much living into a short stay there that the hotel would have been worthy of Hollywood legend if no other movie people had ever stepped through its doors.

In September 1933, Jean Harlow and Harold Rosson drove up Marmont Lane in search of a place where they could live as newlyweds. Each already had a home in the area—hers a large custom-built mansion on an acre-plus site in nearby Bel Air.

But although her place was big, it wasn't big enough: Harlow's mother, also a Jean and therefore known as Mother Jean, lived there with her second husband, and the older couple felt entitled to butt their noses into everything the young Jean, whom they called Baby, did, including her marriages.

The plural is no typo: At age twenty-two, Harlow had just taken husband number *three*, establishing beyond dispute her credentials as Hollywood's premier vixen. In just a handful of years, she had gone from bored young society wife to movie extra to It Girl, style icon, and emblem of female sexual energy. She was famous for her platinum blonde hair; her plunging necklines; her tight-fitting wardrobe (made even snugger by her refusal to wear panties, which she felt disrupted the line of her dresses); her rumored habit of icing her nipples before each take so as to draw attention to her breasts; her love of Art Deco–style white clothes and furniture and cars; and, especially, her torrid chemistry with Clark Gable, frequently cast as her leading man. She had a sensational rise in the movies, from extra to bit player to the sort of star for whom movies are named—*Platinum Blonde, Red-Headed Woman, Bombshell*—in barely three years. She played chorus girls and cheating fiancées and seductresses and gangsters' molls and feckless wives and women with sordid pasts and women who carried on with married men. And she lived a life to match: Just before wedding Rosson, she made headlines for being seen quite chummily in the company of Max Baer, the heavyweight boxing title contender and a married man. Such was her reputation, on-screen and off-, that when she met the English countess Margot Asquith at a dinner party and kept pronouncing her new acquaintance's name with a final *t* sound—"MarGOT"—the older woman felt entitled to reply, "No, Jean, the 'T' is silent, like in Harlow."

For all the sensational roles Harlow played in movies (and not always very well, at least not at the outset—"I was not born an actress," she admitted), her real life was, arguably, just as dramatic. When she first set foot in Chateau Marmont, she was still being whispered about in connection with the death of her *second* husband, MGM production executive Paul Bern, who died mysteriously of a gunshot wound in their Beverly Hills home just a year prior, a mere two months into their marriage. Dark rumors about Bern—sexual dysfunction, adultery, perversity, even a murder-suicide pact involving another woman—swirled around Hollywood. Near his body, police had discovered a note to his wife, apparently in his hand, alluding to something that had occurred "last night [and was] only a comedy," occasioning yet more wild speculation.

But the unvarnished truth would never be known, because MGM executives and fixers were at Bern's house for several hours before the police arrived, staging the death scene so as to put their young star in the best possible light. Creating a domesticated public image of Harlow had been the principal reason MGM encouraged her to marry Bern, a confirmed bachelor more than twenty years her senior. And so, after an appropriate period of widowhood had passed, with Harlow wandering a little too close to the flame of bad publicity with Baer, MGM brass steered her toward Rosson, her frequent cinematographer who, like Bern, had never before wed. If the accounts of the Hollywood gossip press held any truth, they were deeply in love. "I know it's trite," the third-time bride said, "but I want to go on record that ours is one Hollywood marriage that will last!"

�֍

Harlow was born Harlean Harlow Carpenter in 1911 and was first married in 1927, at age sixteen, to Chuck McGrew, a son of Illinois society just twenty years old himself. The couple moved to Beverly Hills, living on the groom's inheritance, and Mother Jean followed, marking her second trip to Hollywood, which she had visited a few years earlier in hopes, quickly dashed, of breaking into movies. On this occasion, though, she would play the role of live-in mother-in-law and play it to the hilt, moving herself and her own new husband in with the young couple, leeching off McGrew's fortune, drinking heavily, shopping incessantly, insinuating herself into all of her daughter and son-in-law's decisions, and generally behaving as if she were the owner of the house. It would be no wonder when Harlow and McGrew split barely two years after they wed.

By then, Harlow had transformed from society wife to movie star. The story was that she had given a ride to an actress friend who was working at 20th Century Fox, and a casting director noticed her sitting in her car. Still a teen, she was a great natural beauty, with sun-bleached hair, a Kewpie doll pout, a bold, inviting gaze, a curvy figure, and an air of worldliness beyond her age. The fellow asked if she wanted to submit to an audition, and she brushed him off but took his card. A few days later, goaded by her actress friend, who suggested that she lacked the moxie to try out for the movies, she drove to central casting and enrolled under a stage name she invented on the spot—Jean Harlow. She soon found herself getting steady work, first as an unbilled extra, then in small feature parts, and then, starting in 1928, as a contract player at Hal Roach Studios, where she was immediately cast in feature roles in a couple of Laurel and Hardy films. The following year she left Roach, claiming that her acting work was wrecking her marriage, but she never completely quit the movies.

She was "discovered" again, almost immediately, this time by someone who knew just what to do with a girl with her looks: Howard Hughes. Four years into his Hollywood career, Hughes was in production on *Hell's Angels,* a silent epic about aerial warfare, when sound was introduced into movies and turned the business upside down. Hughes had to reshoot his not-yet-finished picture with spoken dialogue, and he had to replace leading lady Greta Nissen, whose thick Norwegian accent was unacceptable. One of the actors in Hughes's cast caught sight of Harlow in a talkie and commended her to his boss. Hughes met her, put her under contract, and cast her as the lead in *Hell's Angels,* calculating that the combination of aeronautic thrills and Harlow's sex appeal would mean big box-office returns.

It did. Hughes cast Harlow in a few more pictures, pushing her into sensual roles in which her finite acting skills weren't a liability, and she became such a draw that when he wasn't using her himself, he could lease her out to other studios for fees far beyond what he was paying her in salary. At around this time, Paul Bern noticed Harlow and suggested to his colleagues at MGM that they could use a star with her qualities. When the more prudish voices among his colleagues groused that her image would besmirch the studio's wholesome name, he promised to keep her reputation clean. They accepted both his recommendation and his word, and they hired her away from Hughes.

At MGM, Harlow became one of the top attractions of her time, and in a series of films with Gable she became one of the movies' greatest sex symbols. She might not have been an actress-actress, but she could light the screen on fire. MGM had gotten hold of a force of nature, which left them pleased with their business acumen but anxious, especially after Bern's death and the Max Baer affair, about the sorts of problems Harlow might present them with next. Hence the marriage to Rosson, seen by all as a reliable and stabilizing force.

❈

The Rossons' marriage had been sprung on the world (and, perhaps, on the principals) suddenly—a quickie elopement by airplane to Yuma, Arizona—and plans for the new couple's married life were improvised. It became readily apparent that living under the same roof as the overweening Mother Jean was no option, and so the Rossons sought sanctuary at Chateau Marmont, still largely undiscovered by Hollywood.

Harlow sniffed at the place at first, refusing even to go inside and inspect the suite that Rosson had chosen for them. But after another uncomfortable day in the company of her mother and stepfather, the actress agreed to move into the Chateau—provided that the apartment that Rosson had put on retainer, at $250 a month,* undergo extensive remodeling. The unit that Harlow and Rosson would move into was actually two suites connected by an interior corridor, and the bedroom most suited to serve as the master was equipped with twin beds. That was quickly rectified, and a layer of "Harlow white" was laid on top of the suites' low-key blue-and-beige décor. "She was like a little white rose," recalled a hotel employee. "Her apartment was all white. The carpets, the draperies, the furniture. Even the fireplace." It was a quick makeover: A week or so after their first visit, the Rossons moved in.

It was to be a working honeymoon for Rosson, who had just begun shooting a new film, meaning he had to be at the studio in Culver City early every morning and wouldn't return to the Chateau until dinnertime. Harlow was between pictures, doing publicity for *Bombshell,* the film that she and Rosson had most recently made together, so she was on hand to supervise the work on the apartment. Moreover, because she was in a tussle with the studio over a new contract, she was content to linger over her personal business—her beauty regimen, her interior decorating, even some cooking and reading—while her representatives dickered with Louis Mayer.

But when Rosson came home, it wasn't to a domestic Eden. Moving away from Mother Jean didn't mean escaping her altogether; she and her husband were constant presences at the Chateau, showing up to boss the workers, oversee Harlow's diet, and, as in Bel Air, comport themselves as if they—and not Rosson—were paying the bills. On top of that, a steady stream of friends, reporters, photographers, manicurists, hairdressers, masseuses, and businesspeople came and went throughout Harlow's idle days. The newlyweds might as well have been living in an aquar-

---

* Approximately $4,700 in 2019.

ium. Everything the star did was big, excessive, and, with some sanitizing, reported for public consumption.

Well, *almost* everything. There were other visitors, ones who appeared only at night and whose names were never in the fan magazines. Because of the way the Rossons' two suites had been connected into one large apartment, the master bedroom had a dedicated entrance, and hotel staff began to note that Harlow received visitors—*male* visitors—at *that* door at odd hours, invariably when Rosson wasn't on-site. Additionally, the staff had noticed that Harlow's improvements included a security chain on the door connecting the two suites—one intended to keep the door locked from the master bedroom side. And then there was the damning evidence discovered by housekeepers almost from the start of the Rossons' residency: Maids would make the big bed in the master bedroom every day, but they also had to make the Murphy bed in the living room on the *other* side of the unit. And *that* bed, ostensibly for guests, was the only one that would need making on the nights when Rosson slept at the Marmont alone and, as he explained to switchboard operators trying to put calls through to her, Harlow was with Mother Jean in Bel Air.

The Rossons' marital merry-go-round continued thus for several weeks, the couple rarely in residence in their suite at the same time and comporting themselves more in the manner of colleagues than newlyweds when they *were* seen together. Mother Jean continued to insinuate herself into their lives, finding an ally in, of all people, Ann Little, the Chateau's general manager and, like Mother Jean, a practitioner of Christian Science.

This latter alliance would be tested in October, when the Rossons went out to watch a football game, only to return to the hotel before long with Harlow in very delicate shape. Rosson suggested that his wife had enjoyed herself overly during their outing, but her extremely weak state suggested something more than an excess of drink. Harlow lingered in a feverish delirium through the night, Rosson increasingly worried at her condition. In the morning he made up his mind to call for a doctor, even though he knew that doing so would incense his mother-in-law, whose belief in Christian Science demanded that she forsake medical science in favor of faith-based healing. Rosson phoned Mother Jean to tell her of his plans, and he followed that with a call to Louis B. Mayer, who said he would send a doctor of his own straightaway. The hotel switchboard operator, instructed by Ann Little to listen in on Rosson's calls and inform her if a physician was summoned, heard what was afoot and ratted Rosson and Mayer out to her boss. But before Little could intercede, a doctor managed to make his way to Harlow's bedside, where he diagnosed her with acute appendicitis, sending for an ambulance to take her to Good Samaritan Hospital and the rescue of surgeons.

The episode saved Harlow's life, but it would be at the expense of her marriage. Upon release from the hospital, she returned not to her husband and their suite at Chateau Marmont but to Bel Air and Mother Jean. She didn't come back to the Chateau until New Year's Eve, when she reappeared, in something less than a celebratory mood, beside Rosson. A few more days passed before Rosson, carrying a suitcase, stopped by the front desk to let them know that he could be reached at the studio. Word of his absence from his wife's side made its way into newspapers, the first time that the name of Chateau Marmont would appear alongside the name of a movie star in print.

In the coming weeks, Harlow's mood lifted. Absent the excess baggage of her studio-appointed husband, she was free to entertain guests, and one in particular: Clark Gable. On-screen, Gable and Harlow were absolute dynamite: the hunkiest man alive and the movies' reigning sexpot, connected by a chemistry that you could practically sink your hands into from your movie-house seat. In total they would make six films together, including the hit potboilers *Red Dust, Hold Your Man,* and *China Seas.* He played gangsters, sea captains, plantation owners; she was a prostitute, a B-girl, a moll. He was muscular and rough-hewn and dashing and macho; she was brassy and sensual and liberated and nubile. When their characters met, when they had romantic scenes together, even when they ran screwball comedy lines off each other, they were mesmerizing, arousing, *hot*. There was often another woman in the story with whom Gable's characters had a more traditionally noble-hearted connection, played by the likes of Mary Astor, Rosalind Russell, or Myrna Loy. But he and Harlow projected top-shelf, unashamed sex, and they did so at a time when movies, still not censored or rated for content, were as racy and frank as they would be for decades.

He was about thirty and she was about twenty, and the world was theirs to beckon, and what with both of them seemingly always either marrying or divorcing, it was almost inevitable that they would become lovers—more so that they would take few pains to hide it. Technically, they were both married (he to the second of an eventual five wives), but only technically. Gable was a regular at the Chateau throughout January, arriving in the evening, sometimes after a night out with Harlow, sometimes on his own, and then leaving for the studio in the morning. Rosson never came around.

At the end of January, Harlow and Rosson formally vacated Chateau Marmont, she returning home to Bel Air, he to a room at the Hollywood Athletic Club, about two miles east on Sunset. Accounts in the gossip press reported that the flame between them had burned too brightly to last; by May, they were officially divorced.

Rosson would go on to marry again and divorce again—this time after nine years, not nine months—and to enjoy a distinguished career as a cinematographer, shooting such films as *Singin' in the Rain, Duel in the Sun, El Dorado*, and *On the Town*, and dying in 1988 at age ninety-three.

Harlow would continue to be a major star and enjoy a long romance with William Powell, to whom she was engaged, at least according to the press, for two years without marrying.

In truth, there wouldn't be time for it. In June 1937, barely twenty-six years old, after a lifetime of fighting the likes of scarlet fever, appendicitis, septicemia, and various flus and infections, often without the aid of medical intervention, in accord with Mother Jean's religious beliefs, Harlow died of kidney failure in the same hospital where Rosson had sent her, against her mother's wishes, not four years prior. She was buried in the Great Mausoleum of Forest Lawn Memorial Park under a tombstone that read "Our Baby."

4.

Jean Harlow wasn't the only Hollywood notable who found sanctuary at Chateau Marmont in those early days. Movie people slowly discovered the place in a way that might best be described as subterranean, or else through the back door.

Everyone at the studios knew of the area's more luxurious and fabled hotels—the Beverly Hills, the Beverly Wilshire, the Ambassador—and they would steer the out-of-towners whom they wished to impress or pamper toward them. The Chateau, on the other hand, was where they went when they weren't putting on airs—or hoping to be seen in the act of whatever it was they were getting up to.

The difference was right there upon first impression. Arriving at the Beverly Hills Hotel, you rode up the curved drive, between the palm trees and flower beds, to a grand porte cochere where you were met by a valet or bellman and led through an ornate lobby. Pulling in to the Ambassador brought you along massive lawns and gardens, and the Beverly Wilshire's front door was right out on the street, at the intersection of Wilshire Boulevard and Rodeo Drive, as near as you could get in Beverly Hills to the feeling of pulling up to a luxury hotel in New York, London, or Paris.

Chateau Marmont was something else entirely. The entry was off a side street and belowground, in a garage where you were welcome to park your own car—if you dared risk the paint job to the threading-the-needle path you needed to navigate between the structural pillars. The lobby was smaller than many of the suites—an open space with a tiny front desk and a handsome but not exactly homey sitting area that didn't invite much loitering. The Chateau was more intimate in scale than the area's other hotels, and its lack of a public gathering space like a pool or restaurant or bar made it feel discreet and clubby. Perhaps this was why it became popular with visitors who preferred to feel that they were in an apartment building rather than a semipublic resort. These included Europeans fleeing the tensing political and cultural atmosphere at home and New Yorkers who didn't care for the sybaritic atmosphere of the more posh hotels, which they deemed a little too "Hollywood," or for the raucous carrying-on at the Garden of Allah, which seemed a little too Fraternity Row.

Harlow aside, though, the movie people who lived at the Chateau for any length of time in the thirties were either not the sort whom the gossip press would want to print news of or folks who were actively trying *not* to be noticed. Among them was Lloyd Bacon, who had begun in movies in front of the camera in 1915 and, when acting didn't pan out for him, had become a director, starting in silent movies with short comedies and action pictures and gradually working his way up to features starring Al Jolson (*The Singing Fool, Wonder Bar*) and John Barrymore (*Moby Dick*), as well as the immortal musicals *42nd Street* and *Footlight Parade*.

Bacon would eventually accrue 125 directorial credits, but his prolificacy *away* from the back lot was perhaps even more notable. Between 1921 and 1941, he was wed no fewer than four times, and he enjoyed himself thoroughly when between marriages. In 1935, his separation and divorce from his second wife, Rubey, played out sensationally in the papers—he said that she had carried on a love affair in Los Angeles and San Francisco and, further, was guilty of mental cruelty in the form of "call[ing] him harsh names . . . [being] rude to his guests . . . depriv[ing] him of peace and quiet . . . and hamper[ing] his directorial career." She claimed he deprived her of basic household expenses and threatened to "break every bone in [her] body" and, on another occasion, "break her into so many pieces that they would have to carry her out of the house in a sheet." The two sparred over possession of their seventeen-room Van Nuys estate—where, among other amenities, Bacon kept an elaborate model train set—and Bacon moved into Chateau Marmont while he tried to unseat her from their connubial home.

Ensconced in the hotel's biggest penthouse, Bacon didn't have toy trains, but he did throw an open house nearly every weekend that became more and more sensational with each iteration. The setting and amenities were ideal: a hosted bar, expansive views, lots of famous and attractive faces, and, thanks to the eccentric architecture, a number of little nooks for extra privacy should any of his guests require it. The parties began as a way for Bacon and his fellow Warner Bros. employees to blow off some steam together, but word of the revelries soon spread around town and up and down the corridors of the Chateau, and they became a bona fide scene, only coming to an end in 1938, when Bacon finally pried his by-then ex-wife out of their mansion and was able to move back in with his trains.

Less sensational was the longtime residency of cinematographer Gregg Toland, one of the great innovators in his field, the man who helped create the photorealistic "deep focus" filming technique that came to dominate movies and who would eventually be credited for the look of such classics as *Stagecoach, Dead End, The Grapes of Wrath, The Best Years of Our Lives, Citizen Kane,* and the 1939 version of *Wuthering Heights,* for which he won his only Oscar (he died of a heart attack in 1948 at age forty-four). Throughout their residency of several years in the midthirties, Toland and his first wife, Helen Barclay, frequently hosted dinner parties at their home at Chateau Marmont, quiet affairs that never got more raucous than the occasional need to refill the punch bowl and thus, ironically, more apt to be noted in gossip columns than Bacon's comparatively orgiastic wingdings.

The ability to keep the lid on wild goings-on at the Chateau was quickly deemed part of the hotel's allure for the movie
crowd. The Garden of Allah and the Beverly Hills Hotel had
become must-see sights for tourists to Hollywood, and between
the professional gossipmongers and the amateur rubberneckers
their public spaces could feel exposed and compromised. But the
Chateau, which offered few places for the public or the press to lie
in ambush or ogle celebrities, was, almost accidentally, the perfect blind. Just a few years into its life as a hotel, the Chateau was
being spoken of knowingly by the film world as a place where
the most outré behaviors could go unnoted by outsiders. According to one famed endorsement, "If you want to be seen, go to the
Beverly Hills Hotel; if you *don't* want to be seen, go to Chateau
Marmont."

That—as well as cost—was no doubt why Harry Cohn, the
notorious penny-pinching boss of Columbia Pictures, kept a suite
on retainer at the hotel. Although he was an infamous libertine
in his own right, the apartment wasn't for his use but for that of
his stars. Other studios were known to rent out whole apartment
buildings around town so that their famous employees could
indulge in whatever behavior they wished without turning up
in gossip pages. For the relatively small Columbia, a single set
of rooms at the Chateau would have to do: suite 54, to be precise.

That was where, in the late thirties, two of Cohn's promising
discoveries, Gwyllyn Samuel Newton Ford and William Frank-
lin Beedle Jr., both still in their early twenties, would be introduced to the ways of Hollywood. Each would eventually settle
down with a wife and kids and a career and even a new, marquee-
friendly name—Glenn Ford and William Holden, respectively.
But first they'd sow some wild oats, on Harry Cohn's dime, at the
Chateau.

"Harry really worried about Bill and me," Ford remembered
decades later. "We were constantly getting into trouble. . . . One
day he sent for us and said, 'If you *must* get into trouble, go to the

Marmont.' He made it clear that he had rented the small pent-house there just for us, to protect us. . . . He told us we could stay as long as we were under contract."

The two moved into the suite and immediately made the most of this swell setup, entertaining female companions and playing host to their acting chums and even some of their idols, who would now and again run into marital or logistical problems of their own and require a safe harbor. "It was so very private," Ford said. "You would drive into the garage, get in the elevator, go upstairs, and nobody would see you. People would come and go, in and out, and no questions were asked." David Niven came around a fair bit, because he was then sharing a place with Errol Flynn that had only one bedroom and was often left in the lurch while Flynn entertained guests. According to Ford, Niven was incredulous that two up-and-comers should find themselves the beneficiaries of such a plush living situation, and he frequently rang them up asking if the suite was available for him to do some entertaining of his own. At other times, he'd drop in to have a drink, prepare a meal, or simply hang out with his chums. John Barrymore, his marriage to wife number four, Elaine Barrie, coming to an end, learned about the open-door policy of the suite and would show up at odd hours, strip down to socks and bathrobe, and sit out on the terrace with what he called his "only two friends in this goddamn town . . . Haig and Haig." And Humphrey Bogart, seemingly always engaged in a scrap with his third wife, Mayo Methot, would often come down from his house on Horn Avenue, about a mile west on the Sunset Strip, and drink and chat with the boys until things cooled off back home.

Bogart had another reason for visiting, though. In 1938, soon after he married Methot, he moved his widowed mother, Maud Humphrey Bogart, from Manhattan to live near him in a suite at the Chateau. In her day, Maud Humphrey, as she was known, was a formidable and striking figure: tall, pretty, well dressed, a celebrated artist, an outspoken suffragette, the mistress of a four-story town house on the Upper West Side and a four-acre estate in the Finger Lakes region of upstate New York. Her husband, Belmont DeForest Bogart, was a successful surgeon, and she herself was an artist widely known for her commercial illustrations, especially those of angelic children in advertisements and magazines. Her most famous work was the image of a cherub-cheeked infant that for years graced the label on jars of Mellin's baby food and that was based, at least partly, on her own son. Such was her renown that in 1895 she earned an income of $50,000—nearly $1.4 million in 2019 terms.

When she moved into Chateau Marmont, though, her career was well behind her. In her early seventies, she still put on imperious airs, but she could be dotty and erratic, acting aloof at social functions and falling into a terrified heap if a flying insect, even a butterfly, flitted anywhere near her. She kept a small, tidy art studio in her Marmont suite, drawing and painting for the pleasure of it. Almost daily, she would wander Sunset Boulevard, perfectly attired, approaching passersby to tell them, "I'm Humphrey Bogart's mother, you know." She loved going into Schwab's, where she chatted with the clerks in her regal manner. "She was Lady Maud with a vengeance," her son recalled. "She made little purchases and then strolled grandly home again." In the summer of 1940, she took ill, but she told no one about her discomfort until, in November, she collapsed in her suite and was found struggling and in agony by a hotel maid. Rushed to a hospital, she was almost immediately diagnosed with cancer and fell into a coma; she passed away on November 22 without regaining consciousness. "She died as she had lived," her son said. "With guts."

�֍

That Bogart should have chosen Chateau Marmont for his mother and not, say, the Garden of Allah, where he often lived while between homes or wives, spoke to the sort of reputation the place had accrued in the years that Albert Smith had operated it

as a hotel: genteel, staid, quiet, courtly, just as Lady Maud would
have selected for herself. These qualities were surely amplified
by the sound of British accents in the lobby and corridors of the
hotel. From very early on, performers from the U.K. were fond of
the place. "They were such nice people, so refined and elegant,"
Ann Little recalled. "Everyone was a little envious of the way
they spoke." Stan Laurel, born Arthur Stanley Jefferson in Lan-
cashire, lived there between marriages in the thirties and was
known to keep to himself save for opening the door to his suite
to accept orders of liquor from delivery boys or, occasionally, to
wander into one of Lloyd Bacon's open houses to help himself
to the director's booze. The elegant character actor Alan Napier
(who would gain his greatest fame decades later as the butler
Alfred on TV's *Batman*) frequented the hotel regularly when he
was filming in Hollywood, as did the actress/singer/comedian
Gracie Fields and John Houseman, the British actor/producer
who hired Orson Welles for his first paid job as a stage director in New York and would eventually introduce his flamboyant young discovery to the hotel. And when Laurence Olivier
came to Hollywood in 1933 for a visit that resulted in no film
or stage appearances, he had a note waiting for him at the front
desk of the Chateau indicating that the British old boy network
had anticipated his arrival. "There will be nets tomorrow at 9
a.m.," it read. "I trust I shall see you there." The note was signed
by C. Aubrey Smith, the dean of the British colony in Hollywood
and the founder of the Hollywood Cricket Club, the local home
of the sport for which Olivier was being summoned for a practice
session. Being that Olivier was English, Smith apparently took
it for granted that he was (1) a cricketer and (2) likely staying at
the Chateau.

Continental Europeans were also finding their way to the
corner of Sunset and Marmont, some on their own, some under
the guiding hand of their American employers. Among the latter was a gorgeous and sharply intelligent young woman from
Austria named Hedwig Eva Maria Kiesler, who had gained a

reputation by appearing nude in an arty film shot in Prague in 1933. Known as "the *Ecstasy* girl," after the title of the scandalous movie, she was living in Paris in 1937, divorced, and looking for work, when she was introduced to Louis B. Mayer, who was overcome by her beauty and immediately offered her a job in Hollywood—under the condition that she change her name. And so, when she arrived at Chateau Marmont, where she would spend her first few nights in town before moving out to share a home with the actress Ilona Massey, she signed herself in at the front desk under her newly contrived moniker, which she promptly misspelled. "Hedy Lamar," she wrote, forgetting that Mayer had added a second *r* to her new surname to give it an exotic air.

⁜

Hedy Lamarr had but a brief dalliance with the Chateau. But another Viennese expatriate would dance with the hotel several times in those first years of its operation, and some of his tales of what he did there would have the virtue of *almost* being true.

The thing about Billy Wilder was that he told stories. Some of them he would craft into scripts and direct in one of the greatest résumés the cinema ever produced: *The Apartment, Sunset Boulevard, Some Like It Hot, The Lost Weekend, Double Indemnity, The Seven Year Itch, Stalag 17,* and *Sabrina,* among many others. But he probably told fibs as a child, he admitted to being "creative" with details when he was a newspaperman, and he was writing flat-out made-up tales for the movies as early as his early twenties. Such was the rush of stories out of him that he was credited with twenty-one screenplays in his first five years working in movies—nine of them in 1932 alone.

So it's not surprising that his account of his time at Chateau Marmont is . . . unverifiable. In large part that's because Wilder told it so many different ways over the years, depending, probably, on which way he thought made for a better story.

Some aspects of it are indisputable. By the time he was twenty-three, Wilder was a successful screenwriter in Berlin, enjoying a posh apartment, a handsome car, a collection of Impressionist art, and the company of glamorous women. In 1933, he read the future in the rise of Adolf Hitler—as a Jew from the Austro-Hungarian Empire, Wilder saw that both of those details in his biography would count against him—and he fled to Paris. There, he very quickly resumed his writing career, and within a year he climbed into the director's chair. But even before his debut in that capacity, 1934's *Mauvaise graine,* had its premiere, he fled once again, this time to Hollywood, where his ambitions to reach the top of the movie world would have the best chance of being realized.

Wilder came to the United States on a six-month visa, meaning he had to exit and then reapply for admission not long after he arrived. So even though he had been making small inroads into American movies, he was forced to leave the country, this time to Mexico, before he could return, for good, in August 1934. When he did, he had no place to stay, and a friend recommended a newish hotel where you could cook your own meals and live cheap: Chateau Marmont.

And this was where the stories start to become "Wildered"— that is to say, told differently at different times, with different chronologies, different casts of characters, and different punch lines, as if the teller were working it all out in his head for maximum entertainment value (which, given Wilder's genius and productivity as a screenwriter, might very well have been what was going on).

The best surmise would be this: Between 1934 and 1937, Wilder stayed at Chateau Marmont three times. On the first visit, in the summer and early autumn of 1934, he was put up in the smallest, least expensive room in the hotel: a windowless cubicle, furnished with a desk and chair and Murphy bed and equipped with an electric hot plate on which he could cook. He didn't look down on this lodging; he embraced it. Instead of a view, Wilder installed some of the paintings he managed to bring with him from Europe.* He dined mainly on coffee and canned soup, which meant his tiny tabletop burner was kitchen enough for him. Crucially, he had what he *really* needed—a place to write, which he did like a demon, around the clock. "He stayed in his room and worked till all hours of the night," Ann Little remembered years later. "I can't remember a time when I didn't see a light coming from beneath his door as I would make my evening rounds."

Wilder was a workhorse, no doubt, but he did enjoy a social life. He was still fond of the ladies. He became friendly with other European expats who were struggling to remake their film careers in Hollywood. He spent time idling at Schwab's, practicing his English by reading magazines and chatting with other hopefuls. And he visited the beach at Santa Monica, often by himself, just to listen to voices, ogle swimmers, and breathe the fresh air.

For a while he even had a roommate at the Chateau, or at least he *said* he did: Peter Lorre, the great actor whom Wilder knew from Berlin and Paris and who had also fled to America with hopes of safety and success. If it happened at all, it didn't last long. Wilder claimed that he quickly discovered that Lorre was a drug addict, which was true and might explain the brevity of their cohabitation. But Lorre was a married man when he came to America, and he arrived with his wife *and* a job at a movie studio, neither of which Wilder had and both of which make the idea of the Lorres' moving in with Wilder seem unlikely. (Lorre and Wilder *had* lived at the same hotel during their time in Paris as they passed from Germany to the United States, though, and it's entirely possible that Wilder confused one tiny rented room, and one episode of debauchery, for another.)

By late 1934, Wilder was finding an intermittent market for

---

* Wilder would come to own one of Hollywood's most valuable art collections, including works by Picasso, Miró, Giacometti, and Balthus; a 1989 auction of only *some* of his treasures fetched $32.6 million—nearly $64 million in 2019 terms.

his story ideas, for reworkings of his German and French screen-plays, and for his services as a script doctor. He was getting some-where, in short, becoming a known commodity. At that time, he put his belongings in the hotel basement and left on a quick trip back home, designed in part to see if he could get his widowed mother, then living in Vienna, to leave an increasingly unsettled Europe and live in the sun in California. She refused, and he returned to Hollywood—and to an increasing demand for his writing. He headed straight to Chateau Marmont, where his sec-ond stay would produce even more stories than his first—some of them probably even true.

When Wilder presented himself at the front desk this time, looking forward to moving back into his little bachelor's cell, he was met with disappointing, even shocking news: Not only was his old room not available, but there was *no* room for him. "I forgot to notify Miss Little," he confessed later. "The hotel was absolutely booked up." Wilder was exhausted from travel, haunted by the specter of increasing Nazi influence over his homeland, worried for his mother.* All he wanted was a can of soup and his small room with its familiar Murphy bed, and here was Ann Little in front of him telling him that he couldn't have even that tiny bit of succor.

At first he was furious, reminding the hotel manager that he had announced upon his departure in November that he would return. She remembered that, she explained, but there was a cru-cial omission in his statement: "You didn't say *when*."

She could see what a blow this news was, and she was rack-ing her brain to determine if there was anything she could do for

---

* He would never see her again, and when he returned to Europe after World War II, he was unable to find any definitive proof of her fate. It was virtually certain that she was rounded up with other Viennese Jews, sent to a concentration camp, and exterminated. But he never learned the truth of it, and that mystery only added to his sense of guilt and regret over having failed to convince her to leave Europe with him.

him, when he made a startling declaration: "I would rather sleep in a bathroom than in another hotel!"

With that, a light went off in Little's head. Off the main lobby, there was a women's restroom, and in the corridor leading to that facility there was a bit of an antechamber, little more than a closet. It wasn't a room, per se, but it *did* have a door, and if Wilder would promise to keep it locked so that no one would accidentally walk into it while searching for the bathroom . . .

He took it.

And thus, during Christmas 1934, Billy Wilder lived next to—or, as he sometimes told it, *inside*—the ladies' room in the lobby of Chateau Marmont.

The arrangement only lasted for a couple of days; soon enough, a room that Wilder could afford was vacant, and he moved into more suitable accommodations, resuming what would eventually become one of Hollywood's greatest writing and directing careers. But no matter the glory that ensued—including three Oscars for screenwriting (out of twelve nominations), two for directing (out of eight nominations), and two for Best Picture (*The Lost Weekend* and *The Apartment*) out of four nominations—Wilder would dine out for the rest of his life on tales of the time he lived in a bathroom at Chateau Marmont.

"It was a small room," he would explain, "but it had six toilets." Or he would talk about women wandering into his tiny lodgings and starting to undress before they realized their mistake. Or he'd say that his sleep was interrupted every night by the constant flushing. Sometimes he would get morose: "I could not sleep . . . when women were coming in to pee and looking at me funny, when I was worried about the knowledge that my mother was in danger. . . . I wasn't sure if I fitted in around here in Hollywood. I had the feeling I was not in the right country and I didn't know if there was a right country for me. Right here was the low point of my life." The anxiety and depression were no doubt real, but the setup was all malarkey—or at the very least it contained mere nuggets of truth exaggerated for comic effect. He never tired of the telling.

Wilder left the Chateau in early 1935 and found a proper place to live. He also found time for love: In late 1936, he eloped in Arizona with the artist Judith Coppicus, a tall, pretty New Yorker with connections to European painters and American show business. For a while, when the marriage, which would last a decade, was new, the couple lived in a suite at Chateau Marmont, this time with a view, but they left after a few weeks, moving in with her mother not far away in West Hollywood.

And that was the end of Wilder's connection to the hotel—in real life, that is. In his art, Chateau Marmont would still find resonance. In his 1944 film noir, *Double Indemnity*, the first movie for which he'd be nominated for Oscars as writer and director, the protagonist, a lust-mad insurance salesman played by Fred MacMurray, lives in a bachelor apartment, complete with cramped underground garage and drugstore on the corner that serves meals, designed along the lines of Wilder's first lodgings at the Chateau. Six years later, Wilder created a dark, sardonic tale about a failing Hollywood writer who hangs around Schwab's and dodges creditors until the day he accidentally falls in with a silent screen star who uses him for his body and his craft until . . . well, it *is* told from the point of view of a corpse. That film, *Sunset Boulevard*, was, Wilder often said, based on an idea that originally came to him when he was living at Chateau Marmont, where the ghosts of Hollywood's past seemed as real to him as the hopes and dreams of its present day.

5.

Billy Wilder wasn't the only genius hanging around the corner of Sunset and Marmont at the time. On July 4, 1940, just outside the front door of the Chateau, one of Hollywood's most gifted writers and directors opened a place the likes of which the area—indeed, the world—had never seen.

Preston Sturges was a bona fide one and only. An inventor, entrepreneur, yachtsman, playwright, and boulevardier, the son of cosmetics magnate Mary Desti and sometime husband to daughters of East Coast society, he had come to Hollywood on the strength of his almost accidental success on Broadway and made a significant enough name as a screenwriter as to be allowed the very rare privilege of ascending to the director's chair, from which, starting in mid-1940, he delivered *four* critical and commercial successes in less than eighteen months: *The Great McGinty, Christmas in July, The Lady Eve,* and *Sullivan's Travels.*

Rolling in money and convinced that such would always be the case, he had opened, four years prior, a French restaurant named Snyder's near the Beverly Hills end of the Strip. Snyder's foundered, but it had ignited in Sturges a dream of building a nightspot in Hollywood that would rival the ones he favored in New York and Paris. And so he acquired a worn-down bungalow a few steps to the west of the Chateau and set about creating a fantasia. It was a dilapidated Spanish-style building serving, when Sturges bought it, as a cash-on-the-barrelhead wedding chapel. Rather than raze the place and start from scratch, the mechanically inclined Sturges built a larger edifice *beneath* it, lifting the tiny cottage up onto the roof. The result was a boxy, rectangular two-story building with a small hacienda house on top of one side of it, like a crown worn cockeyed. Sturges named it the Players, after the famed actors club in New York, and it would consume his time, money, and dream life for a solid dozen years.

When the Players opened, the ground floor was a drive-in family-style restaurant, the second floor was a more formal dining room with live entertainment, and the top floor, the former bungalow, was a fine dining establishment (jacket and tie required, gentlemen) serving classic French cuisine. But all of that was provisional. For one thing, Sturges felt entitled to shut the place down on a moment's notice if he wanted to turn the

evening into a private party; the top floor in particular would
sometimes be accessible *only* to the owner's chums, particularly
Howard Hughes, Sturges's fellow gearhead and eccentric and
eventual business partner, who used to bring dates there, especially when he was encamped at Chateau Marmont, and who
insisted that no other patrons use the dining room when he did.

Then there was Sturges's inveterate tinkering. He put a bar-
bershop in a small mezzanine level that his oddball architecture
had created. He built a revolving bandstand so that two ensem-
bles could be seated at the same time and spun back and forth,
with no break between acts. He built false walls so as to alter the
size of rooms as the need arose. He concocted a gizmo that lifted
the tables in the booths so it would be easier for diners to slip in
and out of them. He kept adding onto the structure, eventually
clearing space for a larger dance floor and a cocktail bar, known
as Club Sinister for its dim lighting. After a while, he turned
the top level into a dinner theater, mounting productions of new
plays, including some of his own that were sketches for movies.
He even applied for a permit to build a helipad on the roof, in the
area not occupied by the bungalow, an audacity that L.A. County
officials wisely denied (to what would have been the grateful
relief of Chateau Marmont management and patrons if they'd
had the first clue about the bullet they'd dodged).

The Players was a hit with celebrities, and Chateau Marmont guests regularly dined there when they were looking for
something more refined than Schwab's BLTs and milk shakes.
There was plain American fare on the first and second floors—
steaks and chops and chicken and hamburgers. But the head chef
upstairs was French and specialized in the likes of bouillabaisse
and *tripe à la mode de Caen.* Perhaps not surprisingly, a number of
French cineastes were among the Players' most dedicated patrons:
René Clair, Max Ophüls, Marcel Pagnol, who called the restaurant "une idée poetique," and Jean Renoir, who pronounced the
place "the center of the Hollywood Resistance Movement."

Yet even though it was regularly busy and grossed upwards of

$300,000 in some years,* the Players hemorrhaged money. Sturges would let friends run large tabs and then forgive the debts in moments of emotional generosity, and he would be similarly flighty in turning away cash-paying customers if he didn't like the looks of them. He'd blithely begin a new round of renovation and construction in the midst of what ought to have been the restaurant's busy season. And he paid almost no attention to inventory control or other formal business matters; the Players was notably porous, with exits everywhere, which too many staff members took advantage of to make off brazenly with food and liquor stocks, especially during the rationing years of World War II.

It couldn't last. Though the Players was reliably filled with notable names, though it had a steady stream of customers from Chateau Marmont, the Garden of Allah, and Sunset Tower, though Sturges kept innovating so as to keep his customers intrigued and delighted, creditors kept after him for years, until, at decade's end, he finally saw the truth. "I am very much afraid The Players is past helping at this point," he told a reporter. "The bulk of its customers has formed the habit of going elsewhere, and nothing in the world is so difficult to change as a habit." Not long after, the place was sold for a sum that put only a modest dent in the debts it had accrued.

✻

When he'd bought Chateau Marmont for three-quarters of a million dollars in 1932, Albert Smith provoked skepticism and jeers. But his surmise that demand for quality short-term residential units in Los Angeles would rise turned out to be right. Starting with the 1932 Olympic Games, and carrying on through the decade, the population of the area grew steadily—half a million newcomers moved into the city in the thirties alone—and

---

* Approximately $4.4 million in 2019.

the area around the hotel continued to be developed and filled
in. His decision to turn Fred Horowitz's apartment house into
a hotel proved canny, with a steady stream of guests from the
entertainment world and the worlds of advertising, publishing,
and fashion finding the Chateau a perfect not-too-Hollywood
nest from which to do business with Hollywood studios.

In the winter of 1936–37, Smith increased his investment,
buying the parcel of land immediately to the east of the hotel,
where a series of two-story rental homes were strung together
in a line. He had some renovation and decoration work done on
these units and turned them into a unique feature of the hotel—
stand-alone dwellings, separated from the main building by a
lawn and a copse of trees, that included all the conveniences of
hotel living: maid service, valet parking, day-and-night switchboard operators, a front desk where packages or mail could be
accepted.

Now Marmont guests could opt for a layer of privacy beyond
that afforded by the unusually private setup of the hotel. They
could stay in isolated buildings on the hotel grounds; eventually,
the fencing around the enlarged property was reconfigured so
that guests staying in these stand-alone units could exit and enter
through a gateway on Monteel Road and needn't pass through
the main building at all.

There were other such accommodations nearby. The Garden
of Allah was comprised entirely of such "bungalows," but they
were actually multi-residential units more like garden apartments, and they were right on top of each other; guests famously
complained about the lack of soundproofing and the ability to hear
conversation—and more—from adjoining suites. Smith's inspiration was more likely the Beverly Hills Hotel, where twenty-odd
bungalows, many with multiple bedrooms and bathrooms, stood
on secluded acreage away from the main hotel. Those bungalows, which would become famous in Hollywood lore, were part
of a larger hotel that offered many of the amenities denied Chateau Marmont residents. But what Smith's new facilities lacked

in access to, say, a restaurant or twenty-four-hour dog-walking services, they made up for in atmosphere. Compared with the Chateau, the Beverly Hills Hotel was like a train station, with people bustling in and out every day. Smith's hotel was quieter, more out of the way, and his bungalows were like a den inside an already secret world.

In April 1937 the bungalows debuted in display ads in Los Angeles newspapers:

Chateau Marmont

Announces

CHATEAU MARMONT

BUNGALOWS

Charming secluded hillside homes, with the complete 24-hour hotel
service which has always been an outstanding feature of
Chateau Marmont . . . exquisitely decorated . . . quiet sunny
patios and gardens. Now open for inspection.

They were a hit. Unlike the penthouses, which management continued to advertise as available for rent, the bungalows were occupied regularly, their desirability as super-private units evident from the start. Smith could see the advantage of configuring the grounds to add additional bungalows, but he was increasingly reluctant to invest more resources in the hotel. The flow of traffic, the support of movie studios, the growth in population in the area, the success of Hollywood during the Depression—all of these factors should have made the Chateau a financial windfall. But in striking a balance between keeping the hotel full and keeping it profitable, he was continually landing on the wrong side. He was in fact *losing* money.

Part of it was still to do with the Chateau's low profile, with its being smaller than rival hotels, with its being relatively anonymous, even to locals, and, ironically, with its catering so specifically to long-term residents that it was often understood to be an apartment house rather than a hotel (the rare interviews that Ann Little granted almost always said that she operated an apartment building). Even though it stood right out in plain sight at the eastern end of Sunset Strip, it felt obscure and anonymous, and its bottom line suffered as a result. The novelties of the area continued to draw attention, customers, tourists. Chateau Marmont was, somehow, outside the flow of things—an awful predicament for the owner earnestly trying to make a go of it.

❊

In 1942, a decade into his ownership, Albert Smith, in his late sixties, began to tire of the effort of running a hotel. In the spring of that year, he put the Chateau on the market, and in July newspapers carried word that it had been sold to "an out-of-town buyer" for $350,000.* Not only was this less than half of what Smith had paid for the main building and the original parcel of land in 1931, but it included the expanded parcel to the east, the bungalows that sat on it, *and* a "fully improved estate" of twenty acres in Montecito, a suburb of Santa Barbara.

Smith had correctly predicted that the population of and tourism to Southern California would thrive after the 1932 Olympics. And he had successfully converted Fred Horowitz's luxury apartment house into an apartment hotel. What he hadn't figured on, apparently, was the sheer expense and aggravation of running such a business. Like Horowitz, he would walk away from the Chateau gratified by being proven right, but he would be financially wounded for all his faith and prescience. It would take a new owner with a harder eye for the bottom line to finally put the hotel on steady footing.

---

* About $5.29 million in 2019.

Part Three
AN IDENTITY EMERGES (1942-1963)

The Brettauer Bungalows, the fifties. *Maynard L. Parker, photographer. Courtesy of the Huntington Library, San Marino, California*

Albert Smith had the foresight to recognize that the growing community around Chateau Marmont would find more use for the building as a residential hotel than as an apartment house. And while he correctly predicted the rise of West Hollywood and the Sunset Strip at the foot of the place, he had neither the business acumen nor the physical stamina to make a long-term success of it.

The Chateau's next owner, on the other hand, had both. A mystery man from overseas, he approached the hotel as a garden that had been allowed to grow impractically wild, trimming away at some plants that had become ungainly and gradually adding crucial elements that filled out the design, function, and appeal of the whole. He wasn't necessarily an easy man, but he knew what he was doing.

And under his reign, throughout the years of war and the recovery and boom that followed, as the Sunset Strip darkened for fear of air raids and then lit up more brightly than it ever had with the vitality and spark of youth and even rebellion, Chateau Marmont blossomed with business and energy and a growing reputation as one of the centers of Hollywood's offscreen life. At the head of what was becoming one of the most famous stretches of road in the world, it was a reliable haven, open to all and, more important, safe, welcoming, and secure.

1.

The dreamer who built Chateau Marmont, Fred Horowitz, had a respected name in legal circles in Southern California.

The investor who turned it into a hotel, Albert Smith, had a name in the annals of film history that would one day be engraved on an honorary Oscar.

But the third man who owned the Chateau had a name so obscure that history never quite got it right. In previously published histories of the hotel, he has been referred to as "Dr. Edwin C. Brethauer." On websites devoted to the history of cinema, he is known as "Irving D. Berttauer." In various stories about real estate transactions published during the forties and fifties in newspapers in New York and Los Angeles, he was cited as "Dr. E. O. Brettauer."

That last one would be nearest the truth.

Erwin Oskar Brettauer, to cite his actual name, was born in 1884 in Frankfurt, Germany, the second child of Ludwig Carl Brettauer, scion of a family banking dynasty, and his wife, Clotilde, a Jew from Moravia. Erwin was raised in part in the Brettauer family seat, the Rhine valley town of Hohenems, then belonging to the Austro-Hungarian Empire, today the very tip of western Austria, near the borders with Switzerland, Germany, and Lichtenstein. Erwin attended university in Munich, studying chemistry and earning a doctorate in 1909 for his work on radioactive substances. He continued to pursue a career in science in Switzerland—he was acquainted with Albert Einstein—but he was eventually drawn into the family banking and finance business. By 1930, he was living on the Swiss side of Lake Lugano and working frequently in Berlin, where he became enmeshed in funding political causes (he was a staunch anti-Fascist), and worked to move the family banking interests to Zurich before Hitler's full consolidation of power. Splitting his time between Switzerland and Berlin, Brettauer married and had a son; the boy once expressed interest in joining the Hitler Youth and was threatened by his father with disinheritance. And in Germany, he made two important connections that would shape the future course of his life.

One was to Heinrich Brüning, chancellor of the Weimar Republic from 1930 to 1932; Brettauer supported Brüning with financial contributions to his political works and, after Hitler was elected, by letting him live in his home on Lake Lugano, where the former chancellor wrote his memoirs, oversaw the publication of an anti-Fascist newspaper (financed by Brettauer), and worked to organize resistance to the Nazis, all in the service of what he hoped would be a return to power for his own German Centre Party. Brüning made his way to the United States, then back to Germany, and finally back to America, and during all that time he and Brettauer sustained a correspondence and a financial relationship.

Brettauer's other important connection was in the movie business. In Berlin, he made the acquaintance of Seymour Nebenzahl, son of the producer Heinrich Nebenzahl. The younger Nebenzahl was a prolific producer himself, and his Nero-Film production company worked with such masters as Fritz Lang, G. W. Pabst, and Robert Siodmak on such classics of world cinema as *M, Pandora's Box, The 3 Penny Opera,* and *The Testament of Dr. Mabuse.* Brettauer provided financing for many of these Nero-Film productions, but Nero-Film found itself shut down by Joseph Goebbels, who objected to the clearly anti-Fascist message of *The Testament of Dr. Mabuse,* forcing the younger Nebenzahl, who had been born in New York, to use his American passport to flee Germany for France and, ultimately, America.

Brettauer was himself an occasional visitor to the United States in the thirties, when he started to buy real estate in New

York City, specializing in hotels and apartment houses. By 1941, he was widowed—his wife had committed suicide—and he had relocated permanently to New York. Soon after the U.S. entry into the war, he and his son found themselves among the eleven thousand German nationals held in internment camps in the Midwest; authorities were suspicious of his financial transactions with Brüning, but they soon released him when it became clear where his allegiances were.

Back in New York, he invested and he socialized—he was, per family legend, a ladies' man. In the course of his carousals, he met Lore Lane, a German-born actress some twenty-five years his junior who was living with her family in New York. Lane, who was sometimes credited as Lori Lahner, had been born Annalore Mosheim in Berlin in 1914 and was, by nine years, the younger sister of Grete Mosheim, a star of the German stage and screen who had been married to the actor Oscar Homolka. The Jewish Mosheims had fled Germany with the rise of Hitler, despite Hermann Göring's personal assurance to Grete that the family would be safe if they stayed. Grete passed through England, where she made at least one film, before arriving in New York. Lore had her own acting résumé: She had followed Grete into one of director Max Reinhardt's famed Berlin theatrical troupes, and she made several films before leaving Germany. She also followed her sister to safety, passing through France and England before finally arriving in New York on the strength of a marriage (to a man named Lane) that she appeared to have entered into at least in part in order to gain her entrée into the United States.

Perhaps the movie connection was how Brettauer and Lane met. In the States, he had resumed providing funding to Seymour Nebenzahl, who had surfaced in Hollywood at the helm of a new company, Angelus Pictures. Among its projects, Angelus had begun to support the work of a German immigrant writer-director named Detlef Sierck. In 1942, under the anglicized name Douglas Sirk, he was making a film called *Hitler's Mad-*

man, about the Nazis' recent decimation of the Czech town of Lidice in reprisal for the killing of a German officer by the local resistance; Brettauer supplied just over $150,000 of the film's budget. Among the faces in the cast were two pretty actresses who would be granted little screen time, no lines, and no credit: Ava Gardner and Lore Lane.

Brettauer financed another film with almost the exact same story—Fritz Lang's drama *Hangmen Also Die!*, the only American film for which Bertolt Brecht would receive a screenwriting credit during his lifetime. Brettauer provided the producers with some $212,000 in capital.

By then, Brettauer and Lore had married, and they had begun to visit Los Angeles regularly—partly to facilitate her forays into Hollywood, partly to seek real estate investment opportunities. On one of these trips in 1942, he purchased Chateau Marmont.

❖

Under Brettauer, the atmosphere around the hotel would change, sometimes subtly, sometimes with a tenor that vexed certain longtime staffers. Because Brettauer was a financier and not a property manager, he put the Marmont in the hands of a trusted colleague who had, like him, migrated from the old country, a fellow known to the staff only as Dr. Popper.

Unlike his boss, who had a Ph.D. and was thus entitled to the honorific "Dr.," Popper wasn't a doctor of anything insofar as anyone was aware. He was memorable in other ways, though. Standing maybe five feet two, with a pronounced hunchback and thick, round-rimmed glasses, speaking in a heavy German accent, he was Brettauer's eyes and ears at the hotel and, in the early days, his hatchet man. The Brettauer regime would be remembered by some staffers as one of austerity—partly because it was wartime, partly because it was the new owner's intention to run the hotel as a viable business, partly because Brettauer, still based in New York, wasn't around much and, when he was, could be stern and cool with employees. But it was also remembered for the singular presence of Dr. Popper and for his axe wielding.

In accordance with his money-saving outlook, the hotel's kitchen was closed, and the chef Ann Little hired was let go. The practice of putting vases of fresh-cut flowers and bowls of fruit in rooms to greet new arrivals was discontinued. Various holiday traditions instituted by Little—an Easter egg roll, lavish Yuletide decorations, and a big Christmas dinner for staff and guests—were eliminated. And she herself was gone, having decided, after her mother's death in late 1941 and the change in management the following year, to embark on a new career as a Christian Science practitioner, a layperson who uses prayer to assist the healing of fellow believers suffering from illness.

Popper was the face of all these cuts. And yet because he lived in the hotel and had such a mild, even meek demeanor, disgruntled staffers blamed Brettauer and not Popper for the changes. What's more, Popper surprised everyone with his social life— even at his diminutive stature, with his unlikely aspect and accent, he proved to be something of a roué, dating one woman after another and almost always having a different companion alongside him when entertaining guests at dinner parties in his suite.

By the time the war ended, his most frequent dinner guests were the Brettauers, who had moved to Beverly Hills. Lore appeared in another film that her husband financed: Douglas Sirk's 1944 melodrama *Summer Storm,* a loose adaptation of Anton Chekhov's novel *The Shooting Party,* in which she exhibited lively, winning, and entirely credible acting chops in a feature role as a housemaid who becomes a vital witness to a crime.* But that would be her final screen appearance. In January 1947,

---

* In the film's credits, to complicate matters, she is given the name Laurie Lahner, perhaps because she hadn't yet married Brettauer and taken his name, perhaps because there was another Laurie Lane in Hollywood, a glamour-puss who'd had a run as a bit player at Paramount a few years earlier, perhaps both.

she gave birth to a daughter; a second girl followed in late 1949. During the years of her pregnancies and her daughters' childhood, she was often seen around the hotel, where it was recognized that her husband, who could be so terse and officious with employees, doted on her.

For their part, the young Brettauer girls found the Chateau a little intimidating. "It seemed cold when you walked in," remembered Margo, the elder daughter, "and everyone sort of bowed and disappeared when my dad showed up." More frequent than their visits to the Chateau, though, were Dr. Popper's appointments with their father at the family home. "He would come by every single day," Margo said. "He would say hello, very meekly, and then go into my father's office, and they would have these very loud arguments in German, and then he would leave. He seemed scared to death of my father."

�֎

Initially, the idea of a German owning the hotel frightened some of the longtime staff; America was at war with Germany after all, and Brettauer's icy demeanor didn't endear him. But Brettauer proved a good boss, despite his fiscal severity, and Popper, despite his unconventional appearance, was a sympathetic figure.

In their hands, the hotel began to take on a more European tinge than ever before. The large contingent of entertainers who had fled the rise of the Nazis and the open warfare of the era had been joined at the hotel by many other exiles, including a new sort of guest: Eastern European nobles who'd been deprived of their right to fulfill their family lines by the various upheavals of the century. Two scions of the house of Hapsburg made the Chateau their Southern California seat of exile for a period: the brothers Archduke Felix of Austria and Archduke Otto of Austria-Hungary. Their throne had been rendered moot by World War I, but it wasn't until Otto renounced all claims to his hereditary title in 1961 that the two would cease to be seen by some as kings (or at least pretenders) in exile. For all the showbiz royalty it hosted, Chateau Marmont didn't get a lot of *actual* royals passing through its halls. The pair were greeted and treated with unusual deference and ceremony. They were even welcomed as guests at the Brettauer home, a rare honor.

Another personage who passed through the hotel in the early Brettauer years had a more tenuous claim to royal lineage but carried herself with more courtly hauteur than even the archdukes. Princess Helena Gourielli-Tchkonia arrived at the Chateau with her husband, Prince Artchil, dubious heir to a line of Georgian nobility that itself had only a murky credibility. The pair were rather mismatched—she was in reality a Polish American divorcée more than twenty years his senior—but they were equal in ambition, he to live grandly, she to live under the gilding of a title. They accomplished both aims on the strength of the fortune that the princess had made under her real name, Helena Rubinstein. Founder of one of the greatest cosmetics and perfume fortunes of the century, the princess was a grand and flamboyant character whose entrance into a room, or even a hotel lobby, was a production of color, perfume, energy, and noise. She was courted with great avidity by the Brettauers and Popper, and she was often seen in the lobby lounge in conversation with Lore Brettauer, who was interested in whatever beauty secrets she could pry from Rubinstein.

Yet one more pair of dubious "royals" visited the Chateau in those days: Thelma, Viscountess Furness, and her son Tony, who would soon take a place in the House of Lords. The daughter of an American diplomat, Thelma had been married, decades earlier, to a titled British shipbuilding magnate, but he divorced her when her affair with the Prince of Wales (later Edward VIII and, later still, the Duke of Windsor) became public. (She herself sowed the seeds of that liaison's demise when she introduced her royal lover to Wallis Simpson, whom, of course, he would eventually abdicate the throne in order to wed.) The Furnesses' visit was noted by Los Angeles newspapers, but they weren't shown the same personal attention by the Brettauers as were the archdukes or the princess.

�֎

Erwin Brettauer had acquired Chateau Marmont during parlous times. The Japanese attack on Pearl Harbor had put the entire West Coast of the United States under alert for another such assault, and travel within the country was curtailed, partly because so many people became engaged in the war effort as members of the military or the armament industry, partly because travel itself was seen as a drain on vital resources. Even something as seemingly unrelated to the war as the Chateau was integrated into the fight—and into its neighborhood—almost despite itself. If the hotel had previously stood apart in the midst of the ruckus of the Sunset Strip, it suddenly took on a centrality of purpose, its heavily fortified garage designated by local authorities as an air raid shelter. Like other buildings in the area, it was subject to blackouts, and workers diligently installed heavy shades in all the windows to keep the exterior, from lobby to penthouse, dark at night. Large stores of food, water, and medical supplies took up space in the corners of the garage and storage rooms. And neighbors and other looky-loos who had previously felt unwelcome in or intimidated by the solemn Gothic structure felt entitled—even duty-bound—to walk in and inspect the lobby, the garage, and the grounds, since those could very well be the places where they would have to go if their homes and businesses were threatened by an air attack.

A corner of the lobby was dedicated, as in so many public buildings, to a small table offering enlistment information and selling war bonds, but it wasn't a very busy spot. Indeed, little about the hotel would indicate that there was a war on. The Chateau remained all but unknown to servicemen passing through town, for instance. A booklet for the edification of such fellows,

Sinning in Hollywood, was published in 1943, aimed at telling the many thousands of men and women in uniform who would pass through Southern California during the war years where they could find entertainment (none especially sinful, despite the titillating title), food, USO services (including the famed Hollywood Canteen, where stars danced with servicemen and served them coffee and meals), souvenirs, athletic facilities, sightseeing, and the like. It recommended nights out up and down the Sunset Strip—Mocambo, Trocadero, Ciro's—and it suggested lodging at, amazingly, the Beverly Hills Hotel, the Beverly Wilshire, the Hollywood Roosevelt, and the Ambassador. But it said nothing about Chateau Marmont.

In fact, of all the hotels that could claim some legitimate connection to Hollywood in the era, Chateau Marmont was by some measure the most obscure. Many Angelinos recognized the building but couldn't name it, and newspaper articles about its residents or employees frequently referred to it generically as "a hotel" or "apartment house." In fact, it was barely mentioned in print at all. Between 1930 and 1950, the *Los Angeles Times* carried slightly more than two dozen mentions of Chateau Marmont in its pages (not counting advertisements), whereas in the same era the Garden of Allah was named more than three hundred times, the Beverly Wilshire nearly five hundred times, and the Ambassador more than thirteen hundred times. In an article about the arrival of Helen Hayes in town, published as late as 1954, the *Times* felt it had to identify the hotel for its readers as "a place favored by theatrical celebrities, at the eastern end of the Sunset Strip."* Discreet was one thing; obscure was another— and it was certainly bad for business.

---

* Four years later, when Mann Holiner, the radio personality and musical lyricist—he co-wrote "(It Will Have to Do) Until the Real Thing Comes Along"— killed himself with a gunshot in his Chateau Marmont room, the *Times* didn't even think to mention the name of the place in a story about the death. A blessing in its way, but still . . .

Perhaps this was one of the reasons the Brettauer regime was remembered, perhaps unfairly, as an era of cutting back. There *were* small changes made to the daily operation of the place that might have given the impression of austerity, but Brettauer didn't scrimp on *investing* in the hotel. In the late forties, he commissioned Don Loper, the Hollywood costume designer and sometime interior decorator to the stars, to refurbish the top-floor penthouse, which he did in grand style, installing black-and-white tiles in the entry hall and floor-to-ceiling mirrors around the fireplace.

Brettauer also added signage: a shield, perhaps five by five feet in size, on a post perhaps twenty feet high, down along the southeasternmost corner of the property on Sunset Boulevard declaring,

HOTEL

CHATEAU

MARMONT

in a Gothic font, highlighted in red, yellow, and blue neon. And then, in an identical color scheme, a small neon shield at the start of the rise of Marmont Lane, declaring,

GARAGE

CHATEAU

MARMONT

with an arrow pointing toward the entrance. (This nicely echoed the brown-and-gold shield at the end of the Strip announcing the Beverly Hills city line; the Sunset Strip would henceforth literally begin and end with shields.) It wasn't exactly ballyhoo—the more visible sign was so far from the hotel that it almost seemed to be referring to some other place entirely—which meant that most Angelinos still didn't know *exactly* what the Chateau was or even which building it was.

But beyond such cosmetic alterations, Brettauer made a significant structural change to the hotel that would permanently
transform its culture.

2.

By the end of the war, every newcomer to Hollywood had
heard the old saw about being seen at the Beverly Hills Hotel and
not being seen at Chateau Marmont. The implication was generally taken to be that within the confines of the latter you could
feel free to do the things that would garner you negative publicity and/or a ticket out of town should you be caught engaging in
them at the former. In this interpretation, the Chateau staff, the
press, the police, and your fellow guests would be blind, deaf, and
dumb to whatever trespasses against conventional morality you
cared to practice there, provided you were consenting and adult
and didn't harm anyone else or utterly wreck the joint (or fail to
pay for the damage if you did).

But there was another way to hear those words—not as a cau-
tion, but as a signal of acceptance. In this slightly different light,
Chateau Marmont wasn't a don't-ask-don't-tell zone but rather
a haven, a place where conventional moral judgment held little
or no sway, where guests' proclivities for sex or booze or drugs
or unusual work habits weren't merely abided, as they might be
even at a decorous hotel, but actually *accepted*, where queer guests
and druggy guests and guests with adventurous lifestyles and
guests who banged on pianos or typewriters at odd hours and
guests who cavorted more than they worked were considered not
troublesome invaders but welcome kin. Even the starchiest hotel
favored by Hollywood types would tolerate a certain degree of
excess in its residents' behavior; you couldn't have celebrities staying at your place if your expectations of their carryings-on were
puritanical. But those other places had their limits; the limits at
Chateau Marmont were, comparatively, much harder to reach.

That had long been the unofficial policy of the place: a certain deference even beyond that afforded by other similar hotels. But under the ownership of Erwin Brettauer, who had fled Europe by the good graces of his financial means and acumen but who openly opposed Nazi control of his native Germany, it became a principle. He had witnessed the normalization of anti-Semitism, racism, and hatred, and an ardent tolerance became a keystone of his ownership. Chateau Marmont was more than a hideaway; it was a sanctuary.

So although places like the Beverly Hills Hotel and the Beverly Wilshire might indulge the occasional spree by a famous or wealthy patron, they were by and large more stately—and far more circumspect—than the Chateau. In part because of its location, in part because of its low profile, in part because of its layout, in part because of its traditions, in part because of its characteristic air of East Coast or European worldliness, the Chateau was a more or less open city of fifty-odd rooms. People who might feel exposed in other hotels felt safe there. It harbored misfits, freaks, iconoclasts, outcasts, deviants, seekers, refugees, experimentalists, and anyone else who might feel constrained in the pigeonholes of another Hollywood hotel. It was a home to them all, and they all, in turn, treated it with the affection and loyalty due one's native nest.

Not all of the hotel's guests were appreciative of Brettauer's policy of openness and tolerance. One in particular was so averse to interacting with the hotel's black employees that he would go to rigorous lengths to avoid any contact with them, parking his car out on the street when a black parking valet was on duty in the garage and climbing the stairs to the penthouse rather than share close quarters with the black elevator operator. As it happened, he was as much driven by phobia about germs as he was by racism, but it was a repulsive attitude nevertheless, and it wouldn't have worked for him to complain to hotel management about the makeup of its staff, even if he was none other than Howard Hughes.

Hughes, to be sure, could have stayed at any hotel he wished to, and he spent his money freely to just that end. At any given moment, he would have multiple suites and bungalows on retainer at a variety of hotels, including the Beverly Wilshire and the Beverly Hills, as well as any number of apartments in buildings that he owned, and several houses. He rented the penthouse at the Chateau for months at a time not long after it was renovated, at first to install Mitzi Gaynor, then a teenage singer-dancer under contract to Twentieth Century Fox. Hughes had designs on her, but she moved into the hotel with her mother as her chaperone and hooked up not with Hughes but with a talent agent who wound up being her husband of more than fifty years. When he got wind that Gaynor had another fellow, Hughes moved her out of the penthouse and kept it reserved for himself, on and off, for years. He would drop in without warning, stay for indeterminate lengths of time, come and go at odd hours, eat enormous quantities of ice cream, and, in general, display a lot of the eccentricities that would soon develop into crippling mental illness. He was usually disheveled, wearing frumpy work clothes, unshaven, often unbathed, but he could clean up nicely, especially when he was entertaining guests, particularly young dancers and actresses who were just breaking into show business.

Aside from its vaunted privacy and the spectacular view of Los Angeles and its environs, the penthouse afforded Hughes something that he couldn't have anywhere else in the area: a perch from which to keep an eye on the comings and goings at an amenity that Erwin Brettauer installed, without any ceremony, on the hotel grounds. Behind the curtains of his empty suite, Hughes would gape downward with a pair of binoculars to get a look at bodies sunning and splashing below him where, after nearly two decades, management of Chateau Marmont had finally decided to take advantage of the hotel's place in the California sun and put in a swimming pool.

☼

Despite the many assets that the Chateau boasted, it had always lacked the one thing that would have made it truly perfect: a place to swim. For all the amenities he deemed necessary in building the finest residential apartment house in Southern California, Fred Horowitz had never apparently considered adding a pool. He didn't have enough land for one, to start with. And his tenants seemed not to require one, what with the Pacific Ocean a mere half hour away and with such nearby hostelries as the Garden of Allah and the Beverly Hills Hotel, not to mention the area's many grand estates, equipped with pools to which the Chateau's well-connected residents could gain access. When Albert Smith acquired the property and turned it into a hotel and added additional footage and those cozy bungalows to the grounds, a pool still seemed superfluous and even undesirable—that Black Sea–shaped swimming hole at the Garden of Allah was a magnet for all kinds of hijinks and disruption that the comparatively stately Chateau could, in the view of its owner and his long-term guests, do without.

But after the war, the high-end hotel business in Southern California had become sufficiently competitive that a place without a pool was at a disadvantage; servicemen returning from the Pacific had lauded the balmy climate of Los Angeles to their kin back home, and the lifestyle popularly associated with the region—sun, surf, celebrity, leisure, fitness, the freedom of the automobile, the American dream of the stand-alone home—almost always included a swimming pool on the premises of one's domicile, even if it was a temporary one. To not be able to swim just outside your door seemed . . . eastern. In short, Chateau Marmont needed a pool.

In the summer of 1947, in the copse of trees that separated the bungalows from the main building of the hotel, Brettauer installed a small oval-shaped pool—perhaps twenty feet by forty feet at its largest—that was unadorned with cabanas, an outdoor bar, or any of the amenities that drew crowds to the pool decks of

the Beverly Hills and Beverly Wilshire hotels.* Its petite size and
ovoid shape led to a variety of descriptions—the English writer
Gavin Lambert compared it to a suppository, while Gore Vidal
memorialized it as "a navel filled with sweat." But what the new
pool lacked in surface area, aesthetic charm, and opulence, it
made up for in commodities for which Chateau Marmont was
always known, especially a lack of moral judgment. And because
the hotel had neither a bar nor a restaurant in which its guests
could mingle and boasted only the most minimal of lobbies, the
pool provided something that had never before been on offer at
Chateau Marmont: a gathering place, a focal point—a literal
watering hole.

The Brettauer girls reveled in the pool, often coming over
from their Beverly Hills home for a swim. "My father always
made us wear swimming caps," remembered Karin, the younger
girl, "so that our hair wouldn't clog the filter." But the pool was a
hit from the start for those more interested in two of Hollywood's
prime activities: showbiz and sex.

The pool immediately became as common a spot as the booths
at Schwab's for out-of-town actors and writers to dawdle while
awaiting phone calls from agents and producers. Initially, only
a single phone line was provided in the pool area, meaning that
the ring of an incoming call would prick up the ears of everyone in the vicinity, resulting in a subtle wave of letdown when
it turned out they were not the party being sought. Resourceful
guests lucky enough to be staying in the hotel's bungalows, which
were now poolside units, would bring their room phones out into
the sun with them, meaning that the area would be strewn with
tripping hazards in the form of telephone cords.

The sex, or at least the idea of it, was provided abundantly by
young acting hopefuls—female and male—revealing their bod-

---

* It's possible that Brettauer was inspired to add the pool because yet one more
hotel drawing high-end Hollywood business had just opened: the Hotel Bel-Air,
which began taking guests in 1946.

ies on chaise longues or swimming laps across the modest length of the pool. This was the parade of cheesecake and beefcake that Howard Hughes spared no expense to gander upon from behind the curtains of what became known to Marmont staffers as "the Mitzi Gaynor suite." But even if his technique was singular, Hughes was far from alone in prowling the pool deck at the Chateau for dates. The poolside community was a happy hunting ground for hedonists throughout the fifties and into the sixties, increasingly popular, naturally, as swimwear shrank. From the one-piece to the bikini to the European fashion for topless female sunbathing, the Chateau hosted a parade of styles, sometimes to the dismay of management who had to balance the sensibilities of some guests with the expressive freedoms of others—not to mention keeping the hotel staff focused more on their duties than on the flesh on display at poolside.

This sex-charged atmosphere was especially notable when combined with the nonjudgmental tenor that was characteristic of the Chateau. The hotel had a well-earned reputation for accepting any and all guests without raising an eyebrow or asking questions about how they lived their lives, and this applied equally to the activity at the pool, which became not only a party spot but a popular daytime meeting ground for homosexual actors, writers, directors, and producers, who were still required to keep their identities and orientations hidden from the view of their bosses, the press, and the ticket buyers, TV watchers, and music lovers of the American fifties. Gay Hollywood frequented the Chateau regularly in those years, in particular the pool—the only truly public gathering place on the grounds—and nobody among the staff or the guests much cared as long as simple grown-up decorum was observed.

The pool wasn't the end of Brettauer's investment in the physical layout of the Chateau. In 1951, he acquired a parcel of

land adjoining the northeast corner of the hotel property, along
Monteel Road, and commissioned architect Craig Ellwood to
build two bungalows there. Unlike the bungalows that Albert
Smith had created out of the duplex he purchased in the thirties and that resembled small-town homes, these new buildings
would have a sleek, contemporary look to them. Ellwood was a
significant practitioner of what would become known as the mid-
century modern style, and these two bungalows—the largest, by
square foot, of all the hotel's outbuildings—would adhere to that
aesthetic, low-slung and streamlined throughout, with kitchens,
dining, and living room areas arranged in a flow and large glass
windows and patio doors facing out onto gardens. Although they
were connected to the rest of the hotel by footpaths, they were
most easily reached via dedicated entrances on Monteel Road.
They almost never came to be—a careless neighborhood kid
set fire to them when they were still only framework. But that
damage was easily enough reversed. The bungalows opened by
1952 and were quickly among the most desired units at the hotel,
partly because of their up-to-date appearance, partly because
of the isolation they afforded. The Chateau's guests could now
choose between staying in a French castle, a rustic bungalow, or
a shiny modern apartment almost a block away from the main
building.

Brettauer continued spending money outside the hotel as
well. At around the time he commissioned Ellwood to build the
two modern bungalows, he financed yet another film by Douglas
Sirk, *The First Legion*, a quasi-religious film about a Jesuit priest
suffering a crisis of faith who witnesses what appears to be the
miraculous cure of a paraplegic fellow clergyman. And he continued to make real estate deals in New York and Southern California. If he was a cheapskate, as some of the grumblers among
Chateau employees intimated, he had a funny way of showing it.

❧

During Brettauer's tenure, while rumors circulated about the mysterious foreign owner and the strange hunchback who did his bidding, a quartet of women came to be associated with the hotel, providing it with a set of public faces to replace that of Ann Little. The Marmont Ladies, as they became known to regular guests, arrived at different times, in different phases of their lives, and they became integral not only to the operation of the hotel but to the atmosphere of it. They were joined by a little gang of men—boys, really—who were just as important to the daily business and life of the Chateau.

Of the four Marmont Ladies, Carmel Volti was the first aboard, joining the staff even before Ann Little had. Almost nothing that Ben Weingart did in his couple of years running the hotel made a lasting impression, but hiring Volti was savvy. Volti had come from Wyoming to Hollywood via Salt Lake City in pursuit of a singular goal: Since childhood, when she grew up in one of the few homes in her town that had its own telephone, she wanted to be a switchboard operator, wearing a headset, jockeying wires, literally connecting people to one another. Weingart hired her, and she wound up staying through decades of ownership changes, becoming as much a fixture of the place as the pillars in the garage or the piano in the lobby lounge, so familiar to the streams of guests that they often asked for her by name upon arriving or departing, and she would emerge from her tiny work space behind the front desk to receive a hug and a kiss from a movie star.

A decade into operating the hotel, Brettauer and Popper had gone through a handful of general managers before they finally hit on someone who would go on to hold the title for nearly ten years. Meemi Ferguson came to the Chateau in 1953 as a housekeeper after holding similar positions at a couple of other apartment houses and hotels not far away; before long, she was given managerial responsibilities. She had some of the sinew of Ann Little in her, and she was tall and very conscious of her appearance, carrying an air of gentility to go with her polished professionalism. But she wasn't overly severe or stern: She doted on children, laughed easily, enjoyed a tipple, and was something of a gossip, if a careful enough one to hold such a highly sensitive position. Alas, she made the mistake of taking an extended vacation and leaving herself vulnerable to the rumormongering of an ambitious subordinate who spread dirt about her to management in a successful effort to oust Meemi from her position so she herself could fill it. (Despite firing her, Dr. Popper granted Meemi permission to live in a small suite at the hotel, which she did for almost ten years after being dismissed.)

Corinne Patten was hired by Dr. Popper in 1950 as a part-time bookkeeper, but she quickly proved herself adept at a number of things: operating the switchboard, greeting arriving guests, troubleshooting problems of various sorts. Middle-aged and bubbly, she delighted in making the acquaintance of celebrities and kept several scrapbooks filled with autographs and anecdotes about her encounters with fame over her quarter century working at the hotel. She was known to be free with stories (and with facts; she could be something of an embellisher), and her enthusiasm, professionalism, and stability ensured her not only a long tenure in her position but the honor of having an amenity of the hotel named for her—in the mid-seventies, a portion of the lobby lounge set aside as a breakfast area was dubbed Corinne's Corner. She was even immortalized, eventually, in a manner that no doubt delighted her, appearing as herself behind the front desk in a blink-and-you'll-miss-it cameo in a feature film shot on the premises in the early seventies—a fitting tribute to one of the hotel's longest-serving employees and most public faces.

One of Dr. Popper's last hires proved to be one of his most formidable. Daisy Grossen was believed to be in her seventies, if not older, when she joined the staff as a housekeeper in the early sixties. She was a big woman—tall, muscular, with a booming voice and a no-nonsense manner—best remembered for the giant set of keys she wore on her hip and her habit of sitting in stairwells or the elevator while eating a meal of spaghetti or soup—cold, right out of the can ("Chicken noodle was a favorite," actress Carol Lynley recalled). She liked to work at night, meaning that the sound of her footsteps and jangling keys often awakened guests as she lumbered through the halls. And she liked to be in charge: Those keys opened (and, more crucially, *closed*) every door in the place, and other members of the hotel staff couldn't get so much as a roll of toilet paper for a guest without tracking Daisy down and convincing her to march to a storage closet.

But if the Marmont Ladies were the upstairs face and spirit of the place, it was the men and boys who worked literally below the hotel who, in many cases, were the most important connection that most guests had to the Chateau. Given how large a role the automobile played in the rise of Los Angeles, it seems almost inevitable that one of the most famous aspects of the Marmont, commented upon as frequently as the views from the penthouses or the Gothic colonnade at the entrance, would be its garage. When Fred Horowitz conceived the building as an apartment house, he and his architects allotted a single parking space below-ground to each unit, plus a couple to spare. But given the somewhat small footprint and hillside slope of the building—and the need for robust weight-bearing pillars below the surface—the garage never quite seemed large enough for the number of cars it was designed to hold. It was a notoriously difficult space to navigate, particularly in the early decades, when cars were sizable and automatic transmissions and power steering hadn't yet been invented. (Author Eve Babitz surmised that the garage had been filled with obstacles and narrow parking spaces on purpose: "They must have meant for all the boozers and dopers and midnight drivers to pull into the open field across the street which served as the parking lot for the Garden [of Allah], and for the upright citizens to stay at the Chateau"; she preferred to park on the street because, as a friend told her, "who knows, when you go into the Chateau, in what condition you'll leave . . . never mind what *day*.") Long-term residents might have stood a chance of learning how to cut its corners without ravaging their paint jobs. But when the place became a hotel, it was almost inevitable that the job of getting cars in and out would be given to professionals.

There were always parking valets at the Chateau, even from the first days, but the most memorable era in the garage came in those car-crazy days after World War II, when an imposing fellow named Scotty Thompson ruled over the automotive underworld beneath the hotel. Scotty, as he was known to all, was a hulking combat veteran from Watts, and he was so dedicated to his position that he often slept in the garage rather than commute to and from his home (the rear seats of the Rolls-Royces and Cadillacs left in his charge were just about large enough to accommodate his sleeping frame). Scotty had an assistant, a mechanic, and a posse of neighborhood teens working for him, and he taught them all not only how to negotiate the basement but about the far more delicate matter of dealing with celebrity clientele. The Garage Boys, as the young men were known, learned a lot: how to drive a variety of cars; how to greet famous and/or attractive guests; how to cultivate regulars for tips (or, conversely, how to act coolly but respectfully when they were stiffed by the likes of Eartha Kitt and Jackie Collins, who were known to be tight with money); how to help themselves to loose change and cigarettes; how to sneak off with girls into the very back corners of the garage; and, most of all, how to forget a lot of what and whom they saw. As Scotty and his bosses repeatedly reminded the Garage Boys, they were not only emissaries of the hotel— the first and last employees most hotel visitors would meet—but sentinels responsible for guarding the privacy of guests. It didn't matter how famous the party or what shenanigans they got up to: The watchword was silence. And no matter the antics the young men themselves indulged in, they did a pretty good job of fulfilling their duties, protecting the good names of residents and, when their own activities got a little too out of hand, one another.

One of the great services offered by the garage was a kind of ride sharing for those times when a Chateau resident went off to a bar or party and had a bit too much to drink to attempt the drive back, never mind navigating the garage. A car with two Garage Boys in it would head out to where the over-served guest was stranded, and one would drive him or her back to the hotel while the other drove his or her car. Author Roger Kahn told the tale of a couple of writers who were staying at the hotel and went off on a pretty solid bender one night. When they realized they were in no condition to try to make the drive back, one suggested they call for the ride service. "So they pick up the phone," Kahn said, "and about two minutes into the conversation they discover they've been drinking in their own apartment in the Chateau."*

3.

During the postwar years, the atmosphere of the Chateau and the Sunset Strip in general was spiced with the signature brand of braggadocio, style, and more than a little menace of an honest-to-goodness mobster. Mickey Cohen was raised in New York and L.A. and entered the company of gangsters as a teenage boxer in the Midwest. He returned to California in 1939 after surfacing as a (likely) suspect in a killing in Chicago. There, he became chief lieutenant to Benjamin "Bugsy" Siegel, the New York crime and murder boss who had come out west to find new revenue sources and to indulge his taste for the high life.

Prior to the arrival of these imported East Coast strongmen, the mafiosi of Southern California were a tiny lot who held control over little more than their own immigrant neighborhoods. Ruled by boss Jack Dragna, they were considered so lightweight by their peers around the nation that they were laughed at openly as the "Mickey Mouse mob." They weren't big enough, for instance, to challenge the owners of such Sunset Strip gambling spots as the

---

* In more recent years, the service morphed so that a hotel employee came to the rescue on a small scooter that could be folded into the trunk of the "stranded" party's car.

Clover Club and the Colony, independent operators who worked without paying any sort of fealty to the local Mafia boss, a show of disrespect that would never have gone unpunished back east. And they had no control over Johnny Rosselli, a Chicago mafioso who ran a one-man operation of sorts, leeching a profit for his bosses back home off crooked Hollywood labor unions, making a close chum of Columbia Pictures boss Harry Cohn, and generally dressing and comporting himself like a studio executive rather than the murderous criminal he actually was.

But neither Rosselli nor Dragna compared with the spectacle of Cohen and Siegel, who were exactly the gangsters that the Sunset Strip deserved: oversized, audacious, loud, and flamboyant in the manner of Al Capone and John Gotti. Meticulous clothes-horses, flashy gamblers, tireless ladies' men, the pair were seen alongside the swellest celebrities in the swankiest spots, and they relished their notoriety and reputations.

Cohen was a regular on the Strip, opening as his headquarters a haberdashery on the end of the street closest to the Beverly Hills line, dining and clubbing in several favored locations in the neighborhood, using Chateau Marmont for the occasional mid-day tryst, and, most thrillingly, surviving two wild shoot-outs right out in broad daylight on Sunset Boulevard, not to mention the actual bombing of his home in Brentwood.

Siegel, almost as sensationally, dallied with actresses, got into fistfights in elegant nightclubs, and, famously, muscled his way into one of the greatest coups the Mafia would ever score: Learning of nightclub pioneer Billy Wilkerson's plans to build an elegant hotel and casino on the outskirts of a desert backwater known as Las Vegas, Siegel horned in on the deal, taking it over for his partners back east and turning the initial concept into the Flamingo hotel, the prototype of every successful Vegas venture ever to follow. Siegel wouldn't live to see his (or, technically, Wilkerson's) vision of a desert full of casinos come to bloom: He was assassinated in Beverly Hills in 1947, presumably for the sin of pouring millions of mob money into the Flamingo without authorization (and, maybe, skimming a bit off the top for himself, or at least being suspected of it). But within a few years of his death, his efforts would effect significant change not only on Las Vegas but on the Sunset Strip and even on Chateau Marmont.

Most of the people who came to the Chateau during episodes of legal entanglement weren't gangsters, though. As the hotel's don't-ask-don't-tell policies became commonly known around Hollywood, the trade occasioned by divorces became robust. Whether someone needed a place to stay after a spouse demanded they leave or a refuge in a place less lonely than their former conjugal homes, a number of stars made significant stops at the Marmont as they transitioned out of failed marriages. Much in the way that a trip to Reno or Tijuana was synonymous with "divorce," mere word that a person was staying at the Marmont was enough to signal to gossips that his or her marriage was unraveling.

John Wayne was among those who spent time between homes at the hotel. He had been there once before the war, showing up a little tipsy one evening and asking to be put up in the penthouse because he wanted to see what it was like to live in the most deluxe spot in the house. In 1945, enmeshed in a protracted divorce negotiation with his first wife, he returned to the Chateau with the woman who would soon become his second, Esperanza "Chata" Baur; they left when he was free again to marry.

Desi Arnaz also made the hotel an on-and-off destination over a period of years, chiefly as a result of the many spats and separations incited by his ceaseless infidelity to his wife, co-star, and business partner, Lucille Ball. The two had married in 1940, when she was still emerging from chorus girl roles to proper acting and he was an up-and-coming bandleader and light comic actor. Such was his shameless womanizing that the marriage nearly collapsed less than four years along, with Ball actually being granted a divorce judgment that was vacated when the pair reconciled. That became a pattern in their lives: She would learn he was with other women, they'd fight, he'd leave—often to a suite at the Chateau—and then they'd mend the breach . . . until the next rupture occurred. It got so that, according to one biography of the couple, "Arnaz was a semipermanent resident at the Chateau Marmont."

Some Chateau guests remembered Arnaz being drunk and temperamental when they came across him in the hotel's public areas. Parking valets and bellmen remembered him entertaining a string of desirable young women (occasionally, these employees climbed to vantage points in trees and fire escapes to watch Arnaz disport himself). And at least one legend circulated of Ball and Arnaz having a quarrel on the terrace of his suite that resulted in an attaché case being thrown (at whom by whom was unclear) and bursting open, resulting in a shower of cash raining down on Sunset Boulevard. When the pair finally divorced for good in 1960, Arnaz continued to visit the hotel—and titillate the young boys in the garage with his antics—for several years.

�֎

Despite all the outrageous behavior going on inside its walls, Chateau Marmont was hardly the sort of place that harbored revolutionaries. Hell, it was built along the lines of a castle—a place designed to keep insurrectionists *out*. It was only *gently* bohemian, not a den of iconoclasts and bomb throwers; even with relatively reasonable room rates, it was still more costly than most lodgings in town.

But in the years following World War II, Chateau Marmont regularly played host to the members of an army of sorts who specifically hoped to topple the status quo. They happened to be *attractive* rebels, and they had been deliberately summoned to Southern California by the people who stood to lose most from any *real* rebellion they might incite. So they weren't exactly wide-eyed zealots set on bringing the existing hierarchy to its knees.

On the other hand, they made a lot of noise, they worried a lot of people, they made no bones about wanting to change things, and they brought about a permanent transformation not only in the craft they practiced but in the culture and even business in which that craft was realized. They actually *were* upstarts and saboteurs. And in that light, their migration to the Chateau—on the dime of the very monarchs whose realms they were storming—could be seen as a case of the kings having paved the way for their own downfall.

The revolution in question had its roots in a drafty old church in Manhattan, where a group of actors and directors gathered under the name the Actors Studio to explore new ideas about the representation of human behavior on the stage and the screen. Based in part on the teachings of Konstantin Stanislavski, the titan of the Russian stage whose theories about realism in performance had inspired a fervent collective of New York actors, writers, and directors known as the Group Theatre, the Actors Studio became the great temple of what became known as Method acting, a practice that encouraged actors to impart lifelike realism to their work. Previously, on the stage and the screen, actors had been trained to be what might be called theatrical—larger-than-life, with grand gestures and stylized voices designed to give audiences a sense of wonder and the satisfaction of seeing someone leave everything on the stage, as it were. Method acting, on the other hand, demanded that its adherents seek human truths in their performances and make the characters they played seem more lifelike and ordinary—smaller, more personal, more idiosyncratic—than actors of previous generations ever thought to be.

There were, of course, many actors, before and after the founding of the Actors Studio, whose work could be said to achieve results similar to those sought by students of the Method, even absent any contact with its teachers or their acolytes. And, for that matter, there was more than one strain of the Method: At the Actors Studio, Lee Strasberg and Elia Kazan asked students to infuse their roles with emotions drawn from personal memories and even traumas; at her own conservatory, Stella Adler coached her pupils to build their performances from observation and emulation of real-world role models; Sanford Meisner, doyen of the Neighborhood Playhouse, coached a kind of improvisation that blended elements of these other approaches.

But starting in the late forties, when New York stages began to feature its first adherents, the Method, as an idea in and of itself, became a movement and a sensation. Seemingly every committed young actor sought to train in its techniques, and Hollywood studios sought to get the most talented and comely of them into movies as quickly as they could.

If you were a young actor training in New York City to act in a way that *didn't* seem too much like the Hollywood norm, then when you finally took the bait and came to Hollywood to work, you almost inevitably stayed at Chateau Marmont, which, with its lack of glitz and glamour, made residents feel as though they were signaling to their bosses and one another that they hadn't lost touch with their gritty sides. Virtually every important performer associated with the first wave of Method acting checked into the Chateau on his or her initial sojourn to lotusland, and they were often quite frank about preferring it above all other hotels because it made them feel as if they were still in New York and hadn't yet succumbed to the intoxicating luxuries associated with the movies.

"It was very important in those days to retain your sense of being a 'New York actor,'" remembered Joanne Woodward, one of the reluctant throng. "We'd stay at Chateau Marmont.... There was this community of New York actors.... I guess we were pretentious about it."

Woodward came out to Hollywood in the mid-fifties, along with an actor whom she knew from Broadway and the Actors

Studio and with whom she was involved in a romance, even though he was a married man with three children—Paul Newman. The pair were circumspect and cautious back in New York, but they carried on fairly openly at the Chateau, lounging together at the pool and partying with other movie people and with friends from back east. It's entirely possible that Woodward and Newman never slept together until they were in Hollywood, and that could very well be the reason that they often thought of the Marmont as the place where their five-decade love affair and marriage began.

When they arrived, the path from the Actors Studio to the Chateau had already been well worn. John Garfield, who had been a satellite member of the Group Theatre before the Actors Studio formed, was the first actor with anything like Method training to come to Hollywood—years before World War II. He started to use Chateau Marmont as a base in the late forties and early fifties when he had been all but entirely chased out of the movies and back to the New York stage by the anti-Communist blacklist of movie people who had associations with the political Left. Garfield was resident at the Chateau several times as he tried to make his way back into the top tier of Hollywood through work in small independent movies, a comeback that ended with his death from a heart attack at age thirty-nine.

The next practitioner of the Method to make his way into movies was Montgomery Clift, who attended the Actors Studio while building a résumé on the New York stage and came to Hollywood in 1946 to shoot *Red River,* the classic Western in which his character's clash with the one played by John Wayne, then one of the world's biggest stars, could be read as a battle between the traditional American screen acting style and the newly emergent Method. Most of *Red River* was shot on location in Arizona. But during pauses in the lengthy location shoot, and when production moved to interior sets in Hollywood, Clift could be found at Chateau Marmont—*if,* that is, you knew where to look.

Clift wasn't actually registered at the Chateau himself.

Rather, he was a frequent visitor to the hotel because he was carrying on an affair with one of its residents, Libby Holman, an actress and singer of the twenties and thirties famous for her rendition of the torch song "Moanin' Low" and, even more so, for her sensational private life. In 1932, Holman's husband, tobacco heir Zachary Smith Reynolds—at twenty years old, six years younger than Holman and already on his second marriage—was found dead of a gunshot wound during a party at his family estate. Authorities called it suicide, then changed their minds and ruled the death a murder; Holman and her late husband's best friend were suspected and even indicted, but they were never brought to trial. She was granted a substantial portion of Reynold's $30 million estate,* and seven months after his death she gave birth to his son, Christopher, who was known as Topper and who would himself die at age seventeen in a mountain climbing accident.

By that time, Holman would have buried *another* husband, also younger than she, this time by twelve years: actor Ralph Holmes, whose brother she had previously dated (and who himself died in a flying accident in the war). Holman and Holmes separated in 1945 after he returned from wartime service in the Royal Canadian Air Force, and he, too, died unexpectedly, found in his Manhattan apartment with an empty bottle of sleeping pills by his side.

Clift and Holman knew each other from Broadway, where they met during the war. She had returned to the stage after Reynolds's death, but she was never able to relaunch her career successfully in the wake of the scandals surrounding her. A hardworking young actor on the way up, Clift was *sixteen* years younger than she (she got older, but her beaus seemed always to stay the same age). They were both apparently bisexual, and they shared an emotional vulnerability and a taste for booze and pharmaceutical drugs; their intimacy was immediate and profound. When Clift came to Hollywood to make *Red River,* Hol-

* Approximately $537 million in 2019.

man took a suite at the Chateau and made it clear to the staff that her "Do Not Disturb" sign was to be strictly observed. For his part, Clift would sneak into the place when he came to see her, using the garage entrance if the lobby looked busy, taking the stairs up to the sixth floor if the elevator had other passengers, or insisting that the elevator operator not stop if somebody on one of the floors en route buzzed for a ride. The pair carried on their secretive pas de deux throughout the protracted production of Clift's debut—the first important work by a member of the Actors Studio in a Hollywood film—and they remained closely connected, albeit not romantically, for years to come.

Although Garfield and Clift were trained in the Method, they weren't generally associated with it in the popular view. Studio publicists presented them in the fashion, more or less, of all film stars, and they themselves didn't make their connection to the Method a part of their identities in the marketplace of Hollywood. The Method really *arrived* in the movies, as a concept and as a movement, with Marlon Brando, and in particular with his 1951 breakout performance in *A Streetcar Named Desire*. After that, not only did the studios make increasing efforts to cast actors trained in the new techniques, but the Method and its practitioners became known quantities in the business and in the public eye.

And so they drifted west, scores of them,* and they often stayed at the Chateau, finding in its layout and amenities (or lack thereof) an agreeable facsimile of their New York apartment homes. A room at the Marmont wasn't only affordable and convenient to the studios, to Schwab's, and to the clubs and restaurants of the Sunset Strip; it was, according to the stage and film producer and writer Bob Joseph, a declaration of independence. "The Chateau is where all New Yorkers stay," he said. "It's a way

---

* So many, in fact, that the Actors Studio opened a Hollywood branch, the Actors Studio West, in 1966, eventually acquiring a permanent home on DeLongpre Avenue in West Hollywood, not far at all from Chateau Marmont.

of saying, 'I'm keeping my distance from Hollywood. And I'm going back to New York.'" An unknown young actor named Jack Lemmon was one of the New Yorkers who insisted on staying in the Chateau. "I was sure my place was in the thee-ah-tuh," he remembered. (While not an adherent of the Method, Lemmon, like his peers, saw the Marmont as an oasis of eastern civility amid the barbarism of Southern California.)

The flow of actors to the Chateau in the fifties constituted a true pantheon of postwar American performers: Julie Harris, Ben Gazzara, Kim Stanley, Lee Grant, Lee Remick, and a string of famous couples, including Newman and Woodward, Rod Steiger and Claire Bloom, Eli Wallach and Anne Jackson, and Rip Torn and Geraldine Page. That last pair made quite an impression on the staff; Torn became a regular at the hotel in the fifties and was fond of wandering off into nearby hills and valleys with a hunting gun and bagging game birds—quail, pigeon, what have you—to cook up in his kitchen as the centerpiece of dinner parties, inviting anyone who was staying at the hotel; at his table, you might find the likes of Judy Garland, Miles Davis, or Lena Horne. After he married Page, the two would stay at the Chateau whenever they worked in Hollywood; they would rent a bungalow and more or less trash it, not in a grubby rock star way but in the way any family with three young kids might.

❊

While the Chateau was becoming popular with his peers, Montgomery Clift returned to the hotel under circumstances far different from those that first brought him there. Clift's romance with Libby Holman hadn't lasted, but his memories of the Chateau did. And so, in the summer of 1956, he thought of the hotel as a safe harbor to get him through the physical and psychological trauma he was experiencing as he recovered from an automobile crash that nearly killed him.

In May of that year, leaving a dinner party at the home of

Elizabeth Taylor, who was co-starring with him in Edward Dmy-tryk's *Raintree County,* Clift fell asleep behind the wheel of his Chevrolet Bel Air and careened into a telephone pole, smashing his face on the steering wheel. His actor friend Kevin McCarthy, who was also at the dinner and had left at the same time, had been driving in front of Clift and saw the crash in his rearview mirror. He raced back to Taylor's house to phone for an ambulance, then returned to the car with Taylor and Rock Hudson, another of the guests.

At the scene, Taylor leaped into the wreck, cradling Clift's bloody head in her lap, clearing his mouth of broken teeth that threatened to choke him, sobbing, begging him not to die. Extricated from the car, Clift was taken to Cedars of Lebanon hospital, where his wounds were assessed: deep lacerations on the left side of his face; a broken nose; a broken jaw; multiple missing teeth; a severe concussion. He was taken straightaway into the operating room, where doctors did what they could to repair the damage, snapping his nose into place, wiring his jaw shut, performing plastic surgery on half of his face, clearing out the debris of his broken teeth. It was months before he was discharged. And so, after puttering around his home on his own, unable to return to work and unwilling to see friends, he checked into the Chateau, remembering it as a reliable fortress of solitude.

At first Clift requested the room he remembered from his visits to Holman, but when that was unavailable, he settled for a two-bedroom suite on the same floor. Immediately upon entering, he hung a "Do Not Disturb" sign on the door—it would stay in place without interruption throughout his stay—and ordered the front desk not to put through any phone calls, *especially* not from his mother.

He was there for weeks, lost in darkness both literally and figuratively, the former because he kept the shades drawn at all hours and removed the bulbs from all but one lighting fixture in the room, the latter because he was befogged by pain medication and liquor, a twin scourge that would haunt him the rest of his days. Now and again he would emerge, utterly lost, wandering the corridors or his terrace, swearing, crying, shouting incoherently. One night he pounded on what had once been Holman's door wailing for "Libby," terrifying the people inside. Another night found him naked on the terrace, screaming into the darkness; the hotel only learned about it when a neighbor on Monteel Road called to let the front desk know what was happening upstairs.

With the solicitude of friends and the patience of his employers, he passed through the worst of this living nightmare and finished *Raintree County* and tried to make a go of his career and his life. But there was no happy ending ahead for him. His beauty was gone; he was never without pain; he became addicted to pills and alcohol; and in 1966, after eight more films and a decade of fighting demons, he died at age forty-five.

✣

But even as sensational as that visit was, no Method actors made quite as memorable a splash at the Chateau as did Shelley Winters and Anthony Franciosa, her third husband (she was his second wife), who lived out the volcanic drama of their three-year marriage in a series of visits to the hotel. The two had met during classes at the Actors Studio and became lovers during the debut production of the famed stage play *A Hatful of Rain* in 1955, a milestone in the development and the legend of the Method. Winters had already been making movies for a decade, and she was working in New York while on hiatus from her obligations to Universal Pictures. When she returned to Hollywood, she lured Franciosa out with her by promising that they could stay in Sidney Poitier's suite at Chateau Marmont—even though she already had a place of her own in Beverly Hills, where her parents lived with her daughter from her marriage to Italian actor Vittorio Gassman.

During the months leading up to their 1957 marriage, Winters stayed with Franciosa at the Chateau on and off, and they shared, by her detailed account, a passionately physical and emotional connection. ("If there had been an Olympic sex team," she wrote in one of her autobiographies, "Tony would have been the captain," adding, "It was almost comical. We could not be in each other's presence without feeling desire and touching each other.") The complexities of negotiating a divorce from Gassman and of taking care of her daughter while navigating a career meant that it was best for Winters and Franciosa to live separately for a time. Even after they impulsively tied the knot in Reno, near where Franciosa was shooting a film, he kept his suite at the Chateau rather than move in with her. After some persuading, he finally gave up his beloved bachelor quarters at the hotel and moved into a slightly cramped situation with Shelley, her daughter, and her parents.

Franciosa was then in production on *Wild Is the Wind,* a melodrama based on an Italian film titled *Furia* (*Fury*). The story, as adapted for director George Cukor, concerned an Italian rancher in Nevada who imports a wife from the old country, only to have her fall in love with one of his workers. Anthony Quinn was cast in the lead, Franciosa played the lustful ranch hand, and the great Italian actress Anna Magnani took the role of the woman caught between them. Magnani and Winters were slightly acquainted from Winters's days acting in Rome—Winters kinda-sorta met Gassman through Magnani—and Winters greatly respected the Italian actress's craft, which achieved levels of depth and realism that Method actors strove for without Magnani's ever having any training in the technique. Magnani had won an Oscar as Best Actress just a few years before, for *The Rose Tattoo,* but she was still considered something of an exotic outsider in Hollywood.

When the production of *Wild Is the Wind* relocated from the desert to the studio, Magnani moved into the Chateau, where she became well-known for cooking her own meals, filling the hallway outside her suite enticingly with the aromas of Rome. Cooking, it turned out, wasn't the only way she entertained. As the weeks of filming continued, Winters began to note that not only was Franciosa coming home from the studio later and later after work but he had little appetite for the meals she was cooking him—*Italian* meals, specifically, of the sort he had grown up eating back in New York. One evening, dinner getting cold on the table, she phoned the studio to find out when he might be home, and she learned that he had left hours earlier—*with Magnani.* She sussed out immediately what was going on, grabbed a decorative statuette from a mantelpiece, stomped out of the house, and headed straight for the Chateau.

Increasingly angry as she drove toward the hotel, she left her car in the garage and stormed up the stairs to the suite where a parking valet told her she'd find Magnani. Sure enough, there she was: behind an unlocked door, passionately embracing Franciosa on the sofa, scripts and some articles of clothing in disarray around them.

"I started to scream, '*Puttana!*'" Winters recalled, and she went after Magnani, brandishing the statue she had brought along and chasing her around the suite and into the corridor. Magnani made it to the staircase and was racing downward, Winters in pursuit hollering, when the mood lifted. "Somewhere around the third landing," Winters said, "she looked back at me, and we both started to laugh, hysterically. We sat down on the landing, and when we could control our laughter, she whispered, '*Stupida!* Don't laugh! He kill us both if you laugh! Be jealous and scream!'" Winters knew she was right: Franciosa's ego would be offended if his wife and the woman he was evidently sleeping with were laughing at him, but if they were quarreling, he would feel so proud of his masculinity that he would forget he had been caught red-handed in his adultery. Winters resumed her yelling, the pair of actresses walked down to the garage at a more relaxed pace, and Magnani went out into the street. Franciosa soon appeared in the garage himself, his clothes and hair adjusted impeccably, explaining to his wife that he and Magnani were merely rehearsing a scene. He escorted her to her car, opened the passenger door for her, got behind the wheel, and drove them both back home. "For the rest of the filming," Winters recalled, "Tony came home at 6:15 p.m., and neither one of us ever mentioned the Chateau Marmont again."

�֎

Ironically, despite its strong association with modern actors, the Chateau had a reputation, among the very small percentage of Los Angelinos who could even claim to have heard of it, of being connected to a silent film star. Greta Garbo's first role in a feature film came in Sweden in 1922, and her last, in the comedy flop *Two-Faced Woman*, came in Hollywood in 1941. She was barely thirty-six years old, and she didn't necessarily mean to retire; things just kind of slipped away. And as she faded into myth—the living embodiment of her famous line from *Grand Hotel*, "I want to be alone"—she became the subject of rumors, gossip, and speculation.

Among these was the suggestion, kindled perhaps by Erwin Brettauer's decision to continue living in New York for a few years after he bought Chateau Marmont, that Garbo was the owner of the large, unlikely hotel at the head of the Sunset Strip. And while there was absolutely no truth to the tale, it was fueled by, of all people, Garbo herself, who stayed at the hotel on a few occasions in the late forties and mid-fifties while visiting Los Angeles from her permanent home in New York with the idea, inevitably abandoned, of perhaps appearing once again on-screen.

She registered as Miss Harriet Brown, smoked cigarillos, wore slacks and clunky loafers, and was fond of walking in the hills of an early evening, often returning with a basket of wildflowers to adorn her suite. Ever alert for reporters, photographers, autograph hounds, gawkers—anyone who might give her a second look uninvited—she used the stairs, avoided the lobby, and kept to herself, emerging from her suite only to visit a friend, socialite Virginia Burroughs, who lived with her elderly mother in the adjacent rooms. Such was Garbo's dogged isolation that she didn't bother to stop by the front desk to collect mail and messages for weeks at a time, and she once moved her bed to the dining room of her suite when a family with a young child took the rooms closest to her own bedroom, rather than complain to management that her sleep was being interrupted by the noise.

Garbo socialized—she was especially close to the actress and screenwriter Salka Viertel, who lived in a cottage in Santa Monica Canyon that Garbo used to visit—and she accepted dinner invitations from old friends. And she shopped, often at Schwab's, where she was known to the clerks as Miss Brown, the quiet woman who would stop in for a bottle of wine before going out for an evening or who would often show up just before midnight, when the store closed, so that the doors could be locked behind her and she be allowed to make her purchases in peace. Gossip columnist Sidney Skolsky, whose office was upstairs from Schwab's, certainly knew who she was and recognized her on the occasions when she came in during normal business hours. But he kept her identity close to his vest. Her mere appearance in the flesh, however, could give the shock of a lifetime to an unsuspecting Schwab's regular, such as the starlet who walked out of a phone booth one afternoon, saw Greta Garbo standing before her in unassuming street clothes, and fainted dead away on the spot.

4.

One episode in particular would bring together everything that was happening at the Chateau in the fifties—the swimming pool and the bungalows, the hedonistic tenor, the divorced (or soon-to-be) boldfaced names, the Method actors, the closeted gay performers—and it would also result in the single greatest work of art that was associated with the history of the hotel. One of the most iconic films of the decade was largely written, conceived, cast, rehearsed, and, in some ways, *lived* on the grounds of the Marmont. And the man who orchestrated all of it came to the place in circumstances that themselves could have been the basis of a hair-raising melodrama or classical tragedy.

When Nicholas Ray moved into a bungalow at the Chateau in 1952, he was an accomplished director with a résumé of films that were commercially successful and unusually personal and expressive, including *They Live by Night* (1948), *Knock on Any Door* (1949), *Born to Be Bad* (1950), and *Flying Leathernecks* (1951). He was offbeat and modern and arty, especially by the standards of the big studios. And his movies stood out, drawing the attention of important stars and the praise of critics. He was someone to keep an eye on, and that was true even if you knew nothing about him or his personal life.

Ray had been born Raymond Nicholas Kienzle Jr. in Wisconsin in 1911 and raised in a middle-class household that appeared stable but seethed with turmoil due to the alcoholism and womanizing of his father, who died unexpectedly when his son was in high school. At the University of Chicago, Ray toyed with the idea of becoming an architect and apprenticed himself to Frank Lloyd Wright. Later, he found another mentor, folklorist Alan Lomax, and traveled the South with him discovering and recording roots musicians. Eventually, using the stage name Nick Ray, he made his way into the theater, heading to New York, where he acted and studied directing under the aegis of Elia Kazan, who brought him to Hollywood as an assistant director on his debut film, *A Tree Grows in Brooklyn*.

Refashioning himself once again as a writer-director, Ray became a creator of thrillers and films noir, coming at what could have been ordinary fare with the edge of an outsider. His resistance to the norm was, in a way, a mark of personal expression; for most of his life he was given to depression, to bouts of drinking and gambling, and to reckless promiscuity, with both women and men. He never felt comfortable in his own skin, never felt that he fit in, always carried the scars of his upbringing. Characteristically, in film and in life, he was sensitive to the plights of outsiders, particularly young outsiders, and his films depicted worlds of

moral uncertainty and ambivalence, with flawed heroes, human-
ized villains, and authorities who couldn't be trusted.

In 1948, while directing his second film, *A Woman's Secret*,
he met Gloria Grahame, a rising star known for her work in *It's
a Wonderful Life* (she played the town flirt, Violet) and the film
noir *Crossfire*, for which she was nominated for an Oscar. Grahame was herself married, and a dozen years Ray's junior, but
they fell for each other, and their one-on-one rehearsals became
sexual liaisons almost straightaway. They began to hold hands
on set, to show up at parties together, to appear in gossip columns
as an item.

Ray later claimed to feel an aversion toward Grahame—"I
didn't like her very much," he claimed. "I was infatuated with
her, but I didn't like her"—but they conceived a child together,
which led them to decide to marry. Grahame moved to Las Vegas
to establish residency and get a divorce, within hours of which
she and Ray wed. It was a touch-and-go thing: The reluctant
groom had to be pried away from a casino by his best man, and
he returned to the gambling tables immediately after the no-fuss
ceremony.

As husband and wife, Ray and Grahame worked together
a second time, on *In a Lonely Place*, a critical and commercial
success that gave them the air of a well-matched couple. But
they struggled against imbalances and disconnections in their
marriage: Grahame was prone to anxiety about her weight
and appearance, submitting to plastic surgeries and crash diets
and shopping binges. And rumor had it that she was hun-
grier and more adventuresome than her husband in matters of
sex—which, given Ray's well-earned reputation as a sporting man, was saying something. While he was away shooting
pictures like *Flying Leathernecks* and *The Lusty Men*, she was
widely said to be engaged in a string of affairs.

Still, no rumormonger could have conceived the event that
led Ray to move into Chateau Marmont.

In the spring of 1951, Ray employed private detectives to sur-veil Grahame and catch her with one of her men on the side, but they couldn't get the goods on her, despite tailing her around town and planting listening devices in the couple's Malibu house. And then one afternoon Ray came home early from work and the world collapsed beneath his feet.

He heard noises from the bedroom and stormed in to find Grahame in bed with a lover: his own thirteen-year-old son, Tony, from his first marriage.

Tony had spent the past few summers in Malibu and had just finished his first year at prep school. He decided to surprise his father and stepmother by showing up at their doorstep unan-nounced, and he found Grahame alone. Words, looks, touches, were exchanged, and they found themselves enmeshed.

Astonished, Ray smashed furniture, artwork, dishes— anything he could get his hands on—and screamed oaths and agonies. Tony escaped, fleeing the house, sleeping that night under a nearby porch. And Ray packed up and moved into town, taking a bungalow at the Garden of Allah.*

Before long, as word of the Sophoclean events in Malibu cir-culated through Hollywood, and divorce proceedings were under way—uncontested by Grahame, who admitted everything, which was all captured on a private eye's audiotapes, anyhow— Ray moved again, to a set of rooms behind the Army and Navy Officers Club on Sunset at La Cienega, the former site of the ille-gal gambling den known as the Colony Club. In late January 1952, the place went up in flames in the middle of the night. The only resident, Ray awakened and escaped, but he raced back in to save his pet puppy. Exiting the burning building a second time,

---

* The affair of Gloria Grahame and Tony Ray didn't end with their discovery and shaming. In 1960, when Tony was twenty-two, they married—causing Ray and Grahame's *third* husband, whom she had wed and divorced in the interven-ing years, to pursue custody of the children she'd borne them. Grahame and Tony would remain together for fourteen years, having two children of their own.

he missed the final rungs on a ladder and injured his foot, and then he cut himself by walking barefoot on pavement strewn with broken glass.

Still hobbling from this mishap, he made his way to Chateau Marmont and bungalow 3, where he would live for the next six years, finally departing when he set up house with a new wife. His residency lasted so long that hotel staffers nicknamed his home the Director's Bungalow. In his time at Chateau Marmont, Ray would become a noted Hollywood playboy and bohemian, and he would direct his masterpiece. His new home would figure prominently in both.

·�֎·

If Ray had once seemed an awkward or aloof figure on the Hollywood scene, he came out of his shell at Chateau Marmont, socializing and entertaining guests.

"He liked the Marmont," recalled his nephew, Sumner Williams, who worked and lived with his uncle on and off for decades. "He liked the bungalow, old shingle, wood, with an upstairs and three bedrooms, big kitchen, big fireplace, it was just comfortable. It was not really a hotel service. We did our own cooking. We did have maids for cleaning up, and that was it."

Ray entertained regularly, hosting barbecues-slash-pool-parties-slash-salons that began on Sunday afternoons and often meandered into the wee hours of Monday. These were informal, drop-in affairs that, according to *Variety*, "started at 1 p.m. with Bop, [and] ended at 1 a.m. with Bach"—with plenty of jug wine, a little bit of reefer, grilled burgers, singing, dancing, laughs, and that sine qua non of postwar bohemianism, bongo drumming.

Recovered from the disorienting disaster of his divorce, Ray dove into work, making a pair of Westerns, including one of his best-remembered films, the wild, even surreal *Johnny Guitar*, in which Joan Crawford and Mercedes McCambridge played powerful women vying for the attentions of wandering gunman

Sterling Hayden, who has given up his six-shooter for a six-string guitar.

The idea of being fought over by women resonated for Ray, who was filling his nights with philandering; his lovers of the era included Crawford, Marilyn Monroe, Shelley Winters, Jayne Mansfield, Zsa Zsa Gabor, and some men. Winters would recall spending an evening in Ray's bungalow along with Marilyn Monroe after a preview screening of *On the Waterfront*, sipping strong piña coladas and watching late-night horror movies on Ray's big TV set, on top of which sat a gigantic reel-to-reel tape recorder, the purpose of which she never learned.

Ray had partly chosen a bungalow at Chateau Marmont as a permanent residence because he was extremely sensitive to any intrusions into his personal life, and he was infuriated if the least report of his liaisons appeared in print, as happened once in *Confidential* magazine. "They had this big write-up of Nick and Marilyn balling," recalled a friend. "Nick's really teed off about it, and he says, 'I'll sue the sonofabitch,' and so forth. . . . I said, 'Hey, it's not a bad article. There's thirty million guys in America who want to go to bed with Marilyn Monroe, and you're written up!' Nick could be very humorous at times. 'I'll still sue the sonofabitch,' he said, 'but now that you mention it . . .' "

Besides its function as a trysting spot, Ray treated his bungalow as a private house, frequently hosting friends such as Lew Wasserman, his agent, and his wife, Edie (yet another of Ray's playmates), for home-cooked meals and nights chatting in front of the TV. At one such evening with the Wassermans in late 1954, as the trio sat watching *Dragnet*, Ray expressed a desire to do something important, something topical, something real. "I want to make a film that I love," Ray told his guests. "I have to believe in the next one or feel that it's important." Challenged to name an idea that wasn't highfalutin or overdone, Ray thought for a moment and said he wanted to do "something about kids . . . the kid next door," adding, almost as an afterthought, "like one of my sons."

Wasserman took the idea to Warner Bros., where a project of that sort had been languishing for a few years, a study of juvenile delinquency based on a book of popular sociology—*Rebel Without a Cause: The Story of a Criminal Psychopath* by Dr. Robert Lindner. Several attempts had been made to produce the film, including one that would have starred Marlon Brando. Ray threw out everything in Lindner's book except the title and pitched the studio a thriller about life, danger, sex, and death involving teenagers from the mean streets of a typical American suburb. They told him to develop a script.

Ray began courting screenwriters and young actors, asking them around to his place for parties and meals at which he could get a feel for their personalities and for their empathy for the subject of the film. Veteran screenwriter Jesse Lasky Jr. accepted one such invite to Chateau Marmont. "I drove up to Nick's," he remembered. "I heard jazz coming out as I approached the door, and it sounded like a party. I went in, and the first time I saw Nick, he was dancing with another man. The other man was a young prizefighter, and the two of them were dancing cheek-to-cheek around the room to jazz. Nick waved me to sit down and waved the servant up with a drink, and I sat there and watched the two of them dance. . . . They danced beautifully, very graceful guys, and I didn't for an instant think they were homosexual. This was just having a good time. When it was over, we talked for quite a while and had a lot of drinks."

Ray didn't go for Lasky's work, nor was he disposed to the efforts of a litany of other writers: Dr. Lindner, trying to adapt his own material; Peter Viertel, who had written *The African Queen;* playwright Clifford Odets, who was also living at Chateau Marmont; novelist Leon Uris; even Theodor Geisel, the cartoonist and author better known as Dr. Seuss who had just enjoyed success in movies with his fantasy film *The 5,000 Fingers of Dr. T.*

Finally, the project fell to Irving Shulman, best known for his

1947 teen crime novel, *The Amboy Dukes*.* There was a problem
with Shulman, though: At one of Ray's Sunday shindigs, he got
into a conversation about cars with the young actor who was up
for the part of the lead in the film, during which time the writer
revealed that (1) his MG wasn't equipped with racing carburetors
and (2) he thought that buying and driving a German car so soon
after the war was inappropriate if not downright immoral. The
actor, who was in the market for a Porsche, got quiet, and the chat
dwindled, and within days Shulman was no longer working on
the film. Ray might have thought highly of *The Amboy Dukes*,
but he thought even more highly of—indeed, he was banking
the entire film on—this little-known young actor whose film
debut hadn't been released yet: James Dean.

�֍

Late one evening in 1954, as Ray sat quietly in his bungalow,
there was a knock at the door, and there stood three young Hollywood types, a girl and two guys. Before introductions could be
made, one of the lads scooted past Ray by turning a somersault
through the doorway and into the room. He stood and looked
Ray in the eye and asked, "Are you middle-aged?"

"I admitted it," Ray said later.

" 'Did you live in a bungalow on Sunset Boulevard, by the old
Clover Club?'

" 'Yes,' I said.

" 'Was there a fire in the middle of the night?'

" 'Yes.'

" 'Did you carry a boxer puppy out of the house in your bare
feet across the street and cut your feet?'

"I had."

The acrobat smiled. The girl gave him a look that said, "I told

---

* Ted Nugent's first band was named for the book.

you so." And introductions were made. She was Maila Nurmi, then enjoying a hot moment as Vampira, the host of late-night horror movies on TV. The fellow still in the doorway was Jack Simmons, one of the kids who was hanging around the Strip in those days drinking espresso, playing bongos, riding motorcycles, and trying to break into movies. And Ray's interrogator was Simmons's roommate, James Dean, who had a number of television credits to his name and had only just completed work on his first film.

Ray knew him. They'd met in passing once before, and Ray had seen a rough cut of his debut movie, *East of Eden*, which had been directed by his own mentor, Elia Kazan. Like everyone else to whom Kazan showed the film, Ray was astonished by Dean's raw, emotional, unpredictable work. He was aware that Dean was under contract to Warner Bros., and he hoped to leverage the combination of their common employer and their connection to Kazan to lure Dean into starring in *Rebel*. But he still didn't have a script, and it wasn't worth discussing casting without one. After a bit more socializing, the trio departed, taking with them Ray's encouragement to return for one of his Sunday gatherings.

Dean, as his entrance into Ray's bungalow proved, didn't exactly require a formal invitation to make himself at home. He was an entirely impetuous, spontaneous creature. He had been raised in Indiana and Southern California and had been pursuing an acting career since 1951, when he dropped out of college and moved to New York to attend the Actors Studio. Appearing several times onstage and in live TV dramas, he was pegged as a young acolyte (if not outright impersonator) of Method godhead Marlon Brando, which led to his coming to the attention of Kazan, who had directed Brando on stage and screen and was at work on *East of Eden*. Cast in the role of Cal Trask with the approval of John Steinbeck, the author of the source novel, Dean moved back to Southern California in the spring of 1954.

In Hollywood, Dean immediately immersed himself in the thriving demimonde of the Sunset Strip, roaring around on a motorcycle, disporting himself with both women and men, frequenting the groovy spots of the moment. He was a fixture at Googie's, the twenty-four-hour coffee shop across Sunset Boulevard from Chateau Marmont, meaning that he was often near enough to drop in on Ray if he felt the urge, Sunday or not, invited or not, middle of the night or not.

At one of Ray's Sunday gatherings, Dean met a young actor from San Diego named Dennis Hopper. Infatuated with Dean as both an actor and a man, Hopper spent hours bouncing between Dean's favored Hollywood hangouts, peeking in through the windows to see if he was in residence. ("Oh, for God's sake, Dennis!" snapped Maila Nurmi when she got wind of this. "Don't be so San Diego!")

Another time Dean showed up at the bungalow when Ray was hosting his neighbor Clifford Odets, the celebrated author of such plays as *Golden Boy, Waiting for Lefty,* and *Awake and Sing!,* as well as several significant film scripts, including *None but the Lonely Heart,* which he also directed for the screen. Ray introduced them, and Dean took on an abstract, distant air. "Jimmy was peculiarly silent and retreated to a corner," Ray remembered. Playing host, he went off to fix drinks in the kitchen, learning later from Odets what had happened in his absence.

"There had been a long silence. The distance of the room lay between them. At last, in a grave voice, Jimmy spoke:

" 'I'm a sonofabitch.'

"Clifford asked why.

" 'Well,' he explained, 'Here I am, you know, in this room. With you. It's fantastic. Like meeting Ibsen or Shaw.' "

Ray and Dean circled each other for a few months, *Rebel Without a Cause* always the unacknowledged subject between them. Toward the end of 1954, when it appeared that Ray's inability to deliver a screenplay would doom the project, fate arrived in the form of Stewart Stern, a writer from New York who was spending the year-end holidays visiting his cousin Arthur Loew Jr., a movie producer descended from the founders of Paramount *and*

MGM. Stern forged a rapport with Dean and Ray, whom he met on separate social evenings at the Loew house. Ray put Stern to work on rewriting Shulman's abandoned version of the script, and Dean befriended the writer, admitting to him in confidence that he wasn't sure he should follow *East of Eden* and Elia Kazan with a low-budget teen exploitation film by a genre director, even a hip one. In the coming weeks, Stern managed the delicate job of both delivering an acceptable screenplay to Ray *and* keeping Dean interested in appearing in it.

With the prospect of the film likelier, Ray committed himself more deeply to casting, using his Chateau Marmont bungalow, rather than his office at Warner Bros., as an informal studio for testing new talent. He met a former child actor named Frank Mazzola who was the leader of the Athenians, a gang at Hollywood High School in those days when gangs wore varsity jackets declaring their affiliations. Like Dean, the Athenians became familiar at Ray's Sunday parties and frequently dropped by his bungalow unannounced, rubbing elbows with Hollywood types and hoping to be discovered. Ray loved the mingling of his movie friends, his intellectual colleagues, and the little claque of street toughs, and presided over the constant flow of visitors, "enthroned," as Stern remembered, "as guru."

Another of the regulars was a child actor who was also angling for a part in the film. Natalie Wood was sixteen years old and had been in movies for about eight years, most notably 1947's *Miracle on 34th Street*. Wood was keen to transcend the goody-two-shoes roles that she had been playing and do more grown-up material. She heard that *Rebel* had a big role for a teenage girl, and she kept appearing wherever Ray was—his office, the studio commissary, parties, restaurants—dressed and made up to appear older and more worldly than her years, acting the part of the vamp so that Ray would take note of her.

He did. After several "accidental" encounters, Ray invited Wood out to dinner, where he supplied her with drinks, and then he took her out again, until they became lovers—even though she was a minor just a few months younger than his own son. Wood became a fixture at the Sunday gatherings and often lounged around the Marmont pool for whole days, tanning in a leopard-print bikini, coming and going from Ray's bungalow with her own key. But she still hadn't been cast definitively in the film. Somehow keeping a straight face, Ray told her that she was too wholesome for the part.

Gradually, as Stern's script reached its final form, Ray started to use his home as a rehearsal space for the ensemble he was loosely building. Dean and others would read through pages with Ray, or improvise scenes, or critique Stern's version of contemporary teenage argot or behavior. One of the most remarkable moments in the film was born right there in Ray's kitchen: Dean's character, reeling from the stress of witnessing a death, helps himself to a swig of milk straight out of the fridge and then rolls the cool glass bottle over his forehead and cheek in a touching, intimate, childlike moment of self-soothing.

Wood and Hopper, though neither was signed to the picture, took part in these improv and script reading sessions, and she took a liking to him. One evening, Hopper recalled, she phoned him with the most astonishing declaration: "I'd like to fuck you, but I don't do anything. I just lay there. . . . I have to do a little rehearsing with Nick at the Chateau, but if you pick me up afterward . . ." He was there in a shot, whisking her away, only to realize that he didn't have access to any place where they might consummate the act. "Just go up the hill," she told him. "I know a lovers lane." Once there, Hopper said, "I started to go down on her, and she said, 'Oh, you can't do that.' I said, 'Why?' She said, 'Because Nick just fucked me.' "

Hopper found the situation bizarre, but he was only eighteen himself and wasn't turned off. Rather, he was inflamed. In the following days, just as he had stalked Dean, he began to snake furtively around Chateau Marmont, hoping to catch Ray and Wood in flagrante, to separate them, to have her for himself. Instead, he wound up bringing them closer together.

One night in February, when Wood was bursting with anxiety about whether Ray would give her the role she wanted, she asked Hopper to take her out. They hit Googie's, met some friends, and reckoned that wine was more in the spirit of the night than coffee. Off they went to the Villa Capri, a chic old-style Italian spot in Hollywood, where several bottles of Chianti led them all to think that stargazing—with a bottle of whiskey—would be a good idea. They drove up to Mulholland Drive, swigging away. Wood soon succumbed to all the booze, vomiting by the side of the road, and Hopper decided to take her home. Heading back to Sunset Boulevard, he collided with a car on Laurel Canyon Boulevard. His convertible flipped, ejecting all its passengers. Ambulances were called.

At the hospital, when Wood was pressed for her parents' names and phone number, she insisted that the attendants call Ray. "I just kept repeating the number of the Chateau Marmont," she later remembered, "so that's what they did call." Ray raced to the hospital. He found Wood lying in a bed surrounded by doctors and nurses. He bent over her, and looking right in his eyes, she indicated the hospital staff and whispered, "They called me a goddamn juvenile delinquent. *Now* do I get the part?" She did.

That left only one important role to be filled: Plato, the young loner who hero-worships the protagonist and whose emotional instability leads to tragedy. None of the scores of young hopefuls who'd passed through his office or bungalow projected the right sense of vulnerability to Ray until he met Sal Mineo, a coffin maker's son from Queens who had enjoyed a long run on Broadway as one of the princes tutored by an English governess in *The King and I.* Ray spotted Mineo lined up in a cattle call for the part, and he asked him to come by Chateau Marmont to meet Dean and run through some lines with him.

"I went to Nick Ray's hotel," Mineo remembered, "and he introduced me to Jimmy. It was on a Sunday afternoon. He said, 'I'd just like to go over a couple of scenes.' . . . So I started reading the scene with Jimmy. Then Nick said, 'All right. Now let's put the script away. Can you do improvisation?' Of course I said yes—I had no idea what he was talking about, but I wanted that role very badly. I picked it up from Jimmy, realized that he was doing the scene but making up his own dialogue."

Mineo got more than just an acting class. He got the part and found in Ray both a mentor and, as many observers were convinced, a lover. Ray was, per Gore Vidal, who was then resident at Chateau Marmont while writing a script for MGM, "rather openly having an affair with the adolescent Sal Mineo, while the sallow Jimmy Dean skulked in and out." (Ray would later dispute this claim, but in his time at the bungalow he took as lovers several young men he was ushering into the business of Hollywood, and he was never a very reliable chronicler of his own history.)

In this overheated atmosphere, Stern managed to produce a screenplay that satisfied Warner Bros., Ray, and, perhaps most important, Dean, and rehearsals began in earnest. Starting in February, serious read throughs of the script were held regularly at Ray's bungalow, including a well-attended session captured in a photo that reveals a fairly straight-looking clutch of young actors, a couple of reel-to-reel tape recorders, and the grown-ups Ray, Stern, and Jim Backus, the character actor (and voice of *Mr. Magoo*) who had been cast as Dean's father. So many of these rehearsal sessions were held at Ray's place that the director instructed the film's production designer, Malcolm C. Bert, to reconstruct the living room and staircase of the bungalow on a soundstage at Warner Bros. to serve as the main character's home; the actors already knew the layout after all.*

Filming began in late March and ended at the close of May, about a week over schedule, some of which was due to the studio's decision, mindful of MGM's hit teen picture *Blackboard Jungle,*

---

* The set—or at least one built on very similar lines—appeared once again in a 1960 episode of the TV anthology series *Ford Startime*, "Closed Set." Written by Ray's assistant (and sometime roommate and lover) Gavin Lambert, it concerned the relationship between a lusty film director (John Ireland) and the vainglorious movie star (Joan Fontaine) whom he is directing in a Western.

and appreciative of the terrific footage and performances Ray was capturing, to turn the film from a low-budget black-and-white B movie into a full-color—and, therefore, more expensive— picture. It was a relatively smooth shoot, with the chief disruptions coming not from the work on set but from the sparks still flying between Dennis Hopper and Ray, who were both still squiring Wood. Hopper went so far as to start carrying a gun on his prowls through Chateau Marmont, and he finally confronted Ray, threatening to "beat the shit" out of the older man unless he ceased his affair with Wood. "See, that's your problem," Ray told him. "You have to use your fists. You can't use your brain." Ray continued sleeping with his teenage leading lady, and he added to Hopper's woes by cutting almost every line the actor had out of the finished picture.

Before filming ended, *East of Eden* had premiered, and Dean was the hottest young actor in town. When the final shot of *Rebel* was in the can, Ray rallied the gang of kids and hangers-on for a celebration. "We'll all go to Googie's," he said, which would let him end the night conveniently across Sunset Boulevard from Chateau Marmont. Days later, Dean was off to make *Giant* with director George Stevens. And Ray got to work cutting his film.

He was still editing when he had his denouement with Wood. She had missed her period and had an appointment to see a doctor, the night prior to which she slept at Ray's bungalow. Late in the night, Ray, boozy and half-asleep, stumbled down into the kitchen for a cold drink and tossed back what turned out to be a urine sample that Wood had prepared to bring to her doctor. In the morning, when she learned what happened, she was horrified. And when it turned out she wasn't pregnant, she extricated herself from the entanglement, though she would continue to visit Ray at his bungalow almost as long as he lived there.

In August, as Ray was finishing work on *Rebel*, which was set for an October release, he had dinner with Dean, who had just wrapped *Giant* and hadn't liked working with Stevens as well as he had Kazan and Ray. The pair discussed some projects they thought they could make together and sketched out plans for a vacation together in Nicaragua. Late that night, Dean stopped by Chateau Marmont to borrow a book about how to raise a kitten: Elizabeth Taylor, his *Giant* co-star, had given him a baby Siamese as a gift at the end of shooting.

It was the last time Ray and Dean would see each other.

A month later, on September 30, 1955, Dean, en route to an auto race in Salinas, was killed when he crashed his Porsche Spyder in central California. Ray was in London, preparing with Warner Bros. executives for the overseas release of *Rebel*. He delayed returning to Hollywood, visiting France and Germany and showing up in New York on October 26 for the world premiere, which was a massive success. When Ray finally did return to Chateau Marmont, the memories of working on *Rebel* and the aura of his dead star seemed to haunt the bungalow. He arranged to sublease it and traveled for a while. It was just as well he did: *Rebel* was a smash hit, and the cult of its star grew enormously, with fans kitting themselves out in red Windbreakers just like the one Dean's character wore and making the hajj to Ray's rooms hoping to find the director at home and learn more about their hero.

When he finally settled back into his bungalow, Ray wasn't quite the same man. He went to work on a new film, *Hot Blood*, a melodrama about a gypsy/Romish family in a contemporary American urban setting. He brought his stars—Cornel Wilde, Jane Russell, and Luther Adler—to his home to try to replicate the familial atmosphere he'd generated with the cast of *Rebel*. It went poorly. "We had one rehearsal at his hotel," Wilde remembered. "He was always in control on the set, but at this rehearsal his speech was somewhat broken and slurred. A lot of what he said was incomprehensible, or at least it was way up on cloud nine as far as I was concerned. I know that Nick drank some, but I think he was on something else too."

For his next film, *Bigger than Life*, another melodrama about the dissolution of the American suburban dream, Ray hired an assistant, the English film critic and journalist Gavin Lambert, whom he'd met in London and begun an affair with. Lambert moved into Ray's bungalow and, when it became clear to him that Ray was drinking and using drugs heavily, did a lot of heavy lifting on the film. In addition to lover and chauffeur, he served as Ray's nurse: Wandering drunkenly in the bungalow, the director tumbled on the stairs and reinjured the foot he'd hurt during his escape from the burning apartment a few years prior.

In 1958, Ray was still staggering, still haunted by *Rebel* and the loss of Dean, still overindulging. Then, on the set of the picture he was making, the gangster melodrama *Party Girl*, he reconnected with a young dancer he'd known a few years previously. Betty Utey would become the third Mrs. Nick Ray. And upon marrying her, he gave up his bungalow at Chateau Marmont for good.

Almost.

In 1973, divorced from Utey and married to yet another much younger woman, Ray returned to Chateau Marmont and the Director's Bungalow. He was at work on a new film and thought he could rekindle the heat and magic of that long-ago season that produced *Rebel*. He even threw a Sunday bash, a fund-raiser for his new project, which was attended by, among others, Natalie Wood and her husband, Robert Wagner. But the money never materialized, the film never came to be, and Ray left the Chateau forever.

5.

Nick Ray and his crowd weren't the only people who found sexual freedom in the atmosphere surrounding Chateau Marmont and, especially, the swimming pool. Roddy McDowall, who had come to America in 1940 as a preteen actor and grown up in Hollywood, was in the closet throughout his life but happily entertained a great number of men at the Chateau, where he stayed regularly in the fifties, when he was living full-time in New York. Scotty Bowers, a Hollywood Boulevard gas station attendant who had an active sideline business setting up high-profile movie stars with same-sex dates, remembered bringing many "tricks" up to McDowall's suite and recalled that the star had a fondness for using amyl nitrite poppers to enhance his escapades.

Another young actor from New York who found the place to be a safe haven for sexual self-expression was Anthony Perkins. A tall, skinny, awkward stage and TV performer, he came out to Hollywood in the summer of 1955 to make his second film, *Friendly Persuasion*, a tale about a Quaker family torn between pacifism and abolitionism during the Civil War. Strapped for a place to live, and unsure that he would be in town for very long, Perkins took a suite at the Chateau.

Perkins was twenty-three, the son of the celebrated actor Osgood Perkins, who died backstage in a Washington, D.C., theater after the premiere of a new play when his only son was just five years old. Raised in Manhattan and Boston, Perkins started following his father's chosen career in school, and by the time he was in college, he was a serious stage actor. He'd made one stab at Hollywood in 1952, which resulted in a rickety performance in *The Actress*. The film, based on an autobiographical play written by Ruth Gordon, was directed by George Cukor, and starred Spencer Tracy, Jean Simmons, and Teresa Wright. But even with such a substantial pedigree, MGM didn't care for it and barely gave it a release.* Returning to New York humbled, Perkins continued to hone his craft in a number of live TV dramas and onstage, most notably in the cast of *Tea and Sympathy*, the hit Broadway play directed by Elia Kazan, in which Perkins

---

* Despite the relative prestige of *The Actress*, Perkins for many years disavowed the film and referred to *Friendly Persuasion* as his feature film debut—perhaps because it garnered him his sole Academy Award nomination, as Best Supporting Actor.

took over one of the lead roles, originated by John Kerr, that of a schoolboy of uncertain sexuality who is "rescued" from his proclivities by the wife of a faculty member, Joan Fontaine, filling the part originated by Deborah Kerr (no relation to her co-star). In that much-lauded performance, Perkins was "discovered" by William Wyler for *Friendly Persuasion,* cast as the son of Gary Cooper and Dorothy McGuire, and brought out to Hollywood a second time.

On his first go-round in town, Perkins was just another handsome young wannabe, although one who was able to gain entrée to film studios and the homes of movie stars because of the fondness so many people retained for his father. This time, though, he was given the Hollywood buildup: puff pieces in magazines, appearances at premieres and parties, regular name drops in gossip columns and trade papers. In this burnishing of his brand, he had two advantages. One was the fact that James Dean died soon after Perkins arrived in town and the pop culture machine was searching for the next eccentric New York actor to replace him. The other was that Perkins really was something of a kook, given to walking the streets of West Hollywood barefoot, hitchhiking (and, later, bicycling) to and from the studio, and running with some of the same bohemian crowd that had constituted Dean's circle.

In that world, the fact that Perkins was a homosexual, although a deeply closeted one, wasn't only unimportant; it was even a leg up. A certain cachet was ascribed to anyone who was willing to live outside the societal straitjacket of the day, even someone like Perkins, who wouldn't admit to anyone but his most intimate acquaintances the truth of his sexuality. It wasn't, in that light, a coincidence that Perkins should fall in with several of Dean's old chums, including Maila Nurmi, TV's Vampira and the woman who had first introduced Dean to the Chateau and Nicholas Ray.

To Nurmi it was natural that an actor being given the big star push should be in residence at the Chateau. "That was the center of the universe in those days," she said. But there wasn't a lot of glamour in Perkins's situation, she said. He had been installed in the janitor's quarters, partly because the hotel was overbooked, partly because, still young enough to think of himself as a boarding school student, he wanted to save money. After a time, though, according to Nurmi, "he got a little grander and had a real room upstairs."

The suite that Perkins came to occupy was a rat's nest, with his clothes, papers, kitchenware, and various other belongings strewn about on chairs, the sofa, and the floor. In a series of photographs taken for *Photoplay* magazine, he's shown taking a phone call in the middle of the mess, playing with a paddle-and-ball toy, and retreating onto the balcony to conduct his conversation by literally stepping through the window, dragging the phone and its lengthy cord out with him. (He was serious about his privacy, using the pay phones in the hotel foyer to talk with his intimate friends rather than speak with them on his room phone and risk having a nosy switchboard operator, known to him only half in jest as "Madam Spy," listen in—which, in his defense, she often did.)

Like so many other young bohemian Hollywood types and Chateau residents, Perkins frequented Schwab's and Googie's, where he would often go for early breakfasts—he had to be at the set by 5:00 a.m. most days—and bump into his chums who were still out on the toot from the night before. And like many young gay men in the Hollywood whirl, he found that Chateau Marmont was a place where his private life stayed that way. He was visited there by an on-again/off-again boyfriend from back east; he brought pickups back to his suite with him; he frequently called on Scotty Bowers to bring him exciting new dates ("Who've you got who's different?" he'd ask); and he socialized around the swimming pool, where, wandering by one afternoon in late 1955, he was introduced to another handsome young actor who was also deeply in the closet: Tab Hunter.

Hunter was born Arthur Kelm in New York in 1931 and was

given his mother's surname, Gelien, after his parents' acrimonious divorce. He was raised in California and devoted much of his teenage years to competitive figure skating. After a stint in the Coast Guard, he was discovered by the Hollywood agent Henry Willson, who guided the careers of Rock Hudson, Robert Wagner, and other handsome young men of the era and saw in Hunter the chiseled all-American looks he favored. Willson gave this new protégé a new name and a few roles, culminating in a breakout appearance in Raoul Walsh's 1955 military melodrama *Battle Cry,* in which the nation's adolescent girls discovered Hunter. Hunter seemed destined for big things—he was even making hit records—but his rise was threatened by an exposé that same year in the tell-all magazine *Confidential,* which revealed that he had been arrested in 1950 during the police raid of a homosexual party at a Westside house.* This sort of bombshell might've killed off a young actor's career, but Hunter was spared by studio boss Jack Warner, who refused to knuckle under to the magazine's extortionate tactics. He assured Hunter that the negative publicity involving a minor, long-ago incident would soon vanish, and it did.

But Hunter *was* gay, and whether or not he went to Chateau Marmont that fateful afternoon in search of romance, he found it. An avid horseman who had acted in many Westerns, he had spent the day in the San Fernando Valley riding with his friend and frequent "date," the starlet Venetia Stevenson. Driving home through Laurel Canyon, he recalled, it was his wont to refresh himself with a swim: "I'd go take a dip at the Chateau. It was a wonderful place because of the location and the convenience." Hunter had been introduced to the hotel by Natalie

---

* Likely it was Willson who gave *Confidential* the story—plus a story about the criminal record of another of his clients, Rory Calhoun—in exchange for the magazine keeping silent about the homosexuality of Hudson, the most prominent star on his roster.

Wood, who brought him around to Nicholas Ray's bungalow during the making of *Rebel Without a Cause*. He was fond of the lack of pretension and, especially, the discreet atmosphere: "Despite its prominence, the cloistered Chateau provided plenty of privacy for its tenants, who could laze around the pool without being pestered by starstruck fans."

That particular day, as he toweled off from his swim, an acquaintance approached him in an appropriately low-key fashion and "formally introduced" Hunter to Perkins, who was "tall and skinny, wearing a buttoned-down Brooks Brothers shirt and aviator-style reading glasses. He looked like a gawky New England prep school student who'd taken a wrong turn." The two chatted poolside, and Perkins invited Hunter up to his room.

"My relationship with Tony began that day," Hunter recalled, and it continued for two years, even as Perkins was warned by friends, co-stars, and studio executives that being connected to Hunter could threaten his rising career. Told by one of his bosses that he had to give Hunter up, Perkins retorted, "But I love him!" Stymied, the studio allowed Perkins and Hunter to be seen together in public only on double dates, accompanied often by Stevenson and one of their current female co-stars. The charade, the truth behind which was widely known throughout Hollywood, persisted all through their relationship, which dwindled as Perkins moved on to other romantic partners and, chief of all, chased his professional fortunes. "Nothing," Hunter recalled, "came between Tony and his career."

Hunter continued to visit Chateau Marmont after his affair with Perkins ended. "I remember Anna Magnani going to the market and coming back with sacks of groceries and making her pasta," he said. "And the New York actors, who wanted a simple, comfortable place that wasn't too 'Hollywood.' None of them drove, and they were all lost without cars, but it was no big deal to go pick them up there because it was so close to everything. Geraldine Page stayed there when she and I were appearing together on *Playhouse 90,* and I'd pick her up and take her to CBS Television City. Finally, I taught her how to drive."

Perkins, meanwhile, moved on from Hunter in search of what he considered the sort of company that could aid his ambitions. He met Gore Vidal at Chateau Marmont, and the author invited him around to his suite for a party, where Perkins met the writer Christopher Isherwood and his longtime partner, painter Don Bachardy, who lived in Santa Monica and were as out a gay couple as Los Angeles had. "He was very circumspect," Bachardy remembered of Perkins. "He never talked queer, or in any way acknowledged his queerness to us." But he continued to bring dates back to the hotel—girls that the studio set him up with, who helped him clean his suite and wash his clothes, and boys he met around town, with whom he engaged in more intimate pastimes. He moved out of Chateau Marmont after a few years of intermittent residence and returned to New York, where he had a success on Broadway in *Look Homeward, Angel.* But the hotel remained one of his favored places to stay in Hollywood. In 1964, in the wake of his massive success in Alfred Hitchcock's *Psycho,* Perkins came back to Hollywood for a new film production and once again moved into the Chateau, spending the first night by himself sitting on the balcony of his penthouse suite "eating ice cream and looking at the view." And decades later, married and a father, he was said to keep a room on hold for himself at the hotel so that he would have a place for trysts with young men.

❖

Gay men weren't alone in finding the Chateau an ideal spot from which to carry on adventuresome sex lives. Grace Kelly was known by hotel staffers to have a notable appetite for men— particularly other guests, whose room numbers she would often try to wheedle out of desk clerks. And Warren Beatty, living on the very cheap during his first days in Hollywood, ran up conquests as impressively as he did unpaid bills, finally being asked to leave by management for his financial arrears and returning for a while when he was engaged to Joan Collins and she was in residence—on a movie studio's dime.

But the Chateau held a special symbolic weight in the history of gay Hollywood, and perhaps none of the hotel's many gay residents was better suited to understand and appreciate that fact than Gore Vidal. Starting in the mid-fifties, the blue-blooded novelist, polemicist, and provocateur came to Hollywood repeatedly to do business and, as often, to give the business to a town that he thought equal to Washington, D.C., as a cesspool of ambition, self-absorption, and hypocrisy. On several of those occasions, particularly early in his acquaintance with the town and the movie industry, he stayed at the Chateau.

Vidal had grown up with the benefit of position and money, the only child of a marriage that blended two eastern families of high renown and even higher living and that ended not long after the arrival of its sole issue, young Gore. He was born in 1925 at the hospital at West Point and raised largely in Washington, attending the best schools, one after another, as he was dragged up and down the East Coast by his parents' fluctuating careers and marriages. He had toured Europe as a teen right until the outbreak of World War II, and he developed a taste for the culture and lifestyle of the Continent, Italy in particular and Rome most specifically. He eschewed college for the military, enlisting in the army and serving three years during the war as a warrant officer in Alaska. There, he began writing fiction, becoming suddenly famous in 1948 with the publication of his third novel, *The City and the Pillar,* which was, in part, a frank depiction of homosexual romance. He continued to write seriously: literary fiction, political and cultural essays, mystery fiction (under a pseudonym), and then, in the mid-fifties, plays for live television. Based on his success in this latter capacity, he found himself summoned to Hollywood in 1955 to write a big-screen adaptation of *The Catered Affair*, a family melodrama based on Paddy Chayefsky's TV production of the same name. He checked into the Chateau for an extended stay while he worked on the script.

For Vidal, the Chateau's combination of European self-sufficiency and subdued sophistication made it feel particularly homey. He accumulated friends during that first visit, making the acquaintance of Scotty Bowers. "I introduced him to all sorts of stars," Bowers recalled, "and lots of ordinary guys. He'd hook up for a night or two. . . . This was a lively time for everybody, and nobody thought much about it." Yet despite the liberated environment in which he found himself, Vidal was eventually joined at the Chateau by his longtime companion, Howard Austen, and even by his mother, Nina, which at least partly put the brakes on his carousing.

Around the Chateau swimming pool, Vidal ran into two up-and-coming actors just in from New York, where he'd first met them: Paul Newman and Joanne Woodward. Vidal's open-secret lifestyle coincided with the open-secret love affair between the married Newman and the woman who would eventually become his second wife, and a bond of shared intimacy quickly grew between them all. "Life at the Chateau Marmont was dark and strange," Woodward recalled. "We were closeted together because we were all from New York. . . . It was an odd grouping of people."

"We would meet Paul and Joanne by the pool," Howard Austen said, "and we'd run into all sorts of Hollywood people, hangers-on, stars, producers. We got invited to parties. It was such a creepy place, the Marmont. A run-down fake château, but perfect, too. . . . We got along so well, almost like a family. Those were beautiful days, though everybody drank too much." Vidal loved the company of this glamorous, clandestine pair of future stars, particularly Newman. Bowers assumed there was a sexual attraction between them, at least on Vidal's part: "Gore liked clean-cut guys best. Guys like Paul Newman, only Newman wasn't gay. But that was the look he preferred." But for

Vidal, there was another explanation for the friendship, which would last decades. "One significant thing we had in common was being the same age," he wrote. "This meant that when I was seventeen I enlisted in the U.S. Army; when Paul was seventeen he enlisted in the U.S. Navy. . . . Each of us had missed having a youth, which we later compensated for a bit too long after adolescence had officially ended for us."

There was partying and boozing and socializing and sunbathing and sex during those weeks at the Chateau, but there was also work: Vidal and Newman had met in New York when the actor played the lead in "The Death of Billy the Kid," a live-action teleplay Vidal wrote about the famed outlaw. The pair thought it could be adapted for the big screen, and many of their chats around the Chateau Marmont pool involved strategizing this project. Eventually, Newman succeeded in making the film as *The Left Handed Gun,* but Vidal was squeezed out of the picture by the producer Fred Coe and replaced as screenwriter. Vidal might've resented the failure of his friend to fight for him, but he understood that Coe was the villain: "He sees what he thinks is a stupid movie star in Paul Newman and a scatterbrained playwright who's all over the place in me, and he has an opening to get in and take it over and did."

Vidal was a shrewder observer of the Hollywood scene than many writers who wrote for the movies for their entire lives. He was attuned to everything happening at the studios where he worked and, equally, at the Chateau. He noted the intriguing comings and goings from Nicholas Ray's bungalow and befriended some of the other gay men in residence at the hotel, such as the TV director Ralph Levy, his lover, singer/actor Mike Rayhill, the comedian Paul Lynde, and, inevitably, Anthony Perkins. Always sociable, Vidal made sufficient connections in the Hollywood community to throw himself a birthday party in his Chateau Marmont suite, which the syndicated gossip columnist Mike Connolly, himself a closeted gay man, attended and wrote about without naming any of his fellow guests.

Vidal moved in and out of Chateau Marmont over the next two years, mixing up his visits to Hollywood by renting a house in Laurel Canyon and another in Malibu, where he stayed with Austen *and* Newman and Woodward, the two couples serving as, in effect, beards for each other; Vidal and Woodward were even rumored to be engaged in the gossip press, a ruse that helped to hide the fact that each was coupled with someone else in the house.

In ensuing decades, Vidal would make his home principally in Italy, only occasionally visiting Hollywood and even more rarely stopping by or staying at the Chateau. When he did, he reveled in and bragged about things he got up to there, such as claiming to have had sex with the actor Brad Davis, "a beautiful boy," on the floor of the bathroom in his suite. In 2012, Vidal made the final public appearance of his life at Chateau Marmont, at a party celebrating the launch of Scotty Bowers's tell-all memoirs, reveling once again in shocking people with tales of his youthful debaucheries, then vanishing not long after into illness, hospitalization, and death.

In all those years, with all he did and saw at Chateau Marmont, Vidal remained transfixed by one specific aspect of the hotel, something gaudy and outsized and forever, in his mind, emblematic of the excesses of Hollywood and America and the twentieth century: a statue that stood just outside his hotel window, revolving day and night and beckoning passersby to consider the sexual possibilities of a visit to . . . Las Vegas.

6.

Benny Siegel was murdered for the crime of thinking that a cow town in the Nevada desert would blossom into a deluxe gambling mecca that would earn millions for organized crime. Within a few years, though, his vision had become palpably real. The Flamingo opened at the end of 1946, and within six years the stretch of U.S. 91 that was barren when Siegel first saw it was home to more than a thousand hotel rooms. Las Vegas became a destination, offering guests the chance to indulge in such niceties of Nevada law as legal gambling, ready access to quick marriage and divorce, lax policing of prostitution, liberal liquor laws, and a dependably warm and dry climate. For Hollywood people, the proximity to Los Angeles and Vegas's relative dearth of newspapermen and gossip columnists also proved alluring.

But there was an even more compelling incentive for entertainers to make their way to Las Vegas than hedonism, isolation, or arid weather. The resorts along Highway 91, now christened the Las Vegas Strip, all had show rooms and lounges where the most famous names in entertainment—musicians, dancers, comedians, even straight actors—were booked as feature attractions, luring visitors to the hotels and, of course, the casinos. Such was the spirit of competition in Vegas, and such were the immense profits made off gambling, that resorts started to pay astronomical fees to performers. By 1952, the Vegas Strip had become an entertainment capital to rival the Sunset Strip.

It was almost inevitable that the jostling between the two Strips should be exploited, and in 1953 the Sahara Hotel and casino created a sensation in West Hollywood by erecting what could only be described as a live billboard to advertise itself. A large deck and aboveground pool were installed, actual human bathing beauties were employed to dive, swim, and lounge around it, and prominent signage for the Sahara topped it all off.* The thing made headlines for a few days and drew some additional notice when the comedy star Red Skelton, under contract to the Sahara, dove into it a few times to promote an upcoming engagement. But it disappeared before long, a mere novelty. And then the owners of the Sahara decided they needed to keep

---

* In another of those only-in–West Hollywood things, the use of live models in an advertising display was illegal in the city of Los Angeles but perfectly okay in the county. Voilà.

their place in the public eye with an even more audacious bit of advertising, one that would change the image of—and the view from—Chateau Marmont for years.

�֍

Like so many girls before her, she breezed into Hollywood without fanfare; caught the attention of everybody with her beauty and her brass; became famous for, more or less, being famous; danced and smiled ceaselessly; changed her look cheekily with the seasons and the times; and vexed her most staid and priggish critics with the sheer fact of her existence.

Unlike any of her predecessors, though, she was some forty feet tall.

She rolled into town in May 1957, unannounced but foretold, if you knew what to look for, by a construction crew installing concrete supports for a "spectacular," as oversized billboards were known in the ad trade. Before she arrived, the crew had already placed a large advertisement for the Sahara Hotel on the small stretch of scrub that sat between the corner of Marmont and Sunset and the building that had once housed Preston Sturges's Players Club.

The Sahara was well-known for gaudy promotions, and this one was shaping up as a lulu: At ground level, a theatrical marquee announced the current and upcoming performers; above that sat a rendition of the hotel's logo that itself was larger than any of the billboards farther west on the Strip; topping *that* was a giant silver dollar. That was plenty monstrous, but for a few days one last structural piling, taller still, remained unused, threatening. And one benighted morning, the residents of Chateau Marmont awoke to the racket of a flatbed truck and a crane settling into place to deliver . . . *her.*

She was a giantess, with a bouffant hairdo, elfin features, a gleaming smile, an hourglass figure. She was poised like a Rockette, her right thigh raised to parallel with the ground, foot bent inward; her left arm extended as if to receive a kiss on her hand, in which she held out, like a cocktail tray, a cowboy hat. From bosom to hips and on her feet, she wore the costume of a cowgirl or, rather, the costume that a lonely cowboy on the trail might dream of encountering a girl dressed in: a bikini top, short-shorts, and cowboy boots.

She was lit up from dusk until well past midnight.

And she revolved.

All day.

All night.

Endlessly.

Forever.

She stopped traffic on Sunset Boulevard, which was exactly what the folks who put her on that spot had hoped.

And inside Chateau Marmont, she made blood boil.

Trying to sleep on the busily trafficked Sunset Boulevard side of the hotel was hard enough for some guests. But with the advent of the Sahara showgirl, they had a new vexation: They couldn't look out their windows without being overwhelmed by the spectacle of "the outsize floozie," as *The New York Times* called her. They complained to management, who said that they had no recourse against the garish thing. It was built on private land and conformed to Los Angeles County's (very lax) regulations for advertising signage. There were whispers—unproven—that the Sahara had made an under-the-table payment to the Chateau's owner to keep silent about the monstrous showgirl. And when certain long-term residents put together a petition to have the thing dismantled, their signatures added up to naught. The billboard was there to stay—and to vex the hotel's clientele.

Paul Muni, for one. Nearing the end of his acting days, the great star made the curious decision to appear onstage in Los Angeles in *At the Grand,* a musical adaptation of the film *Grand Hotel,* and moved into a penthouse suite at the Marmont for the duration of rehearsals and the actual run. It started as a happy experience for him; he was agreeable and polite with staff and the occasional hotel guest who would approach him for an autograph. But the production quickly became troubled, and Muni's bonhomie dissipated. Muni was unhappy with the script, according to playwright Luther Davis, and continually ad-libbed lines, making the rehearsal of musical numbers almost impossible. The lines he *did* know, he learned by pacing the balcony of his suite at night, barking into a tape recorder, much to the annoyance of fellow guests who joked that they'd heard the script so often, *they* could play his part. But that was nothing compared with his response to the Sahara showgirl, spinning ceaselessly just in front of him, a living reminder, he felt, of the worst aspects of his profession. "It's the whore Hollywood! The whore show business!" he bellowed into the night. Visiting the actor in his suite, Davis was alarmed at the star's obsession with the spinning figure. "He pointed to the window," Davis recalled, "and said, 'They put that there just to taunt me,' and I thought, 'Uh-oh.' "

Writer Roger Kahn remembered what an imposition the revolving billboard had been to his friend screenwriter Ring Lardner Jr. "There he was," he said, "working on a screenplay, a portable typewriter on his desk and the venetian blinds drawn. It was a lovely November day. I said, 'Ring, why are you working with the blinds drawn?' Ring opened the blinds and there in his face was this gigantic, spinning, plastic showgirl. Every 15 seconds these massive plastic boobs came past the window. Ring said, 'Makes it hard to work,' and he closed the blinds."

A few years into the showgirl's tenure, Brooks Atkinson of *The New York Times* seemed to encourage vandalism against her, so riled was he by her very existence: "She has not lost any of her fingers. They would make a good target for enterprising boys with guns." (And Chateau Marmont legend held that Brandon De Wilde, the teenage star of *Shane* and *Hud,* who occasionally lived in an upper-floor suite with his parents, took target practice at her erogenous zones with his air rifle.)

Another visiting New Yorker, however, found her not only comforting but even inspiring. John Cheever stayed in one of the nicer penthouses at Chateau Marmont in the fall of 1960, when he was hired to adapt a D. H. Lawrence novel for 20th Century Fox. Cheever wasn't a natural for Hollywood. He was embarrassed by the studio's largesse, writing to friends with chagrin about being regularly reminded by hotel staff that he was staying in the famed "Mitzi Gaynor suite," sighing that he felt déclassé in his worn-out dressing gown, dotted with cigarette burns. His letters bragged happily about the carnations and watercooler in his suite, but he was put off by the Lincoln Continental convertible that the studio had stowed for him in the hotel garage. He was entirely out of his element: One afternoon, relaxing by the pool, he heard somebody whisper, "There he is; that's Cheever." Aghast at being recognized, he dove into the water and immediately lost his swim trunks.

But the specter of all of these awkwardnesses vanished when he considered the gigantic Sahara showgirl twirling outside his window. In 1961, she appeared in a story that he published in *The New Yorker,* "The Angel of the Bridge." In it, the narrator, a neurotic business traveler, finds himself in an unnamed Sunset Strip hotel staring out the window at a mysterious fistfight in the street below and, later, at a drunken woman in a sable coat being helped into a car. Most prominently in view, though, is the Sahara showgirl: "She revolves slowly in a beam of light. At 2 a.m. the light is extinguished, but she goes on restlessly turning all through the night. . . . I wondered if she had a family—a stage mother, perhaps, and a compromised and broken-spirited father who drove a municipal bus on the West Pico line?"

There were no such winsome fantasies in the mind of Gore Vidal, who detested the twirling giantess. Encamped at the Chateau while trying to write *Ben-Hur,* among other scripts, he found her to be just another of the cursed aspects of life in Hollywood. "Oh, God," he remembered, "to wake up in the morning with a hangover and look out and see that figure, turning, turning, holding the sombrero—you knew what death would be like." He would, in time, get his revenge for these horrors.

7.

No matter what was spinning on the street in front of it, the Chateau maintained its reputation as a haven for movie stars who were riding the carousel of marriage and divorce. Rita Hayworth was in and out of the hotel as her marital status evolved over the years, and staffers who remembered her as a glamorous dancer, actress, and pinup girl were quietly aghast at her sometimes decrepit appearance and befuddled manner. Those same staffers were on tiptoes when Marlon Brando showed up at the hotel after his divorce from the actress Anna Kashfi. (She herself had checked into the hotel with her infant son, Christian, the previous year after a row with Brando at their Mulholland Drive estate.) Brando's reputation as a bad boy and roué was significant. But he was at a low point, both personally and professionally—he was engaged in the marathon ordeal of directing the psychological Western *One-Eyed Jacks*, his only foray behind the camera—and he passed a great deal of his extended visit in brooding isolation, having the switchboard intercept all his phone calls, ordering food deliveries rather than going out for meals, and talking long into the night with hotel staffers, who found him a surprisingly sympathetic and vulnerable character. He finally left only when he set off for Tahiti for the production of *Mutiny on the Bounty*, during which, almost inevitably, he found a new woman to wed.

A similarly somber aspect was presented by Vivien Leigh, Brando's *Streetcar Named Desire* co-star, who appeared at the hotel with twenty-two pieces of luggage, her Siamese cat, Poo Jones, and authentic Renoir and Picasso canvases that she had brought from England "to brighten my hotel rooms" while on tour. She was in town to appear onstage—she hadn't made a film in Hollywood in nearly a decade—and also, it was clear to everyone who met her, to nurse the wounds of her recent divorce from Laurence Olivier. Olivier himself had been at the Marmont just the year before, separated, it was assumed by one and all, from Leigh and hoping to marry another actress, Joan Plowright. Leigh was involved in a romance of her own, with the actor Jack Merivale, and it appeared that she and Olivier would part and move on in their lives without much fuss. But while Olivier continued to thrive both professionally and romantically, Leigh did neither. Struggling from what at the time was called "madness" but would likely be known as bipolar disorder decades later, she chattered constantly to hotel staffers about "my Larry" and had framed photographs of her ex-husband looking back at her from shelves and tables throughout her suite.

In her attachment to a man who had moved on, Leigh reminded some old Chateau hands of Rose Cohn, ex-wife of Columbia Pictures boss Harry Cohn (he of the famed adage "if you *must* get in trouble, go to the Marmont"). She had come to the hotel after her divorce on the advice of Nellita Choate Thomsen (a.k.a. Pauline Payne) and found herself unable to cope with life there on her own. In the mansion she shared with Cohn, there were maids and cooks and other servants to make the tasks of life seem effortless or even invisible to her. At the Chateau, even with much of the housework done for her by hotel staffers, she was helpless, unable to cook a meal without burning it and speaking constantly about Cohn, who she was certain would return to her, even though he had remarried within days of their divorce becoming official. To his credit, he remained attentive to her, supporting her with alimony and even solicitous phone calls during her long stay at the hotel. But she cut a sad and lonely figure, incapable in any way of enjoying her new life, however pampered it might have been.

Marilyn Monroe wasn't fleeing a bad marriage when she arrived at the Chateau in 1949, but she had one in her past, and her relationship with her manager, Johnny Hyde, resembled one.

She wasn't at the hotel on her own, but rather as the overnight guest of Milton Greene, a young New York photographer whom she met at a party when Hyde was out of town and with whom she immediately struck up a friendship; the two spent several weeks in close proximity, much of that time within the walls of the Chateau. She returned to the hotel a few years later, when she was on the rocks with husband number two, Joe DiMaggio, and living in New York City, where she was studying at the Actors Studio. This time, she took a suite of her own while she filmed the interior scenes of *Bus Stop* at Twentieth Century Fox. And once again she spent time in her suite with a young man from New York, although, by his testimony, it was entirely chaste: Brad Darrach was a writer with *Time* who had come to interview Monroe for a cover story; they were in the living room of her suite when she asked him if they could move into the bedroom. "My heart lurched," Darrach recalled, but she quickly calmed it: "I'm completely exhausted. It would help if I could talk lying down." And so they did, her head at one end of the bed, his at the other, for an hours-long chat that yielded a great amount of material for his story and a great yarn to dine out on years later.

One woman who visited Chateau Marmont several times in the wake of failed marriages neither sought nor needed anyone's sympathy—and would likely have thrown it right back in the face of anyone who had the nerve to proffer it. Bette Davis was among Hollywood's most formidable personalities—both in her art and in her temperament. One of the greatest actresses in the history of the cinema, she was also one of the most outspoken, unafraid to defy her employers publicly, to take extended hiatuses from the movies to appear onstage, or even to make her permanent home in New England, as far as physically possible from Los Angeles. The steel and craft she demonstrated in her work and in her continual wars against her bosses carried on in her marriages, which tended not to last more than a few years.

She became acquainted with the Marmont in the mid-fifties, when she was with her fourth husband, Gary Merrill, who had co-starred with her in *All About Eve*. Davis was having trouble finding film work, and so her visits to Hollywood were often short, either because she was coming away without the parts she hoped for or because she was performing on TV and thus didn't need to be in town for very long. Merrill was with her on some of these visits, and the impression the couple made wasn't rosy. Guests and staff members could hear their quarrels throughout the corridors and in the lobby. And that was the least of the ruckus they caused. In early 1958, when they were staying in a bungalow, they forced the whole hotel to empty when Davis, watching one of her old movies on late-night TV, fell asleep and lit the room on fire with a cigarette. "Had not someone in a nearby room seen the smoke billowing out our window," Davis later recalled, "we would have been asphyxiated." (That someone happened to be actor Lou Jacobi, who was staying in an adjacent bungalow.) Davis and Merrill raced out in their nightclothes and immediately bumped into Gig Young, an old friend whom they hadn't seen in a decade. A few years later, this time separated for good from Merrill, Davis caused yet another commotion at the hotel when an electrical short in her bungalow set off an alarm, once again sending all guests from their rooms. That was the last straw for her. "[She] said she'd never be back," said Carmel Volti, the Chateau's longtime switchboard operator, "and she has kept her word."

❈

One of the first guests to return to the hotel repeatedly because of TV work was Boris Karloff, who, after many years in Hollywood, had made what he thought would be a permanent retirement to his native England when new opportunities arose for him on the small screen back in America. In 1955, he and his wife, Evie, arrived at the Marmont expecting to stay for three weeks. They wound up living at the hotel on and off for seven years.

Karloff only once in all that time had a TV series of his own—

The Veil, a horror and suspense anthology program that ran but eleven episodes in 1958, with Karloff serving as host and appearing in several featured roles. But he acted in many other anthology series, dropped in as a guest star on several long-running shows, performed in a number of made-for-television movies and plays (some broadcast live), acted on local stages in his signature role of Jonathan Brewster in *Arsenic and Old Lace,* got surprised and biographied on TV's *This Is Your Life,* did a little work on radio, and even provided the voice of several children's albums of poems and stories, including one that was nominated for a Grammy.

It was a tremendous run, and the Karloffs managed to sock away enough of the money he was paid to secure retirement back home in England once and for all after it was over. Not that they didn't enjoy their time in the sun, or at Chateau Marmont. Karloff was a much-remarked presence in the hotel, startling his unsuspecting fellow guests when, for instance, the elevator doors would part and they would find themselves face-to-face with a fellow who looked like, well, Boris Karloff. Another time, Karloff drew attention to himself at the front desk while complaining loudly and angrily about a parking ticket he'd gotten for parking on Sunset Boulevard—Frankenstein brought low by a meter maid.

He might have cut a menacing figure, but he was a pussycat. He made friends with many of the hotel employees and found it especially easy to talk to Meemi Ferguson, then working as general manager. One evening he came home from the studio and tossed a glance at Meemi as he got into the elevator. A few minutes later, he called down from his suite and told Meemi, "Go to the elevator. I'm sending something down for you." She did as he instructed, and when the elevator door opened, she found herself confronted by a chilled, freshly made martini, complete with an olive on a toothpick. She put it aside—she never drank on the job—and called to thank him. Assuming he had done good, he proceeded to dispatch a martini similarly to her every night for the rest of his stay.

Toward the end of Karloff's never-ending short visit, another out-of-town performer made a longtime part-time home of the Marmont. Shirley Booth was principally a stage actress in New York and made only five movies—winning an Oscar for the first of them, *Come Back, Little Sheba*, in 1952. But in 1961 she started a five-year run as the star of the sitcom *Hazel*, playing the wise-acre maid of a suburban family (and winning an Emmy in her first season). Throughout the filming of all 154 episodes of the series, she lived at the Chateau, where she seemed from the very first to be like one of the family, coming down to the front desk in her robe, slippers, and curlers to check her mail, asking female staffers to help her get into dresses, kibitzing in the lobby and around the pool like somebody's maiden aunt visiting town to attend a wedding. She was adored.

❁

One of the hallmarks of Erwin Brettauer's ownership of Chateau Marmont throughout the forties and fifties was the hotel's tolerance—not only for the behavior of its rowdier guests, but, more important, for populations marginalized by the larger culture. Hollywood was run by moralizing hypocrites who were quick to preach the virtues of home and hearth in their films and public appearances while abetting right-wing anti-Communist witch hunts, excluding women and people of color from positions of power and/or dignity, and comporting themselves in their personal lives like debauched medieval princes. Similarly, the Hollywood community would grant lip service to the concept of inclusion, but its most prominent hotels—the Beverly Hills, the Beverly Wilshire, and the Hollywood Roosevelt—outright refused to book black guests, no matter who they might have been in the firmament of the entertainment world.

But Chateau Marmont was a different place. Having seen firsthand what Fascist intolerance had done in Europe, Brettauer was determined that his hotel would refuse nobody on the basis of race, religion, sexuality, or anything else, not even when a bigoted guest like Howard Hughes, who kept multiple rooms on retainer at full price, made it clear that he didn't care to have contact with blacks.

The open-door policy of Chateau Marmont under Brettauer became known throughout black show business after the war, and in subsequent years it would result in visits from any number of black American and African entertainment luminaries. Previously, the premier destination for black travelers was the Dunbar Hotel in South Central Los Angeles. In business since 1928, it was originally named the Somerville, and it had hosted the first national convention of the NAACP to be held in a western state. It was luxurious and elite, but it was far from Hollywood, and it was born of segregation. So when someone running a place like Chateau Marmont made it clear, as Brettauer did, "we have no color barrier," one black entertainer after another made a visit to the hotel, and often they would become regulars.

By most accounts, the first marquee name to switch permanently from the Dunbar to the Chateau was Duke Ellington. In 1958 and 1959, the great bandleader and composer was at work on the score for Otto Preminger's drama *Anatomy of a Murder* and made the hotel his base then and henceforth. He was a creature of habit, according to the director Martin Ritt, who visited Ellington at the hotel and would soon work with him on the film *Paris Blues*. "He'd get up late, have a steak for breakfast, always be [*sic*] a broad around," Ritt remembered. Ellington would literally lie about the hotel, receiving visiting reporters while he reclined on a sofa, and his collaborator Billy Strayhorn stayed busy answering phone calls, fixing drinks, bringing Ellington the California grapefruits he adored, and so forth. In the evenings, Ellington would occupy himself composing, in an idiosyncratic fashion.

While at work on a jazz interpretation of Edvard Grieg's *Peer Gynt Suites,* according to his producer Irving Townsend, Ellington would roam the corridors of the hotel deep into the night: "Duke concocted his arrangement of 'In the Hall of the Mountain King' while strolling around the halls of the Chateau Marmont." The album that resulted from these nocturnal voyages around the halls was named for Grieg's work but also punningly referred to the hotel in which he wrote it: *Swinging Suites.*

Once Ellington had made a home at the Chateau, a staggering roster of black entertainers followed. Just from the worlds of jazz and popular music, there were the likes of Pearl Bailey, Quincy Jones, Nina Simone, Harry Belafonte, Lena Horne, Della Reese, Hugh Masekela, Odetta, Miriam Makeba, Eartha Kitt, Sarah Vaughan, and Carmen McRae. Their stays at the hotel generated stories that enhanced the legends they were making with their music and their public personalities. On the carpeting of Erroll Garner's suite, Dizzy Gillespie learned how to putt a golf ball and proved a natural, rolling one shot after another into a water glass lying on the floor; "I just imagine that I'm the ball and I want to be in the cup," he explained. Josephine Baker, the great American dancer and singer who rose to fame in the twenties, when the sensual daring of her act made her the red-hot star of the *Folies Bergère* in Paris, spent several uneasy weeks in a small room at the Chateau during a late-career return to America, even though her manager, William L. Taub, "lived," according to an article in the *Los Angeles Sentinel,* the city's foremost black newspaper, "in a swell-elegant hotel and was driven around town in a chauffeur-driven automobile." Not surprisingly, the tour collapsed in lawsuits and counter-lawsuits.

Miles Davis and his first wife, dancer Frances Taylor, lived at the hotel while he was doing some recording, and they socialized actively with other guests. The pair went out almost nightly to see jazz performances on the Strip, and Miles rolled up his sleeves to cook pheasant with Rip Torn after one of the actor's hunting forays. Frances, who fancied an acting career, made the acquaintance of Michael Macdonald, the casting director of an adaptation of *Lord of the Flies*. When Macdonald rang the Davises' suite to invite Frances to an early screening of the film, he got Miles, who hissed, "She isn't here, motherfucker." Macdonald, abashed, stuttered a good-bye, hung up the phone, began to dial another number, and said to a friend standing beside him, "Gee, Miles called me a motherfucker"; he put his ear to the phone to continue his next call, only to hear Miles, still on the line, hissing, "No, I called you a *cocksucker.*"

There were black sporting figures among the Chateau's clientele during these years, including the boxer Archie Moore and the tennis star Althea Gibson. And there were black actors, naturally, many of them, none more famous or influential than Sidney Poitier, who made the hotel his base of operations in Hollywood for many years.

Poitier's residency at the Chateau stirred up headlines, although not the sort one normally thinks of when one hears the hotel's name mentioned. In 1960, on the heels of an Oscar nomination for *The Defiant Ones*, Poitier, along with his family and his fellow cast mates and crew members from the upcoming film adaptation of *A Raisin in the Sun*, couldn't find a hotel—or even a rental home—in Hollywood or Beverly Hills that would accommodate black residents. The star was willing to pay $1,500* for a three-month rental, but nothing appropriate was made available.

"I speak about this with pain," Poitier told *The New York Times*. "Hollywood has been extremely good to me. . . . But show business is not Southern California. The show business community is just a small portion of Southern California. The rest of the area yields only to time and to pressure. There is not one ounce of altruism." As Poitier explained, his family had at one time considered moving permanently to the Los Angeles area

* Nearly $13,000 in 2019 terms.

but decided against it because his children were comfortable in their New York–area home, where "they attend multi-racial schools. . . . We don't want to barter that kind of atmosphere for something hostile." So, instead of a rental home, Poitier, his wife, Juanita Hardy, their three children, and their traveling retinue took three adjacent units at the Chateau.*

But that wasn't Poitier's first visit to the Chateau, just the first one he cared to publicize. He had stayed at the hotel a couple of times in the preceding years, most notably when he was in production on the film version of *Porgy and Bess*. At that time, Juanita and the kids stayed in New York. And at that time, Poitier saw a lot of his co-star Diahann Carroll, who was in residence at the hotel as well while her husband, musical producer and manager Monte Kay, also stayed in New York, where he had founded and continued to operate the famed jazz club Birdland.

Poitier's suite was on the third floor, Carroll's on the first, and, as often happened at the Chateau, they were working together for a few weeks before they realized they were staying at the same hotel. Poitier invited his co-star to dinner, and a spark struck between them. Dinner turned into a semi-regular thing, they went to movies and nightclubs together, they started to take evening strolls in the hills behind the hotel, and they fought themselves to stay true to their marital vows. It was a battle, Poitier later wrote, "we both lost. . . . We fell in love." Their affair continued after *Porgy and Bess* had wrapped, in New York and, in Los Angeles, at the Chateau. Within a few years, both were divorced and they were talking about marriage. But there were too many bumps—including a fair bit of squabbling, complete, in at least one instance, with a flying hairbrush—and their romance dis-

---

* As it happened, the article about Poitier's awful situation was the *first-ever* story in the *Times* to mention Chateau Marmont, referring to it as "an apartment hotel here that caters to men and women in show business and is such a favorite with visiting New Yorkers that it is sometimes known as 'Hollywood-on-the-Hudson.'" (Um . . . ?)

solved. Both continued to stay at the Chateau when in town, but they were never seen there together again.

❈

By the late fifties, in the wake of Marlon Brando and Montgomery Clift and James Dean and the arrival of Actors Studio alumni in the movies, after the birth of rock 'n' roll and the teen culture that nurtured it, against the ascent of Las Vegas, the rise of television, and even the growth of passenger air travel and the faraway vacations it enabled, the Sunset Strip transformed once more.

Not long before, the Strip had been synonymous with Hollywood glamour and style, a deluxe destination for men in dinner jackets and women in gowns and jewels rolling up to the Trocadero, Ciro's, or Mocambo after attending a movie premiere. But that way of life seemed stiff in comparison to the new energies blossoming in fashion, music, and, in truth, the broader popular culture. The Strip still had its famed nightspots and restaurants; it still had its rows of talent agencies; it still had Schwab's and the Garden of Allah and Chateau Marmont; it was still the most sensational stretch of road in the region. But the nature of those sensations was changing, the tenor was getting younger and less formal, and the novelties and styles that were born there and that captured the global imagination were harder than ever for entertainment companies to predict, package, and commodify.

Up and down the Strip there were new beatnik-ish coffee shops—the Bit and the Unicorn and the Fifth Estate and Fred C. Dobbs's. And there were space-agey drive-ins and diners—Googie's and Ben Frank's and Tiny Naylors, with their parking lots, booths, and soda fountains crammed with kids from the San Fernando Valley or Orange County or the beach towns or from clear across the country, all hoping to follow in the footsteps of their movie idols. The Sunset Strip had once been an adult playground of sophistication, indulgence, and vice. Now it bore a palpable air of youthful activity, recklessness, novelty: Kids were everywhere. The spectacle of a young actor like James Dean roaring down the Strip on his motorcycle might have turned heads and provoked disapproval in 1954. By 1959, it was a cliché, even if an undeniably cool one.

The nightspots that had made the Strip famous were roiled by these changes. "There was definitely a feeling of death on the Strip," remembered singer Andy Williams. "Las Vegas had set a salary standard for new talent that the nightclubs could not come near matching. Rock 'n' roll was coming in big. It was the end of the era of small, intimate clubs. Things had changed to people performing in large palaces." In 1957, Ciro's was sold by its longtime owner, Herman Hover, in an effort to thwart bankruptcy; a string of new management teams kept changing the sorts of acts they featured and even the name of the place, desperate to grab hold of the times. Mocambo shuttered the following year, resurrecting under new management with the ungainly name Club Renaissance #2 and a booking policy emphasizing jazz.

The Chateau Marmont continued to be above it all, protected from some aspects of this sea change by its slight but significant physical remove from the scene; by its intimate size, which meant that it was usually well occupied; and by the unusual loyalty of its customers, who continued to check in for lengthy residencies. No matter the vicissitudes down below, the Chateau remained a bastion of the familiar. But everyone associated with the hotel surely felt a twinge when it was announced in 1959 that the Garden of Allah, the legendary bungalow colony and hotel more venerable even than the Chateau, had been sold and would be leveled.

❋

Time had devastated the Garden of Allah. Almost nobody connected to show business stayed there any longer, and it had become a den of prostitution and drug sale and use. Alla Nazimova herself had passed away there in 1945, broke, unfashionable, and living in her former home as a guest (at a reduced rate, in a gesture of magnanimity from the people she'd sold it to).* It was estimated that she had spent $250,000 acquiring and developing the estate and hotel during her years of ownership and that she had walked away with $7,500[†] when she let it pass from her hands, a sum that was itself gone when she checked in for her final stay.

In 1956, the Garden was sold once again, and the new owners tried to revive it by dividing each bungalow in half, doubling the capacity. But they could do nothing to stop the sordid goings-on. The actor John Gilmore recalled those years as a horror show:

> Wine and beer bottles, cigarette butts, tampons, used rubbers and crumpled paper sacks were piled against the peeling sides of the bungalows. Cops had fished a stiff from the weeds behind the swimming pool—he'd been dead a few days. . . . One garage door was nailed shut. A woman had been strangled and found with a branch pushed into her vagina. . . . [H]ookers paced the lobby, the hallways and the restaurant bar . . . [A] pair of pimps jobbed them out of a broom closet. A Negro pickpocket named Simms had a scam going in the men's room, where he faked the role of porter with a whisk broom. The world-famous Garden of Allah on Sunset had somehow died overnight, and all that was going on was the scavenging of its remains.

Finally, in April 1959, it was announced that the Garden of Allah had been sold and would be razed to become the new headquarters of a bank, Lytton Savings and Loan. That August,

---

* Coincidentally, Robert Benchley died that same year, in New York, of complications of dissipation.

[†] Approximately $3.62 million and $109,000 in 2019 terms, respectively.

a final party was held on the grounds. Among the three hundred or so guests was Francis X. Bushman, the silent screen idol who had been present at the *opening* night party, and a number of others who turned up accoutred as various old-time movie stars. Nazimova's notorious "queer" silent film of Oscar Wilde's *Salome* was screened on a wall; a few of the young ladies in attendance agreed to let themselves be tossed in the pool one last time; and by 2:00 a.m., the hour at which Robert Benchley might just be getting his second or third wind for the night, the party was over. Within a few weeks, the furnishings were all removed from the various buildings and sold in a single lot to the actor Denver Pyle, who held a rummage sale right on the sidewalk outside the grounds.

One of the hotel's final residents, the English actress Patricia Medina, tried to rescue her own portion of the faded paradise, offering to buy her bungalow outright and have it lifted and rolled away to a piece of land she owned near Malibu. Assured that such a transplant would be impossible, she finally capitulated and moved out—and right into Chateau Marmont. "I made several trips carrying my clothes in my arms," she recalled, "with tears streaming down my face, out of the Garden of Allah and across the street." She checked into a penthouse that overlooked her former home—she would be courted by and wed to the actor Joseph Cotten while living at the Chateau—and watched the destruction of the famed hotel and the rise of a generic bank building with a deep nostalgia.

Writer Eve Babitz would have none of that. She had become acquainted with the Garden of Allah while a schoolgirl at Hollywood High, showing up at the bar with a classmate, both of them dolled up and sporting fake IDs, sipping forbidden drinks, and trying "to be clever around men twice as old as us." It was never a glamour spot or source of nostalgia for her. Quite the contrary: Understanding that Hollywood is essentially a town of the walking dead, she later wrote, "You can't tear down places like the Garden of Allah and just expect them to cease. All that

Hollywoodness has to go somewhere." And she knew just what happened to it: "In the end it took refuge in the Chateau. . . . The ghosts and furies from Alla Nazimova's garden just wafted across Sunset."

✳

The passing of the Garden of Allah foreshadowed dark times for Erwin Brettauer. In 1961, at age forty-six, his wife, Lore, suffered an aneurysm that forced her into the hospital for more than a year. Her husband, then seventy-eight, became intensely involved in her recuperation, hiring round-the-clock nurses to see after her, a tremendous drain on his resources. After about eighteen months in the hospital, she returned to the family home, still incapacitated, still requiring full-time care. On Valentine's Day 1964, only forty-nine years old, she suffered a second aneurysm, a fatal one.

During the years of Lore's illness, the mysterious Dr. Popper also died, without warning, and Erwin Brettauer began to lose interest in running Chateau Marmont. He'd owned it for more than twenty years and had seen it through a world war, the postwar boom, the building of the swimming pool and Craig Ellwood's bungalows, and the principled defiance of racial barriers. In that time, he'd also continued to work in film financing, in other real estate projects, and in philanthropic efforts. He had become father to two girls, who were nearing adolescence. Now, almost eighty years old, with less than a decade left to him, he decided to part with the Chateau. "I don't think he had too many passion projects," one of his daughters reflected years later. "He saw it as a business. He was done with it." After more than two decades of ownership, he sought a buyer for his most famous investment.

Part Four
TUMULT AND DECAY (1963–1975)

Cheap advertising, the sixties. *Bison Archives*

When Erwin Brettauer walked away, unsentimentally, from Chateau Marmont, he left it with an identity and a legacy that carried it through a decade-plus of upheaval, inside and out, even as the owners who followed him treated the place neglectfully. On the streets below, a youthquake that began to rumble testingly in the fifties became a full-strength temblor, and it shook the inside of Chateau Marmont as surely as it did the wider world. The owners of the hotel—and there were several, almost all entirely indifferent to its condition—were content to coast on the work done by their predecessors, on the renown of the setting, and on the loyalty of a cadre of regular customers to keep the place afloat. But afloat was just about all it was. And even as the neighborhood where the Chateau sat was thriving, there was a sense that the hotel itself was holding on to life with a shaky grip.

1.

In March 1963, with neither fanfare nor even a newspaper mention, Erwin Brettauer sold Chateau Marmont to William Weiss, a Los Angeles real estate developer who was then building an office tower down the Strip at the corner of Sunset and La Cienega and who was seeking to get into the hotel business not only in Southern California but in Las Vegas, where he hoped to build a hotel/casino in the downtown area. Weiss's plans were more than he could tackle, though, and he wound up selling the Chateau within two years to Guilford Glazer, another Southern California real estate man.

Glazer, a son of Eastern European émigrés, was a World War II vet with a background in engineering who turned his father's Knoxville, Tennessee, scrap metal business into the Glazer Steel Corporation and used some of the immense profits of that enterprise to build apartment houses and shopping centers near his birthplace. When he saw opportunities in Los Angeles in the late fifties, he relocated and went to work on a variety of projects with an eye toward building what would eventually become one of the largest shopping centers in the world, Del Amo Fashion Center in Torrance, south of Los Angeles. When he acquired Chateau Marmont, Glazer was married to a Parisian native named Françoise Wizenberg who had survived the Holocaust as a girl by pretending to be gentile. They had two young children, but Glazer was a workaholic, "completely neglectful of his family and . . . preoccupied with business—even on weekends and holidays," as his wife complained in divorce proceedings, which reached court soon after Glazer purchased the hotel. Glazer moved into the Chateau when his marriage dissolved, and he took an interest in improving the place. "We added some touches and upgraded to some extent," he recalled, "but it became a pain in the neck. I poured a lot of money into the place . . . [but] it became an expensive project and a losing proposition."* Glazer sold the hotel in late 1965 to Loughridge Ltd., a holding company that immediately sought to sell it but was unable to find a buyer. Chateau Marmont wasn't yet forty years old, and it had lost almost all of its appeal as an investment.

⚜

Ironically, the troubles at the Chateau coincided with a stupendous rise in the fortunes of the neighborhood in which it sat.

In 1958, Dean Martin, who'd become famous as a handsome singing straight man alongside yowling comedian Jerry Lewis, was part of a group that acquired the Alpine Lodge restaurant on the 8500 block of Sunset Boulevard. Redubbed Dino's Lodge, it sported a sign with a gigantic cartoon image of the co-owner, who never bothered much with the place. In October of that year, the joint became famous, not because of its owner's celebrity, but because of a kid who never even worked there.

77 Sunset Strip was an ABC-TV series about a pair of detectives (Roger Smith and Efrem Zimbalist Jr.) who had an office

---

* Glazer remarried, continued to develop large properties, and financed a variety of political and philanthropic endeavors, including such Jewish-related causes as resettling refugees from the Soviet Union, bringing Nazi war criminals to justice, and funding studies at Tel Aviv University. His ex-wife, Françoise, though, had the really impressive résumé. Her next husband was Albert S. Ruddy, whom she would work alongside during his years as producer of *The Godfather, The Longest Yard*, and other successful films. After she split from him, she paired with . . . a guru: Bhagwan Shree Rajneesh, whom, under the name Ma Prem Hasya, she served as personal secretary through the tumultuous years in which he built a massive commune in rural Oregon and was eventually forced to leave the United States under threat of prosecution for breaches of immigration law. Hasya, as she became known, joined the Bhagwan on his final flight from the States, worked by his side until his death in 1990, and remained an important member of the Rajneesh community until her own death in 2014.

at the titular—and entirely fictitious—address. In the opening credits, above a finger-poppin' theme song, their make-believe workplace was shown to be right next door to Dino's Lodge, where the show's breakout character, the pompadoured hepcat Kookie (Edd Byrnes), parked cars in between sessions of hair combing and girl watching.* Kookie brought big audiences to the series and new customers to Dino's Lodge, which thrived, even though management inevitably disappointed tourists by telling them their cars would have to be parked by somebody who actually existed.†

The address and carhop might have been phony, but the juxtapositions they embodied were real. The Sunset Strip was undergoing yet another transformation. You could still see old-time Hollywood stars filing into some of the famed clubs and restaurants, but they did so less often and less to feed the publicity machine than simply to enjoy a meal or a night out. At the same time, the younger stars who haunted the new coffee shops and no-frills eateries had evolved into a much larger cohort of kids who were turning the Strip into a mecca of youth.

Not long after *77 Sunset Strip* premiered, the Sea Witch, at the corner of Sunset and La Cienega, became the first venue on the street to feature a rock 'n' roll–style act as the house band and to book rock performers regularly. The success of this new policy was noted by the owners of neighboring clubs, which were

---

* The character had originally appeared in the show's pilot as a hit man—hair-combing fetish and all—but he was so popular with preview audiences that he was written into the series as a sidekick and, after a few seasons, as a junior partner in the private eye business.

† Martin retained his stake into the early sixties, when he sued, unsuccessfully, to have his name and likeness removed from the place, which stayed in business into the eighties, when it was made over beyond recognition. In 1962, Jerry Lewis, seeking to imitate Martin's success, opened his own restaurant, named Jerry Lewis's, three blocks west. Without a TV series to buoy it, it barely lasted two years and only became profitable under its subsequent owners, who transformed it into the strip club the Classic Cat.

struggling to survive with menus of jazz bands and singers of standard American popular songs. They too began to fill their stages with acts that played the new sounds, and they too started to see a rise in business. But the youth scene on the Strip didn't truly ignite until a club owner named Elmer Valentine visited a bar in the South of France and decided to replicate it back home in Southern California.

Located in Juan-les-Pins, a seaside town not far from Cannes, the Whisky à Gogo* was among the very first places in all the world to replace live music or a jukebox with records selected by a disc jockey and to provide the spectacle of paid dancers— who came to be known as go-go girls—to encourage patrons to cut a rug or simply to treat as eye candy. Licensing the name, Valentine and his partners opened their own spot, a discotheque as it was known, near the Beverly Hills end of the Sunset Strip; because the space was tiny, they chose to exhibit their dancers in cages suspended above the bar and the small stage. They opened the doors on January 11, 1964, and started spinning records.

The Whisky was an overnight sensation, almost immediately being ballyhooed on national radio and television, in *Time* magazine, even on the BBC, and spawning a slew of imitators up and down the Strip, around Los Angeles, across the nation, all over the world.

One month later, the Beatles appeared on *The Ed Sullivan Show*, and the Sunset Strip, like every place on earth connected to the popular culture, changed forever. Clubs that had been booking old-style entertainment died off or reinvented themselves; the spot once known as Ciro's, which had been discarding one name and identity after another, was renamed It's Boss and hired a Beatle-ish local group named the Byrds as its house band. Discotheques, including the Whisky, began mixing live rock acts

---

* The name was taken from the French title of the English comedy *Whisky Galore*, which had been known as *Tight Little Island* in the United States.

in with the disc jockeys. Boutiques featuring new look clothes from London and New York began to dot the Strip. New joints taking advantage of lax county regulation started to feature top-less dancers and waitresses. Local and national record companies opened offices on the Strip for the same reason that film agents had previously hung their shingles there: It was where the talent was. At the end of the year, Hugh Hefner, who had moved Playboy enterprises to the Strip for more or less the same reason, opened a Playboy Club at the top of his office tower at 8560 Sunset Boulevard, providing old-school hedonists an island of swank privilege laced with a bit of newfangled naughtiness.

All this activity proved attractive to Southern California teenagers. Boys with long hair and girls with short skirts started clogging Sunset Boulevard, and many businesses along the Strip simply weren't prepared to handle the influx. The owners of linen tablecloth restaurants saw reservations plummet; haberdashers and vendors of antiques lost customers to rivals on streets less clogged with traffic. And things only got worse for them when a county ordinance made it legal for underage patrons to attend venues where dancing was taking place without being accompanied by a parent or guardian. If the influx of teens onto the Sunset Strip had begun as a rising tide, this change of policy occasioned a tsunami; every night became as busy as a weekend night and every weekend night was like Mardi Gras. It was a stunning transformation and not entirely positive. "The value of the homes above the Strip dropped about 30 percent," said Francis Montgomery, whose family had built the Strip's first night-clubs. "A lot of people just stopped coming here." In the words of another longtime owner of swank Sunset Strip nightspots, "It was almost impossible to travel from Crescent Heights to Doheny. Business dropped overnight."

It might have hurt some people's bottom lines, but this youth-quake drew massive attention to the area. "The Sunset Strip is the Via Veneto of Los Angeles," said a national magazine in 1965, invoking the name of the famed Roman boulevard where movie stars, royal rakes, fashionistas, and paparazzi cavorted and where Federico Fellini set *La Dolce Vita*. But that film was made in 1959, when teen culture was still embryonic. The decadent revelers it depicted were grown-ups in dinner jackets and evening gowns who drove luxury cars and indulged in fine food and wine before relatively sedate evenings at nightclubs. The kids who fueled the Sunset Strip were much more akin to the hip young things crowding Carnaby Street and the King's Road in London: fashionable, sexy, inexhaustible, teeming, and legitimately frightening to the traditional stakeholders in the area.

❖

In 1963, as the Sunset Strip was transforming into an internationally known youth destination and cultural stew pot, two hotels opened mere blocks from Chateau Marmont that would play important roles in its story and that of the neighborhood in the coming decades.

The Gene Autry Hotel (before long, renamed the Continental Hyatt House) was the bigger of the two, and the closer to the Chateau—just two blocks west. Featuring 239 rooms and standing fourteen stories high right out on Sunset Boulevard, it was built by and named for the cowboy star of singing and acting fame whose offscreen empire also included the Los Angeles Angels of Major League Baseball and the Melody Ranch, a working cattle ranch that also served as a location for Western films. Farther west yet, just on the other side of La Cienega Boulevard, was the Sunset Marquis, more modestly scaled in size (it had approximately 100 rooms when it opened) and designed, according to its original owner, George Rosenthal, along the lines of the Garden of Allah or the Chateau itself, with each room a self-contained suite or villa including a kitchenette. Those two hotels—along with the Tropicana Motel, a lower-rent and even more louche spot about half a mile south on Santa Monica Boulevard—formed a troika of havens where musicians indulged in bacchanals and reveries when touring through—or sometimes lingering for as long as several years in—Southern California. The history of rock 'n' roll, at least the sensational, nonmusical parts of it, was largely written inside their walls.

These spots were all different from Chateau Marmont in crucial ways. Movie people would always favor the Chateau, along with the Beverly Hills and the Beverly Wilshire, in large part because those hotels—through their size or the cost of staying in them or their vigilant security staffs or a combination of all three—kept outsiders outside. No autograph hounds, snooping journalists, pushy photographers, or buttinsky civilians threatened the privacy of its celebrity guests. They were oases of isolation, a luxury that so many movie people craved.

Rock 'n' roll people were different. For one thing, they were, literally, bands: trios and quartets and more, with entourages that included managers and stage technicians and road crews and record company operatives and personal associates. An excessive movie star might be attended by a confidant or companion, a dresser, an agent, a manager, a publicist, a bodyguard—a group that you could squeeze into a limo. A band like the Rolling Stones or Led Zeppelin would have three to four times that cohort in tow, often more. These cavalcades required a lot of rooms to house them all—more rooms than the relatively tiny Chateau could provide; Zeppelin, for one, would sometimes rent out as many as *six entire floors* of a hotel when they settled in.

Musical acts were also far more itinerant than actors. Movie people might settle in for as much as three or four months at a time, twice that if they were shooting a TV series. Musicians would pass through Los Angeles on tour, perform a few shows, maybe have some rest and recreation or do a bit of recording, staying a few days or maybe a week but usually not much longer. If they were in town for a full recording session, they'd often rent homes, which made it possible to set up rehearsal spaces and work together. Or, like most movie people, they made permanent homes in the L.A. area and didn't need to stay in a local hotel at all.

Most of all, at least in the days when the Sunset Strip and its hotels were most excitably occupied by modern kids and the people who made the music they danced to, rock 'n' rollers *wanted* to meet their public, specifically their *female* public, and most particularly the species of their female public known as groupies: the young, sexually available women who made a quest of becoming intimate with their musical heroes. When the Sunset Strip evolved into a charm bracelet of rock 'n' roll clubs and discotheques, the musicians who played in them wanted to stay right there, in the middle of it all. The big, noisy hotels like the Hyatt House and Sunset Marquis were perfectly situated for all that.

To be fair, Chateau Marmont was part of the conversation about rock 'n' roll on the Sunset Strip, and a home away from home to some great lights of popular music. But, as ever, it was slightly off to the side and slightly ill-suited to the scene, even as it sat virtually in the middle of it. Most obviously, it lacked the restaurant or bar that would enable casual encounters between musicians and their fans. It was also so small that uninvited guests couldn't easily loiter on the grounds. And it was characteristically sedate, more like a sanitarium than a caravansary—not, in short, the most hospitable environment for the sort of carrying-on that was a standard of the rock 'n' roll lifestyle. You could write there, you could sleep there, you could hide there, and, yes, you could drink and smoke and snort and cavort there. But you had to provide your own amusements. In those larger hotels, the ones where musicians got up to some of their most legendary adventures, those latter activities were practically amenities of the place, like tiny bars of soap and complimentary buckets of ice. The Chateau, even with its deep bohemian cred, even with the likes of Jim Morrison and John Phillips and Gram Parsons and Pink Floyd among its guests, seemed quaint and dainty in comparison.

Over time, the rock hotels adapted to their famous, raucous clientele in ways the Chateau never could. At the Hyatt House—inevitably known as the Riot House—the most egregious behaviors from stars went unpunished save for the expense of repairing the damage done to the premises. When John Bonham of Led Zeppelin rode a motorcycle through the hallways (a stunt long said, incorrectly, to have occurred at the Chateau), management didn't ban him, nor were Alice Cooper and his entourage evicted for playing football nude in the hotel's public spaces, nor were the famous Keiths—Moon and Richards—exiled for throwing TV sets out of the windows of their rooms. The policy was similar at the Sunset Marquis; you almost couldn't get kicked out so long as you could pay the bill for any damage you'd done.

That didn't cut it at the Chateau, where a certain sedate reserve was assumed. Over the years, a few visiting musicians—including Bob Dylan and Richie Havens—were put on notice for leaving their bungalows in disrepair, as close to an outright ban as hotel management was generally willing to impose. (The actor and singer Richard Harris actually managed to get eighty-sixed in the early sixties. After shutting down the bars on Sunset Strip, he staggered back to the hotel some time after 2:00 a.m., and instead of heading for his room, he wandered the corridors banging on guest room doors and bellowing that a nuclear bomb had been dropped. The only thing dropped was him: In the morning, he and his belongings were on the curb, waiting to be taken to another hotel.)

But most of the havoc wreaked on the Chateau was low-key: Some musical acts over the years were scolded for parking their vans and trailers along Marmont Lane and Monteel Road in such a fashion as to make it difficult for neighborhood residents to get in and out of their driveways. And loud late-night carousal was generally discouraged. The message from management and the other guests was clear: We don't want that sort of thing going on here. Most of the musician guests of the hotel complied.

"I once stayed next door to the country rock star Gram Parsons," recalled journalist Anthony Haden-Guest, a frequent guest at the Chateau, "a man whose consumption of drink, drugs, and women was legendary, as were his good manners. Indeed, he was very pleasant in the corridor, and for all the sound I heard from his rooms he might as well have been at prayers." Famed drummer Jim Keltner was often inside Parsons's suite and remembered it as a serene scene: "We'd all sit around the edge of the bed while Gram played and sang." That deference to decorum was largely respected, according to Ann Little, who had set the tone for the Marmont in a previous time; as she said, nobody staying there misbehaved much, and "if they had, out they'd have gone." That wasn't the case at the other rock 'n' roll hotels. As a musician of a later generation, Dave Navarro of Jane's Addiction and the Red Hot Chili Peppers, put it, "For some reason, behavior at the Chateau that would end up in the tabloids, you take that same behavior and go over to the Marquis and you're pretty much right as rain. I've been escorted off that property a number of times and then allowed back the following night."

Led Zeppelin, who would become one of the bands most famously associated with let's-throw-the-TV-out-the-window-style hedonism while on tour, treated the Chateau with relative reverence on their first visit there in late 1968, posing for some iconic photos by Jay Thompson in which they looked more like pixies than satyrs. That was just appearances. After a brief stay in the main building, the group were moved into bungalows because of the tenor of their partying, the flow of girls in and out, and their constant calls for more booze from room service. Even still, by their later standards, their stay was relatively tame. There was a hijacked food cart used to transport nude girls (and, in one case, guitarist Jimmy Page) from one bedroom to another, and there was an episode in which cold cans of baked beans were poured out onto a bed where the band's road manager was entertaining a guest. But there was also a traditional Christmas dinner, cooked by the band's maddest member, drummer John Bonham, for his homesick companions. Led Zeppelin felt at home at the Chateau, and they were welcomed back when they returned the following year. They stayed only briefly, however, because the Manson-family murders made them feel unsafe living in a bungalow on the edge of the Hollywood Hills; they decamped to a more secure hotel farther down the Strip.

Safety from homicidal maniacs wasn't the only reason that rockers gravitated toward the newer hotels. The fact was that in the sixties and seventies, when the Sunset Strip was at its height as a mecca for musicians, the Chateau was fairly dilapidated. As music executive Paul Fishkin explained, "The Chateau Marmont was cool as shit and had incredible history, but it was sort of a dump." For rockers to wreak havoc on a place, apparently, it had to meet certain standards for decor. So the Chateau, deemed dowdy, was, ironically, spared the disasters that accompanied the arrival of supergroups and their supergroupies at other, sleeker hotels.

Which is not to say that it didn't host its share of music world guests or that it couldn't claim for itself some significant moments in rock 'n' roll history. Probably the best-known rock star of the sixties to call Chateau Marmont home was Jim Morrison, the charismatic, self-destructive lead singer and lyricist of the Doors who had a history of flitting from rental home to rental home and from hotel to hotel. In addition to houses in Laurel Canyon, Morrison spent some time at the Tropicana and at the Hyatt House before arriving at Chateau Marmont in 1970, about a year before his untimely death in Paris. He had been there previously, and he was back in part because he'd burned his bridges elsewhere and because, frankly, the hotel's standards had sunk, even in comparison to its nearby rivals. "I had to move here," he told a journalist, "because the people at the Continental Hyatt House didn't like the idea of me swinging off the tenth-floor balcony."

At the Chateau, Morrison had a poolside bungalow that was strewn with books, mostly poetry, and unwashed clothes, its refrigerator filled with beer and no food. Visitors would rap on the door using a secret knock, and Morrison would poke his head out an upper-floor window and come down to let them in. Sometimes it was bandmates, sometimes it was women, sometimes it was journalists, sometimes it was collaborators on a screenwriting project that Morrison was noodling with. Once it was the photographer Art Kane, who captured a memorable shot of the singer sitting in his bedroom closet with a TV in his lap, the image of a woman crackling seductively on it in black and white.

Inevitably, a visit to Morrison's bungalow turned boozy and druggy: vodka, pot, cocaine, and anything else the motley crew could get their hands on. The impromptu parties would last until dawn, with old movies playing silently on the TV, music from a Mexican station blasting from the radio, and a cuddle puddle of stoned friends and hangers-on lying about the living room as lifeless as the dirty laundry. And there was plenty of dirty laundry: Hotel maids found blood on the sheets and the walls in the master bedroom of Morrison's bungalow after he was visited there by one of his more adventuresome playmates.

That business about him swinging off balconies wasn't a joke, by the way: Morrison was a genuine thrill seeker, especially when he was drunk or high, which, at the point in his life during which he was living at the Chateau, was practically always. He was known to rush into traffic on the Strip waving his jacket like a toreador, for instance, and to play threateningly with knives and guns. And he really did indulge in what he called his "Tarzan act," swinging between upper-story windows and balconies by grabbing hold of drainpipes, gutters, and tree limbs. At Chateau Marmont, he had a bit of a slip. According to a witness, Morrison "got up on the roof and tried to swing into his bedroom window off the rain gutter. He lost his grip and fell two stories. Only reason he didn't get killed, he bounced off the roof of the

shed attached to the back of his cottage. It was outasight, man."
Morrison was injured in the fall, and he walked around gimp-
ily for days. The following week, in a rehearsal studio, Doors
drummer John Densmore noticed the singer limping and asked
guitarist Robby Krieger what happened. Krieger told him the
story, and Densmore was surprised. "He never used to get hurt. I
thought he was indestructible," he said. "Not any more," replied
Krieger.*

Janis Joplin, like Morrison doomed to die at a tragically
young age as a result of her lifestyle habits, was far more low-key
when she stayed at the Chateau in 1968, endearing herself to staff
with her politeness and friendliness; a desk clerk recalled her
stopping by frequently to chat in a "dainty voice" that was nothing like the sound she made onstage or on recordings. Another
giant of music appeared at the front desk one evening in the late
sixties, with an appearance that portended some kind of trouble.
He had long hair, loudly colored clothes, and high-heeled boots.
"He looked very bizarre," recalled Carmel Volti, who was called
to reception to vet the new arrival. But there was a reassuring
detail about him. "He had a cage with two cats in it," she said,
"and people with pets are always stable. So we let him in." He
turned out to be Phil Spector, the notoriously eccentric record
producer whose Beverly Hills mansion was being remodeled. His
stay was brief and uneventful. (Spector's acquaintance with the
hotel went at least as far back as 1964, when he flew the New
York songwriters Barry Mann and Cynthia Weil to L.A. and put
them up in a suite at the Chateau to work on the composition of a
single song, which turned out to be the classic "You've Lost That
Lovin' Feelin'," so perhaps the producer wasn't as far gone as he
looked—at that moment, anyhow.)

* In director Oliver Stone's 1991 film *The Doors*, Morrison is depicted as staying
in an upper floor of the main building of the hotel and engaging in similar antics
with the added peril of extreme height.

Other musicians who were based in Los Angeles would use Chateau Marmont as a pied-à-terre when they couldn't be bothered to drive all the way home to Malibu or Topanga Canyon, or when they found themselves involved in impromptu parties or trysts after a night out on the Strip. John Phillips of the Mamas and the Papas was one such, often partying late into the night in a suite booked on impulse or stopping in to visit friends such as Roman Polanski, with whom he got into more than a little devilry. Phillips's bandmate Cass Elliot lived closer, right in Laurel Canyon, but liked to rent a suite at the Chateau sometimes when she wanted a change-of-pace setting for an acid trip. Near-lifelong Southern California resident Jackson Browne stayed at the Chateau as a wunderkind teenage songwriter in the mid-sixties when he was between more permanent homes; he included an image of the Sahara showgirl statue, which rotated outside his bedroom window, in "The Birds of St. Marks," a song he wrote in the sixties but wouldn't officially record and release until 2014. The hotel became a kind of backyard tree house for L.A.'s musical elite of the era—a place to get out to when they were tired of staring at the same old walls in their permanent homes.

2.

By 1966, the novelty of a Sunset Strip crowded with kids from all over Southern California and indeed the world had worn off for businesses in the area, Chateau Marmont included. Formerly, the eastern edge of the Strip was dominated by the Chateau, the Garden of Allah, and Schwab's. But time and the sixties had changed the landscape considerably. The Chateau still stood above the main road, witness to the tumult but disassociated from it, and Schwab's was still a mainstay. But where the Garden of Allah once sat edenically across from the Chateau, some of the moment's most vital businesses were operating: the Plush

Pup hot dog stand; the Fifth Estate coffeehouse, where, among other things, the alternative newspaper the *Los Angeles Free Press* was headquartered; and Belinda, a boutique run by a tastemaker named Charles Lange. Just east, at the corner of Sunset and Crescent Heights, a small triangular real estate lot hosted Pandora's Box, a minuscule club that had started life as a jazz joint more than a decade before under a set of owners that included the actor Tom Ewell.

Pandora's Box wasn't much, a squat pink-and-purple cube with a tiny stage that was one of the very few on the Strip that *didn't* launch some world-beating new rock act. But it was situated right at the threshold of the Strip, the first hip teen spot you saw as you cruised Sunset Boulevard westward from Hollywood or came down from the Valley through Laurel Canyon. It wasn't important, exactly, but it was iconic. And it stood at the intersection of a land development scheme and a cultural moment that made it, almost accidentally, a flash point.

For more than a decade, civic and business interests had envisioned a highway running from the San Fernando Valley south to Los Angeles International Airport. The Laurel Canyon Freeway would serve as a direct line from the population center north of the Hollywood Hills to the airport and create the opportunity to develop business districts at key interchanges along its course. None of those would be more important, in the eyes of developers, than the area where the freeway would cross Sunset Boulevard—just east of Chateau Marmont and right through the front door of Pandora's Box. Officials of both the city and the county of Los Angeles imagined a vital commercial and business district growing up around the intersection. And many landowners on the Strip were also keen on the plan, perhaps even the owners of the Chateau, who were doing little to maintain the hotel, likely with an eye toward razing it altogether.

Steadily, since the end of World War II, the Laurel Canyon Freeway kept trying to emerge into the world. In some areas of the proposed route, homes, small businesses, and other parcels were readily acquired from their owners, and some portions of the freeway were actually laid out and paved: Several miles of La Cienega Boulevard cutting through Culver City and Baldwin Hills were widened and divided into what was intended to be the middle stretch of the future highway. On the Sunset Strip, the decline of certain businesses was seen as an inevitability that would lead to yet more of the crucial pieces of this puzzle falling into place. Elected officials seemed actively to encourage devaluation of the land around the proposed route. They even floated the idea of annexing the Sunset Strip—not all of West Hollywood, just the Strip—into Los Angeles, which would have provided them with a means to institute zoning regulations favorable to their development scheme.

But nobody had foreseen the rise of rock 'n' roll or youth culture. The Sunset Strip had lost its golden age luster, but it hadn't died, as many predicted and hoped it would. Tiny, low-rent clubs like Pandora's Box were actually proliferating; a string of teen-oriented nightspots, eateries, boutiques, and coffee shops extended from one end of the Strip to the other. Far from dying of financial starvation and welcoming the bulldozers, the freeway, and the proposed commercial district, the Strip was thriving. And thriving not with movie stars and their fat wallets but with kids from the suburbs who couldn't afford more than a burger and a Coke but who were content to spend hours walking up and down the road from Crescent Heights to Doheny and congregating in small mobs outside spots like Pandora's Box. "It's not a pleasant thing to see them walking around," said Bruno Petroletti, owner of the La Rue restaurant, of the kids. "I don't know what to do. It's not nice for us. Can you imagine someone coming here from Europe and taking movies of these kids and showing them back home? What would people think of America?"

The thriving of the Sunset Strip was a real vexation for the interests behind the freeway plan, and they continued to use whatever means they could to push their project forward. One weapon at their disposal was law enforcement, specifically the enforcement of curfew laws, laws against unsupervised minors, and laws governing the activity inside entertainment venues. In 1966, as clubs along the Strip pulsed with the sounds of L.A.'s most iconic bands—the Byrds, the Doors, the Mamas and the Papas, Love, Buffalo Springfield, the Mothers of Invention, the Seeds, the Leaves, the Turtles, and more—authorities decided to crack down on the teen activity on the Strip, partly to deal with real problems growing out of the crowds, the traffic, and the drug use, but partly, too, to squelch the growth of the area and make it available for development.

Throughout the spring and summer of 1966, sheriff's deputies began enforcing laws that nobody had bothered with for years, emptying clubs for being filled beyond their legal capacity, or for allowing dancing without a permit, or for not complying with restrictions on underage patrons. New parking regulations, designed to curtail masses of kids from congregating on the Strip, were instituted. And kids on the street were being rousted with increasing vigor, forced to produce identification and, if found to be underage, taken into custody and remanded to their parents. In the clubs, coffeehouses, and pages of the alternative press, an antiauthoritarian sentiment brewed, with calls for organized protest against what was seen as police brutality becoming louder and more common. By October, the situation had reached such a boil that the *Los Angeles Times* ran a five-page illustrated story about the county sheriff's deputies' twenty-four-hour job of patrolling the Strip and dealing with the young offenders.

On Saturday, November 12, four days after Californians elected Ronald Reagan as their new governor, the lid finally burst off the situation. At about 10:00 p.m., the hour of the new curfew, police began rousting some of the hundreds of young people milling around the corner of Sunset and Crescent Heights, right in front of Pandora's Box and across the street from Chateau Marmont. The kids responded with defiance. A group of them sat in the street to block traffic. A city bus was stopped in the snarl, and a small swarm of young people boarded it, forcing the driver and passengers to flee; they broke the bus windows, ripped the advertising signs from its flanks, tore out its fuel line, and tried to light the entire vehicle on fire. The thirty sheriff's deputies on the scene, overwhelmed, called for reinforcements from city police, and nearly two hundred officers from all over the county responded. Together, they pushed the crowds back with force, an assault that was met with hails of rocks and bottles and cries of "Gestapo!" and "Heil Hitler!" Some teens trying to escape the melee ran into Schwab's, where they were locked in place by authorities. Farther east, the traffic snarl resulted in an attack on another bus and a fistfight after a fender bender between a pair of on-leave marines and a young scenester. It was hours before order was restored, and approximately a dozen people—including the two marines—were arrested.

The following night, Sunday, the thirteenth, both the kids and the police hit the Strip in increased numbers. This time, the kids were prepared with protest signs sporting, among other mottoes, "We're Your Children! Don't Destroy Us!" "Stop Blue Fascism," "End Police Brutality," "Ban the Billyclub," "Rights for Youth Too!!!" and (best and most telling) "Leave Us Alone."

But the authorities were prepared, too. Some fifteen months previously, the African-American community of Watts exploded in a shocking episode of civil unrest ignited, at least in part, by the rough tactics of police in arresting an intoxicated black motorist. During the six days of rioting that ensued, thirty-four people died, more than three thousand were arrested, and a wave of arson and looting spread as far as Hollywood, resulting in more than $40 million in property damage.* State officials had compared the fighting in the streets to the Vietnam War and vowed never to let it happen again. The mess on the Sunset Strip was their first chance to put their resolve in motion.

---

* Approximately $314 million in 2019.

The augmented police force did its work that second night; the kids were easily corralled and dispersed. But for the next month, every weekend brought more crowds to the Strip, on both sides, and more trouble. Skirmishes between police and kids were regular, and arrests grew more numerous each week. Celebrity allies of the kids would show up to join the fray, and some, such as Peter Fonda, wound up in handcuffs. Others who wished to help forestall trouble by encouraging talk between the two sides suffered public relations hits; Sonny and Cher, whose hippie haircuts and outfits were spreading the Sunset Strip style around the nation, were disinvited from the Rose Parade for appearing at the scene and seeming to take the side of the kids.

The ongoing unrest—"'Riot' is a ridiculous name," said musician Stephen Stills, an important witness. "It was a funeral for Pandora's Box. But it looked like a revolution"—grabbed national attention. The letters pages of the *Los Angeles Times* were filled with the voices of readers taking opposing sides. Stills, then playing guitar and singing with Buffalo Springfield, wandered down from Laurel Canyon into the ruckus one evening and found himself inspired to write a song, "For What It's Worth," about the confrontations between the kids and the cops. With its low-key, slightly menacing tenor and its evocative chorus—"It's time we stop / He-ey: What's that sound? / Everybody look: / What's going down?"—it would eventually become one of the standard references for sixties unrest, appearing in documentaries and feature films about the protests and uprisings of the era for decades to come.

The spectacle of these disturbances, of armed policemen waging battle with unarmed—and, it must be stressed, *white suburban*—kids made for terrible PR for the authorities. It was one thing, in the minds of the white majority of Los Angeles residents, to respond with force to the Watts riot, which was an occasion of significant death and destruction. It was another to bash in the heads of high school and college students who were guilty simply of wanting to hang out. Yes, the crowds on the Sunset Strip had been a nuisance. But few outside the scene saw them as a genuine threat. Public sympathy for the protesters increased as the authorities became more strident in enforcing the curfew and other laws.

For local businesses, the situation was a nightmare. Pandora's Box simply shut its doors by late November; it reopened for a single show on Christmas night,* at which Stills debuted his soon-to-be-famous tune. Merchants and restaurateurs petitioned their elected representatives for better enforcement of curfews. A ban on dancing by people under twenty-one years old was voted into law, and several of the nightclubs that had mushroomed during the previous three years saw business plummet as a result.

❖

At Chateau Marmont, the disturbances rose to little more than a nuisance and even provided some entertainment for guests. The first-floor windows facing Sunset Boulevard were boarded up for safety and to help keep stray protesters from wandering in. A guard was placed at the front door to verify the identification of anyone trying to enter. "It was like a war zone," complained one guest rather dramatically, but the checkpoint did manage to snare one hippie, namely Dennis Hopper, who was staying at the hotel and did, to be fair, look just like the troublemakers across the street. Most of the guests, however, treated the disruptions as a bit of entertainment. Reports circulated of Chateau residents repairing to their balconies and terraces as curfew approached with wine and cheese to watch the commotion. "The peasants are revolting," came an anonymous cry during one night's disturbances. "Let them eat cake,"

---

* Somebody had figured out that the club didn't need any sort of special license to open on Christmas or New Year's Day.

replied another nameless wag.* Hotel guests even hosted riot-viewing parties for their friends, inviting them for cocktails and meals and the show on the street below; the actor and filmmaker Griffin Dunne, then an eleven-year-old in the tow of his father, Dominick, attended one such gathering and never forgot the thrill of tossing firecrackers from a fifth-floor penthouse into the action below.

It being Hollywood, there were several professional movie cameramen on the scene of the disturbances, including the Hungarian émigrés László Kovács and Vilmos Zsigmond. Some of the footage they captured in front of Pandora's Box would be employed in the climax of Arthur Dreifuss's *Riot on Sunset Strip*, a dreadful melodrama shot in January and February 1967 and hurried into theaters the following month like a quart of milk about to hit its sell-by date. It tells a preposterous story of youth gone wild—"Let's all go to Pandora's Box tonight!" one cackles—and lays blame for the titular insurrections not on authoritarian sheriff's deputies but on a cop (Aldo Ray) driven to retribution against hippies when his daughter (Mimsy Farmer) is dosed with LSD and gang-raped. The rest of the film came about as close to depicting true events as did that inane plot, but there were a couple of real glimpses of the unrest and a worthwhile soundtrack of Sunset Strip bands to recommend it.

Even more images of the disturbances appeared in an actual documentary, *Mondo Mod*, which spends a far greater time painting the scene, with the Plush Pup and Pandora's Box clearly visible behind protesters carrying signs. The film, a kind of travelogue of life along and around the Sunset Strip, wandered into

---

* Tongue-in-cheek though these might have been, they evinced a certain disconnect from events on the part of many Chateau residents. In 1972, novelist/memoirist Eve Babitz would publish a semi-fictional account of spending the 1965 Watts riots boozing and making love with a new beau at the hotel. "It was nice spending the Riots in a penthouse," her alter ego mused. "We slept in separate beds and changed channels to mostly watch old movies. We only turned on the Riots during commercials."

the Fifth Estate coffeehouse for a visit, ogled go-go dancers at the Whisky, and stopped in at the Belinda boutique to leer at girls trying on barely there clothes and chat with proprietor Charles Lange. In the uprising scenes, and in much of the footage shot inside Belinda, Chateau Marmont sits imperially in the background, impassive to the newfangled tumult below.

⚜

The Chateau might have looked prim and stately in the midst of the commotion going on all around it, but it was enmeshed in a dire financial crisis. The holding company Loughridge Ltd. had acquired the hotel in 1965 and was unable to turn a profit operating it. In November 1966, almost as soon as the agitation in front of the hotel's doorstep began to make headlines around the world, Loughridge had had enough. That month, an ad appeared in the *Los Angeles Times* announcing that the Milton J. Wershow Company would be auctioning off the hotel—the main building, the bungalows, the pool, the sixteen-thousand-square-foot lot, all of it—on December 16 at the Statler Hilton hotel near downtown L.A.

In advance of the sale, the *Times* published a story that consisted of two dull sentences, identifying Chateau Marmont as "a Sunset Strip landmark" but having nothing else to say about it. Come the day of the sale, there were bids, but none met the reserve the Loughridge group had set. Sitting right in the midst of one of the most exciting spots in the world, Chateau Marmont went begging for owners who could see its value, its history, its potential. It was almost an entire year before a new group would materialize to purchase the place: three Beverly Hills attorneys who had combined their fortunes to seek investment opportunities. Forming a corporation named Chateau Marmont Ltd., the trio—Harold Klein, Paul Levinson, and Marvin Rowen—would run the hotel for approximately eight years with an indifference that could easily have spelled its doom.

⁂

By then, the protest kids had dissipated. The sheriff's department braced for an influx of hippies during the summer of 1967, but it never quite materialized, perhaps because so many of the underage dance spots had shut down in the wake of the so-called riots, but more likely because young people had been drawn north to San Francisco and the Haight-Ashbury in the Summer of Love, and who could blame them?

The Sunset Strip was still lined with trendy venues and the promise of sex, drugs, and rock 'n' roll, but Pandora's Box was no longer part of the scene. In August, not ten months after the disturbances began, it was bulldozed by the county, which had acquired the property ostensibly to realign the intersection of Sunset and Crescent Heights ("Hippies Pout, Politicians Cheer as Pandora's Box Is Wrecked," read the headline in the *Los Angeles Times*). A contingent of politicians actually showed up to watch the demolition—"I think they want to win the Croix de Guerre or something for tearing this down," muttered a construction worker—among them Ernest Debs, the supervisor whose vision of the Laurel Canyon Freeway and a modern commercial business district at Sunset Boulevard all but died with the previous year's uprising.

When the Garden of Allah had been razed, it lived on as a miniature model in the lobby of the bank that replaced it. Pandora's Box didn't even get that much: The land it stood on was turned into a literal part of the road. Tor Olsen, then managing Chateau Marmont, wasn't necessarily thinking of the tiny club that created such a racket when he lamented Los Angeles's habit of erasing its past, but he could have been. "This is a sad town," he said. "One can be here 10 years and not make enough friends to count. Anything with any character, any *history*, they will tear it down and they will put in a neon sign. Or something in plastic."

⚜

Nothing was more plastic than the Sahara showgirl, who had been spinning in front of the Chateau for about a decade when, without warning, she was dismantled and carted away in 1966, to the infinite relief of the hotel and its guests.

John Cheever was one of the very few with a soft spot in his heart for the statue, and he was saddened to learn of its demise, writing to a friend, "How sorry I am to know she is gone. How vividly I remember those evenings when she revolved and I sat in the window, chain-smoking while her old father—a bus driver on the West Pico line—ate his sandwiches under a palm tree. . . . With her gone I think I never want to return."

But his wouldn't be the lasting literary impression of her. That honor would go to the image of the Sahara showgirl that would grace the cover jacket of *Myra Breckinridge*, the scandalous novel published by the pirouetting pixie's nemesis Gore Vidal in 1968.

Myra Breckinridge takes the form of a diary kept by the title character, a transsexual woman, formerly known as Myron, who has come to Hollywood to finish her gender reassignment and to indulge her appetites for old-time movie glamour and sexual dominance over the most robust heterosexual specimens she can find. For most of the novel, she lives at Chateau Marmont, and from her suite she gazes endlessly on the spinning statue of the Sahara showgirl:

> From where I sit, without turning my head, I can see a window covered with venetian blinds. The fourth flat from the bottom is missing and so provides me with a glimpse of the midsection of the huge painted plaster chorus girl who holds a sombrero in one hand as she revolves slowly in front of the Chateau Marmont Hotel, where Great Garbo stays on her rare visits to Hollywood.

Three in the morning again. Joy and despair, equally mixed, as I watch, hypnotized, the turning statue, and think for the first time how lonely she must be out there, ten times life-size, worshiped but not loved, like me.

"For me," Myra writes most definitively, "she is Hollywood, and mesmerizing."*

The novel, filled with outrageous sex scenes and wicked Hollywood in-jokes, was a huge hit, and in 1969 Twentieth Century Fox set about doing the unthinkable—filming it for the big screen. They hired a nearly untested young hippie director from England, Michael Sarne, and signed an oddball cast: the celebrity journalist and film critic Rex Reed; the director and occasional actor John Huston; the seventy-five-ish-year-old Mae West, who hadn't appeared on-screen in a quarter century; such Hollywood stalwarts as Jim Backus, John Carradine, and Andy Devine; and a pair of newcomers, Farrah Fawcett and Tom Selleck. Playing Myra—and doubling as the spinning Sahara showgirl—would be Raquel Welch, then at the height of her fame for her own physique.

As Welch (along with the rest of the world) remembered it, the film was, from the screenwriting stage to the final on-screen product, "a nightmare." The production blasted through its initial $4.5 million budget because Sarne, admittedly overwhelmed by the complexity of the job, appeared to be uncertain, confused, and cowed by working on such a big Hollywood production. He constantly fiddled with the script; he got lost in creating arty sequences that added nothing to the final product; and he seemed, according to some witnesses, to encourage conflict between cast

* As for the hotel, Myra was less complimentary, explicitly complaining that her $87.50 monthly rent (approximately $639 in 2019) was "much too much" and taking deflating note of her broken venetian blinds and a water stain on a white wall that "resembles an upside-down two-leaf clover—or heart—or male scrotum as viewed from behind."

members. (Not that they needed much encouragement; West, for one, absurdly, saw Welch as a *rival*.) It was a calamitous recipe.

Quite a bit of the film was shot and set in Chateau Marmont, with Welch and Reed chatting in bed, on the floor of an elaborately decorated penthouse, and on a terrace, beyond which was visible a reproduction of the Sahara showgirl statue, smaller than the original and temporary, but spinning endlessly in front of a billboard just as she had in Vidal's hungover nightmares. She stayed up for the length of the shoot and appeared again when the billboard was given over to an advertisement for the film.

That wasn't necessary for very long. Released with a well-deserved X rating in June 1970, *Myra Breckinridge* was met with some of the worst reviews ever hurled at a major studio film: "a tired, smirking elephant with nowhere to go" (*The New York Times*); "both dirtier and more aberrant than *Beyond the Valley of the Dolls*" (*Los Angeles Times*); "about as funny as a child molester" (*Time*). It would go on to be "celebrated" as one of the worst films ever made, and for the rest of his life Vidal blamed it for killing off sales of what had been a popular novel. (Of Sarne, he said, "I believe he is working as a waiter at a pub in London where they put on shows in the afternoon. This is proof that there is a God and, in nature, perfect symmetry.") The final blow was the cruelest: Sarne had chosen to liven up the film campishly by intersplicing it with short snippets of scenes from classic Hollywood films, and the producers were sued by Shirley Temple and Loretta Young, both of whom objected to their images being used in such a vulgar context (and both of whom succeeded in having their work removed).

Myra Breckinridge is, arguably, best remembered for the poster image of Welch showing off her famous body in the clothing and posture of the original Sahara showgirl—complete with red, white, and blue barely one-piece swimsuit, white boots, red gloves, and cowboy hat. And it provided one delicious treat to

Chateau Marmont nerds: The scenes on the balcony afford full-color evidence of the brief spell in the late sixties when management thought they'd bring attention to the hotel by having its name spelled out in gigantic letters on the side of the eastern wall of the topmost terrace—a folly that likely did nothing to increase business or even clear up for the locals just what the place was.*

⚜

Despite inspiring Cheever and Vidal, despite the iconic image of Raquel Welch dressed in a bikini and posed in imitation of her, the Sahara showgirl would live on longest and most memorably in parody. In the late fifties, the animator Jay Ward, who created *The Adventures of Rocky and Bullwinkle,* among other successful TV series, leased office space for his studio across Sunset from Chateau Marmont, eventually adding a retail gift shop, the Dudley Do-Right Emporium, to the premises. In 1961, seeking at once to mark his spot on the Strip and cock a snook at the setting, he erected a statue of his own, a fifteen-foot-tall Bullwinkle J. Moose, dressed in an old-timey two-piece striped gentleman's swimming costume, right leg bent in dance, left arm extended to hold aloft a statue of his chum, Rocket J. Squirrel. It stood for decades. In 2013, long after the Sahara showgirl was disassembled, long after the Ward studios and the gift shop were gone, Bullwinkle finally came down.†

---

* They had a few other schemes, including a pair of print ad campaigns. One touted the hotel as "A little bit of France in Hollywood . . . Easily best in Southern California . . . Convenient to Mountains, Seashore, Studios, and Golf Courses . . . Must be seen to be appreciated)." The other declared, "CHATEAU MARMONT HOTEL—HOME OF FAMOUS ARTISTS."

† But that wasn't the end of him. After fifty years along the eastern edge of the Strip, Bullwinkle had become so iconic that he wasn't scrapped. Rather, he was restored and then moved to a variety of spots in West Hollywood, finally destined to settle down farther west on the Strip, although that site has yet, as of this writing, to be determined.

3.

The McGraths, Earl and Camilla, were one of those insider-ish couples who could be found in the most elite corners of the twentieth century, and for much of the mid-sixties one of the corners they were most frequently found in was their fifth-floor penthouse at Chateau Marmont. The McGraths had enviable connections to the worlds of art, popular music, film, literature, publishing, and even international royalty, and they collected celebrity friends and important works of art with affection, taste, and largesse. During their long tenure at the hotel, they held an endless series of open houses at which all their circles mingled: a legendary Southern California salon at which you might meet anyone and after which anything might happen.

Earl McGrath was born in 1931 into a blue-collar Wisconsin family, but he had a bohemian streak in him from a young age. As a young man, he traveled the world on his own and in the merchant marine, and he had no qualms about ringing the doorbells of his cultural heroes—Aldous Huxley, Henry Miller, Gian Carlo Menotti—in an era when an earnest visitor could be welcomed as a guest and even become a friend. He socialized constantly in New York and traveled widely, often in the company of the century's best-known artists, musicians, and writers. In 1958, while attending Menotti's Spoleto Festival in Italy, he met Camilla Pecci-Blunt, the Paris-born daughter of an Italian papal count and a Spanish-Cuban noblewoman. Camilla was also of an artistic temperament, raised in a household where Jean Cocteau, Salvador Dalí, Arthur Rubinstein, and Igor Stravinsky were familiar faces. The two sparked and a courtship began, culminating in a marriage in 1963.

By then, Earl was working in the offices of Twentieth Century and had made two friends who would remain close his entire life: Ahmet Ertegun, the Atlantic Records co-founder and chairman, who would hire McGrath away from the movies and launch him into a career as a music executive, and the writer Joan Didion, whom he knew from a time when neither was yet married or known outside a small circle of friends in New York.

Not long after marrying, the McGraths set up a home in Manhattan, opposite Carnegie Hall; at the same time, they took a suite at Chateau Marmont, and it would have been impossible to say which one was the more impressive. The walls in both places were covered with art by their friends—Larry Rivers, Isamu Noguchi, Andy Warhol, Cy Twombly—as well as photographic portraits of their celebrity and socialite chums taken by Camilla, who worked with a camera seriously throughout her life. They threw regular open houses on both coasts, parties at which elite figures from all creative fields and social classes intermingled: Gore Vidal (*bien sûr*), Audrey Hepburn, Mick Jagger, Francesco Clemente, Christopher Isherwood, Michelle Phillips, Bernardo Bertolucci, Dennis Hopper, Prince Rupert Loewenstein, Marella Agnelli, and any number of star makers, billionaires, and European royals—an endless parade of gilded lilies. And they were not snobs: Harrison Ford would later recall that when he arrived in Los Angeles in the mid-sixties, working as a carpenter while trying to get started as an actor, Earl McGrath befriended him, introduced him around, and lent him money to buy the tools he needed to start his fledgling handyman business.

The McGraths never had any children of their own, but they adored kids (Earl was named godfather to more than twenty of his friends' offspring, including three of Harrison Ford's five children). Their parties, even in the relatively intimate confines of their Chateau Marmont suite, were always open to their friends' whole families. And so, throughout the sixties, Dominick Dunne, by then Joan Didion's brother-in-law, and his wife, Ellen, known as Lennie, would turn up regularly with their bouncy brood of three: Alexander, Dominique, and Griffin. Griffin Dunne would always remember that his first visits to the hotel were as a guest of the McGraths—the sorts of friends of your parents whom you were encouraged to call "aunt" and "uncle"—and his lifelong connection to the place began on their enormous terrace, overlooking the Sunset Strip. "It was very kind of exotic to us that there were people who lived year-round in a hotel," he remembered. "It felt kind of a bit of an adventure every time we went there. If you're a kid, it's like going to a castle. Earl and Camilla's place was very much like being in the turret of a castle." The young Dunne always felt not only welcome at the McGraths' gatherings but actually a part of them. The McGraths, he remembered, "would invite one and all to their parties where we'd be seated next to anyone from a Rolling Stone to Harrison Ford, Larry Rivers, Terry Southern, or [the sculptor] Bob Graham."

Earl and Camilla eventually left Chateau Marmont for a proper house in West Hollywood, which they turned into a significant art gallery and, yes, a salon. And even though the cast of characters didn't change, they never again could afford their guests the same enviable view.

⚜

One actor who was resident at the hotel never fell into the McGraths' orbit, and while he surely could have used the boost to his social life, he might not have felt entirely comfortable in the fashionable company of those get-togethers. Dustin Hoffman was another of the acting hopefuls to have squeezed himself into tiny quarters at the Chateau in hopes of breaking out into something bigger. In fact, when he moved in, he had already begun work on the film that would make him a star for the rest of his life, Mike Nichols's *The Graduate*. Hoffman had grown up very near the Chateau, in the hills off Mulholland Drive, and he had moved to New York to pursue a career in acting. Being cast in Nichols's follow-up to his sensational debut, *Who's Afraid of Virginia Woolf?*, was a tremendous coup for an unknown actor, but Hoffman was taking no chances on being an overnight success. When the production called for him to be in Los Angeles, he moved into his boyhood bedroom in his parents' house and commuted to the studio just as his father, a furniture salesman who had started as a film set decorator, once had. That lasted about a week. Smothered at home and unable to focus adequately on his work, Hoffman moved into the Chateau, taking a cheap room and spending his days off lounging by the pool.

He was miserable. "I was so aware of people sitting around the pool and of how different I looked from them," he remembered. "This was how I felt when I'd moved out of this town 10 years [earlier]. . . . I was right back where I didn't want to be." He stayed at the hotel throughout production and beyond. And, in fact, he was there long enough to start collecting unemployment checks: Until the film was actually released and became a hit, his ability to sustain himself as an actor was still a touch-and-go thing.

But there were other residents at the time who knew exactly how to fit in in the groovy new world that was blooming in and out of the Chateau.

They first met at a cocktail party at the Dorchester hotel in 1966 during the acid-and-paisley days of Swinging London. He was a Holocaust survivor and film student from Eastern Europe who had made his name as a director of claustrophobic dramas and had turned his mind toward a change-of-pace movie: a sex-horror spoof. She was an American military brat who had been raised in part in Italy, where she began a modeling career that took her to Los Angeles and, inevitably, appearances in commercials and television. They were under contract to the same production company, and at a meeting in its offices he had first heard her mentioned as someone whom he might want to cast in his comedy: a girl he knew only by what he took to be a French name—Charontais or maybe Charontait.

At the Dorchester, they were introduced and chatted and exchanged phone numbers and soon then met again for dinner, during which they discussed LSD, which she was familiar with but he had only tried once, disastrously. They decided to trip together, moderately, sharing a single dose. They stayed up all night and then made love and then she left, explaining that she was due on set. She kept putting off a second date, still too attached, he reckoned, to her former boyfriend, a hairdresser back in L.A. For a while they saw each other only at social gatherings, and there was a chill between them. But then he cast her in his film, which would be shot in Italy, and when she showed up on set the frost thawed, and their romance was rekindled and caught fire.

The film they made together was enough of a hit that they both got career boosts out of it, each getting the chance to be part of the motion picture adaptation of a gigantic best-selling novel. She would appear in a scandalous melodrama playing the role of a sex object trying to be taken as a serious actress—hardly a stretch—and he would direct a potboiler about a woman raped by a demon and forced to bear its child. Officially a couple, they began to visit Los Angeles in preparation for these films, and since neither of them felt secure enough professionally to acquire real estate in the area, they started to stay regularly at Chateau Marmont, where, one of the most fashionable items of the moment, they made at least a temporary home. In January 1968, they married—not in California, but in London. She was just about to turn twenty-five; he was ten years her senior. She decided to continue to work under her own name, the one that he couldn't quite make out when he first heard it—Sharon Tate—though she sometimes liked to refer to herself by her married name: Mrs. Roman Polanski.

Even though Roman Polanski was as European as anyone who had ever checked into Chateau Marmont, even though it was his new wife's favorite place to stay in all the world, he didn't quite cotton to it. He had grown up in Kraków in decaying apartment houses, and they had fed his imagination as he made such films as *Repulsion*, *Cul-de-Sac*, and the picture he had come to Hollywood to direct, *Rosemary's Baby*. The Chateau was a little too much like his nightmare/fantasy of back home. But his beloved's enthusiasm for the hotel's bohemian atmosphere trumped his distaste for its condition:

> Sharon loved its rundown appearance and old-world atmo-sphere, not to mention the crazy layout of its shabby rooms; she felt at home among the actors, musicians, and writers that constituted its regular population. You could sense, sim-ply by walking down its corridors, that the place had had its quota of real-life dramas, of slashed wrists and overdoses, just as you could almost get stoned from sniffing the haze that seeped through the various keyholes.

Despite his assessment of its upkeep, Polanski was happy at the Chateau. He was youthful, in love, working, in demand, and surrounded by friends. Also in residence at the hotel were his chums and colleagues Richard Sylbert, the production designer on *Rosemary's Baby;* Brian Morris, who had founded the classic Swinging London nightclub the Ad Lib (and was visiting L.A. to open a less successful spot called Bumbles); and the aspiring Moroccan-born filmmaker Simon Hesera. Sylbert, a New Yorker who had begun what would be a legendary career in Hollywood, also loved the hotel: "It was a congenially seedy, reasonably priced apartment hotel that we found sympathetic to our way of life. You could always find familiar faces." The Polanskis often had Morris and Hesera over for breakfast, which the pair attended while still in their bathrobes. And they were regulars at Earl and Camilla McGrath's open house afternoons on the weekends.

The Polanskis themselves got into the party-throwing feeling of the Chateau, hosting semi-regular Friday night get-togethers that would be attended by their friends among the residents as well as the likes of Warren Beatty, Jack Nicholson, and a couple with whom they were to grow close in the coming months, Mia Farrow, the star of *Rosemary's Baby,* and her new beau, Peter Sellers. The two had gotten together not long after each had been party to a splashy divorce, he from Britt Ekland, she from Frank Sinatra (who actually had his lawyer serve her with papers while she was working on Polanski's set). This quartet of fabulous faces spent many days together at the Chateau, launching off on a memorable string of trips to the beach or the desert. Sellers, a congenial cutup, perennially announced his arrival at the Chateau with some sort of improvised performance or bit, to the alternating delight and embarrassment of Farrow. It was a time of pure pleasure.

In early 1969, with Polanski looking for the appropriate follow-up to *Rosemary's Baby*, which had been a critical and commercial hit, Tate became pregnant. She had already committed to a new film, a sort-of-caper story called *13 Chairs* (or, in some markets, *12 + 1*) that would be filmed in Europe, Italy primarily. Polanski, still not settled on his next project, decided to travel with her for some of the shoot, which would last into the summer. Before they left, they decided to give up their apartment at Chateau Marmont; Polanski, who was intimidated at the thought of fatherhood, reckoned they'd need more space for the coming child, while Tate simply thought it would be inappropriate to bring a newborn baby to live in a hotel rather than a proper home. In February 1969, they signed a lease for 10050 Cielo Drive, a sprawling ranch house previously rented by their friends actress Candice Bergen and, fatefully, the record producer (and son of Doris Day) Terry Melcher. Those two had recently split up, and the place, which was situated in a quiet nook off Benedict Canyon, was available quickly and cheaply. It was large, isolated, ideal.

The Polanskis went off to Europe for Tate's shoot, and then, as she neared full term, she decided to return to California to prepare to have the baby. Because she was approaching her eighth month of pregnancy, no airline would fly her, so she traveled on the *Queen Elizabeth 2* out of England; Polanski stayed behind to continue pursuing potential film work. Tate wouldn't be alone on Cielo Drive, though. Besides the caretaker, William Garretson, who lived in a small cottage in the back of the property, she had regular guests, among them Polanski's old schoolmate Wojciech Frykowski and his girlfriend, coffee heiress Abigail Folger, who had been house-sitting in the Polanskis' absence, and Jay Sebring, the hairdresser boyfriend with whom Tate had broken up soon before meeting Polanski and who had remained on friendly terms with both his ex and her new husband.

On the evening of August 9, 1969, Polanski, still in London trying to land a contract for a new project, was about to leave his flat for a dinner engagement when he answered a phone call. There was horrific news from Cielo Drive, where it was about noon that same day. During the preceding night, somebody had come to the house and slaughtered—there was no other word for it—Tate, her unborn baby, Frykowski, Folger, Sebring, and a fellow named Steve Parent who was visiting the caretaker. It was a scene of unimaginable savagery and carnage. And there was no explanation for it; none.

In the coming months, amid baseless rumors of the Polanskis and their circle being involved in drug dealing, orgies, and satanic rituals, the truth would be uncovered. Charles Manson, a charismatic madman who had spent half his life in prison, had used sex, drugs, psychological manipulation, and threats of violence to build a cultlike commune around himself in the desert northwest of Los Angeles. Manson had aspirations toward a musical career, and he had become acquainted with, among others, Terry Melcher in that pursuit. Melcher introduced Manson to the likes of Beach Boys drummer Dennis Wilson and to the members of a band that the producer was nurturing but never quite fully brought to life, the Gentle Soul. During the time he was steering the Gentle Soul, Melcher rented a house for them to live in on Monteel Road, just behind Chateau Marmont. "It was a pretty cushy deal for us on some level," recalled band member LeRoy Marinell. "They gave us a food allowance, and they gave us a pot allowance." The house became a popular hangout, and among those who wandered in and out of it were Manson and a few members of his "family," as his acolytes called themselves. (Inevitably, some of them floated through the hotel, just across the street, but without incident.) Eventually, Melcher stopped entertaining the thought of helping Manson with his music, which apparently motivated Manson to plot bloody revenge on him. Manson believed that Melcher still lived at Cielo Drive—he went and scoped it out earlier that summer and was asked to leave by Garretson—and it was Melcher, not Tate or Polanski or their guests, who was the target of the madman and his minions that awful night. There was no connection whatsoever between Sharon Tate and her killers . . . unless they had incidentally exchanged gazes one ordinary evening at the Chateau.

4.

The Manson murders changed the atmosphere around the Hollywood community forever, even inside the otherwise insulated enclosure of Chateau Marmont. They even occasioned some grim comedy. Bud Cort was a baby-faced comedian and stage actor from New York, not quite twenty years old, when he first came to the Chateau in the late sixties to work with Robert Altman on *M*A*S*H*. He continued to return to the hotel as he sought other opportunities—"I think I've done everything but get laid there," he once said with a sigh. "It was just too holy an environment for me." One afternoon, his agent sent over a script by an unknown writer named Colin Higgins that would turn out to provide him with his most famous role: *Harold and Maude*, the story of the strange and dark romance between a death-obsessed young man of means (Cort) and the eccentric septuagenarian who becomes his friend, confidante, and lover (Ruth Gordon).

Director Hal Ashby made the film in the Bay Area, after which Cort returned to the Chateau, with visits back and forth to New York, where his musician father was dying. The film was released in 1971 to a mixed reception, but it was immediately embraced by a cult, both of which results rather terrified Cort.

His compelling performance led Hollywood studios to offer him one neurotic part after another. "The only roles being offered me were nuts," he complained. It was years before he could break the cycle and get better parts.

Almost worse, the few fans who embraced *Harold and Maude* from the start were overzealous in expressing their affection. They found out that Cort was living at the Marmont, and they haunted him, leaving tiny tombstones and coffins and pictures of dead babies outside his room and hovering around Marmont Lane in hearses, waiting to offer him rides. "I tried to talk to them, tell them they missed the point of the movie," Cort lamented, but they wouldn't be discouraged.

The one ray of light came when he returned to the hotel one night and found a message from an acquaintance who was managing Groucho Marx, inviting him to dinner at Groucho's house. On the appointed evening, he took a taxi to the place and was about to knock on the front door when it suddenly opened and he was faced with Groucho, looking back at him from beneath a beret. "We both at the same time gasped," Cort recalled, "and he slammed the door in my face." Presently, the door opened again, this time revealing a record industry executive, who introduced them. "Groucho," he said, "this is Bud Cort. He just made a film with Ruth Gordon." "Ruth had the hots for Harpo," Groucho replied, "I'm sorry, I thought you were Charles Manson. Come in."

Not only did the two hit it off that night, but Groucho was sympathetic to Cort's twin plights of being typecast by producers and stalked by ghouls. He invited Cort to live in a spare room in his house, and the younger man did, leaving the Chateau and staying with Groucho on and off for nearly seven years.

❋

If Cort felt overly exposed to his fans while living at the Chateau, others found it a peaceful enough environment for them

Dream castles: Chateau Marmont (above) and the Château d'Amboise in the Loire valley, which inspired it. *Bison Archives, Wikimedia Commons*

ABOVE: The famed Black Sea–shaped pool at the Garden of Allah, just across the road from Chateau Marmont and, for decades, more famous for hijinks. *Bison Archives*

RIGHT: Headquarters: The Sunset Boulevard Schwab's, studio commissary for Hollywood hopefuls and de facto dining room for Chateau residents. *Bison Archives*

The accidental hotelier: Albert E. Smith (right) with his partners in the pioneering Vitagraph Studios, William Rock (left) and J. Stuart Blackton (center). *Everett Collection Inc./ Alamy Stock Photo*

Loving couples: Jean Harlow and Harold Rosson, who called Chateau Marmont home during their brief marriage; Robert Benchley (left) and Billy Wilder, who lived in hotels across Sunset Boulevard from one another. *Photofest*

Ann Little: The cowgirl with the gift for hospitality. *Photofest*

ABOVE: In Nicholas Ray's bungalow, the cast and crew of *Rebel Without a Cause* read through the script. Ray is at the far left, lighting a cigarette; James Dean is in front of the TV; Jim Backus and Natalie Wood are in chairs, center.
Author's collection

LEFT: Erwin Oskar Brettauer: The mystery man who created so much of what Chateau Marmont became.
Brettauer family

LEFT: Before the Bates Motel: Tony Perkins's sloppy bachelor pad at Chateau Marmont. *Photofest*

BELOW: The girl who twirled: The Sahara Hotel showgirl, a staple on the Sunset Strip through the late fifties and sixties. *Bison Archives*

BOTTOM: Prelude to a bomb: Rex Reed and Raquel Welch in *Myra Breckinridge*, in the penthouse with the Sahara showgirl, resurrected in the form of Welch, behind them. *Bison Archives*

Even bad boys do chores: Led Zeppelin, on one of their first U.S. tours, in the hotel kitchen. *ZUMA Press, Inc./Alamy Stock Photo*

Shacked up: Marsha Mason and George Segal in a typical bedroom in 1973's *Blume in Love. Photofest*

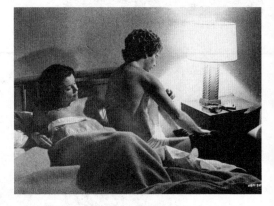

Dark day: Paparazzi await the removal of John Belushi's body from his bungalow, March 5, 1982. *Associated Press*

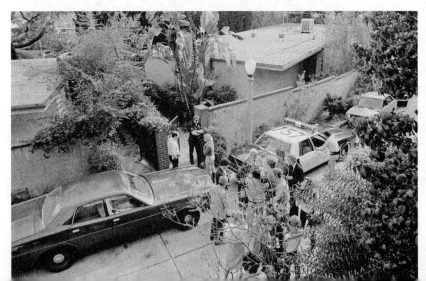

The man who saved the castle: Raymond Sarlot at the hotel he fell in love with. *Author's collection*

BELOW: The snapper snapped: Helmut Newton during one of his winter residencies in the late eighties. *David Fahey*

Hotelier in the fast lane: André Balaz steers his then fiancée Uma Thurman through the paparazzi. *David Long/Harlequin/ Camera Press/Redux*

Still not quite the Ritz: Madonna and James Russo in *Dangerous Game* (1993). *Photofest*

Two gentlemen of the Marmont: Dominick Dunne shows Billy Wilder the portrait painted by Sacha Newley. *Al Seib /* Los Angeles Times *via Getty Images*

to focus on their actual work. The Canadian-American musical quintet who called themselves the Band left the rusticity of their home in West Saugerties, New York, to stay at the hotel in late 1967 while finishing work on their debut LP, *Music from Big Pink*, which was named for the house they shared back in the Catskills; several of the members of the group went on to use the Chateau as a base during visits to the area thereafter.

The Velvet Underground, the New York rockers led by Lou Reed, shared a bungalow at the hotel in 1968 when they were at work on their third album, *The Velvet Underground*. Doug Yule, the guitarist who had just joined the band, remembered it as a homey time: "The band were like a little family during this period. We'd go to the studio together, we'd go to the Chateau together, we'd go out and eat together. It was kind of like we were a little band of gypsies. Normally we all lived in New York and went home over the weekends to live our own lives. I wouldn't see them again until it's time to go out on the road again. But for this period of time, we lived and worked as a group. We were very close and warm." During their stay, the band performed a few gigs at the Whisky a Go Go to pay bills and keep themselves fresh; no less than Jimi Hendrix stopped in to see them one night. And there were other thrills, as the band's drummer, Maureen Tucker, recalled: "I was up at four in the morning—still up, not up after sleeping—and I had the radio on, and it was announced that Lars Onsager, the father of our road guy, had just won the Nobel Prize."

Graham Nash moved into a bungalow in 1971 after his breakup with Joni Mitchell, bringing along an electric piano from their Laurel Canyon cottage to bury his heartache in songwriting. "I went there for a night," he recalled, "and stayed for five months. . . . There's something womb-like about it." Nash wrote a number of songs during his stay and even found love. "I was sitting up in a big tree in the garden," he remembered. "I used to spend a lot of time in that tree." And he was perched in it when he met a woman who would become his second wife.

Nash's sometime bandmate Neil Young was another occasional visitor to the hotel. He first stayed there in the early seventies, when he injured his back and had to wear an uncomfortable
brace that made it painful for him to drive long distances, even
if that only meant his Topanga Canyon ranch. He became fond
of the place. In 1974, he was staying in a bungalow and recording an album called *Homegrown,* with which his record label
hoped to have a commercial hit on the scale of his best sellers
Harvest and *After the Gold Rush.* One night during the recording
sessions, Young was entertaining guests, including Rick Danko
and Richard Manuel of the Band and various members of his
own backing group, Crazy Horse. They were all, by all accounts,
very high—booze, pot, methedrine—when Young offered to let
them hear the tracks he was recording. "It was late at night,"
Young remembered. "We were all pretty fucked up . . . on the
edge." The *Homegrown* sessions happened to be on the same
tape as some songs that Young had recorded but not planned
to release—dark, druggy, moody songs about two friends who
had died of overdoses. The music was bold, raw, searing. "Danko
freaked," recalled Crazy Horse drummer Ralph Molina. "He
said, 'If you guys don't release this fuckin' album, you're crazy.' "
Young saw that as a dare and decided to take it up. The record,
Tonight's the Night, came out in 1975, recognized by critics for its
brilliance but almost entirely shunned by the audience Young's
label hoped to capture; *Homegrown,* on the other hand, was left
unfinished and unreleased, various of its songs turning up, like
refugees, on other of Young's albums over the years.

Carly Simon stayed at the Chateau when she was a brand-new
recording artist performing at the famed Troubadour club on
Santa Monica Boulevard. She was pursued (and, it would seem,
snared) by Warren Beatty during her residency at the hotel, even
though she was already connected to the man she would marry,
fellow singer-songwriter James Taylor. It was a touch-and-go
relationship: Taylor wanted to commit himself to Simon, but he
was using heroin and couldn't see a way to be true to both his

heart and his drug habit. One evening at the Chateau, the night before she was to return to New York, Simon was called by Taylor into the bedroom of their bungalow, where she found him sitting beside a small suitcase, tying a rubber hose around his arm as part of the ritual of shooting up.

"OH SHIT," she remembered thinking, "what was he doing?"

He was, he explained, showing her his darkness in the hope that the light of their connection would wash it away. "This is what I do," he said. "Watch. I can't have you and the habit at the same time. I just can't. I've got to get rid of this. Maybe if you see me do it, it will take away the cat-and-mouse games. You have to watch me. I have to let it all go." He went through the entire ritual and shot up, while she looked on, aghast.

When it was over, Taylor flushed the remaining heroin down the toilet and threw all the gear into an incinerator chute outside the front door of the bungalow. For the rest of the night, she remembered, "we clung to each other like apes, and closeness got hold of us in a painful but towering way." She left in the morning, putting faith in his words. He would have relapses, but that night at Chateau Marmont marked a milestone and a breakthrough, and the pair married later that year.

It wasn't all sex and drugs and insanity. Sometimes the music history made at the Chateau was ironic: The comedian and filmmaker Christopher Guest was sitting in the lobby lounge one night when he overheard an anguished conversation in which a jet-lagged musician tried to explain to his manager how it was that he came to leave his bass guitar at the airport; the scene helped inspire Guest to create his fictitious rock band, Spinal Tap. And sometimes it was intimate. One of the homiest features of Chateau Marmont had long been the piano in that same lounge, which was used by musicians of all stripes to work on new material, rehearse for performances, spend idle hours productively, or simply pass lonely evenings by making music and, in the bargain, entertaining staff members and fellow guests. Over the years, the likes of Duke Ellington, Erroll Garner, Judy

Garland, George Shearing, Annie Lennox, Rickie Lee Jones, and the original stage cast of *Hair* were seen at the keyboard (a guest checking in late at night and witnessing the latter lot writhing around in a big, friendly pile and various states of demi-dress thought he had stumbled on an orgy and alerted management). Van Morrison, staying at the hotel one Christmas season, played a number of holiday songs for a dazzled staff one winter's night. Actor Maximilian Schell, who also made full use of the pool during his many visits to the hotel, was also fond of the piano, which, it was said, he played surprisingly well—and used more than once as a bit of a tease when engaged in an episode of seduction.

⁂

In these years of rock 'n' roll tumult and psychedelic devilry, the Chateau sufficiently maintained an air of gentility to continue welcoming the sorts of guests it had thrived on for decades: a staid actorly crowd seeking the comforts of medium-to-long-term homes without the expense of actually buying and maintaining property in Southern California. Beatrice Lillie, also known as Lady Peel, was a lively fixture of the hotel throughout the sixties, contributing a slightly bawdy but never quite naughty spice to the atmosphere. Her more acid-tongued compatriot Hermione Gingold was another Chateau regular, as was, just to confuse matters altogether, another English actress, Hermione Baddeley, who was in residence for many years.

The Chateau's reputation as a haven for those in the throes of dying marriages persisted and was even polished in 1973 by the release of Paul Mazursky's film *Blume in Love,* in which the title character, a divorce attorney (George Segal), is caught by his wife (Susan Anspach) in flagrante with his secretary and forced to leave home. His missus sets out to seek her own bliss (which takes the form of, in part, Kris Kristofferson), and, almost inevitably, Blume checks into the Chateau, where, among other things, he begins an affair with a friend (Marsha Mason) of his soon-to-be ex.

The hotel is never identified by name, but it is shown in some great detail: Blume and his sweetie walk in one night through the colonnade; Blume checks for messages at the front desk (with Corinne Patten, the hotel's reigning jack-of-all-trades, making a cameo as herself); and many scenes of lovemaking, chat, and conflict are staged in a bedroom decorated with the cheap, generic furniture that characterized the Chateau of that era. Like its cheeky narrative device of balancing scenes in Venice, Italy, with scenes in Venice, California, the film's use of the Chateau itself is a knowing wink by the filmmaker to his Hollywood chums, many of whom had spent time at the hotel under very similar circumstances.

⚜

"Sha...teeeaaauuuu..." was how it sounded to people who called the hotel in the seventies and eighties at certain hours of the late afternoon, evening, and night.

"You had to know what he was saying," remembered *Washington Post* TV critic Tom Shales, a frequent caller, of the voice that so often answered the phone at the front desk, "because the way he said the word 'Chateau' was so bizarre."

The voice was compared to Tony Perkins in *Psycho,* to a crypt door opening, to "Dracula answering the phone at the morgue." A journalist familiar with it thought you could hear "the rustle of bats' wings in the tower and the groaning of the ropes on the drawbridge" when it spoke its creepy greeting.

"It was like performance art," said actress Jennifer Beals. "He was like a European aristocrat—he would tolerate you, but let you know that you were calling a place that was very wealthy, and old, and weren't you lucky to be calling! And yet it was not a put-off; it was incredibly charming. I would love to know what that guy's name is."

It was Daniel—no surname has attached itself to his legend—a switchboard operator, front desk clerk, and "Alice Cooper look-alike" whose manner was so singular that, legend had it, habitués of the Marmont would call from all around the world just to hear the voice or to share it with their disbelieving friends in New York or London. (Sometimes, it was said, he was too wrapped up in watching a tiny TV to even bother to answer.)

What Daniel lacked in polish he made up for in character, and there was a certain poetry to having so macabre a voice answering the phone at the hotel in those days, since, amazingly, the old-time telephone switchboard that was installed when the hotel was first built, though updated, was still in place until it was finally ripped out in the mid-seventies. The contraption had been a cause of eternal frustration; outgoing calls could be delayed for so long that one Chateau regular, playwright and director Burt Shevelove, joked, "I would never dream of using the phone here without a magazine to read." For decades the switchboard had been run by Carmel Volti, hired by Ben Weingart back in 1930, and she had operated it with as much equanimity and efficiency as was possible, and she was beloved. But she retired in the early seventies, and like so much else about the hotel in that era the quality of telephone service was left to devolve into Daniel's (perhaps appropriately) gothic "*Sha… teeeaaauuuu….*"

The hint of the tomb in his voice wasn't merely a joke; it wouldn't have taken much at that moment in the hotel's history for it to have died—or been transformed into something unrecognizable—altogether.

Part Five
RESCUE AND RESTORATION
(1975–1990)

The seedy seventies. *Bison Archives*

Finally somebody came into possession of Chateau Marmont who appreciated it fully: the architecture, the history, the special place it held in the firmament of Hollywood, Los Angeles, and the popular imagination. Like Erwin Brettauer, he bought it as an investment and saw more potential than his predecessors. He restored, rebuilt, expanded, burnished, babied, and revived the hotel. He wasn't a showman—he didn't rebrand, relaunch, reimagine the place—but he was exactly the savior that was called for. Under his hand, the name Chateau Marmont would finally become known all around the world. Unfortunately, it would be for a reason that nobody ever remotely wished for.

1.

After its sale by Erwin Brettauer in 1963, Chateau Marmont began to show the toll of the benign neglect practiced by a succession of owners. The last of these—the trio of attorneys who'd established Chateau Marmont Ltd.—had acquired the property at a bargain price and managed it for more than seven years without putting much more than the bare minimum into running and maintaining it (although they did once insinuate to *The New York Times* that they would be building an annex—a "twin . . . right next door"). But in many ways, they had succeeded in keeping the hotel occupied not because of its location, its history, or its respect for guests' privacy but because they kept it cheap. And that cheapness came at a price.

The photographer Dewey Nicks, who would one day conduct commercial shoots at the Chateau, remembered visiting it during these years with his father, a St. Louis advertising executive, and making note, even at a young age, of the state of disrepair. "One day I was in the elevator with my sister, and Keith Richards's son got on," he recalled, "and he carved a gash into the woodwork with this knife he had in his pocket. And we came back like a year later and that mark was still there."

Actress Carol Lynley lived at the Chateau with her daughter in the early seventies, and she remembered it during that era as a place "run by eccentrics for eccentrics. . . . It's the kind of place where something gets broken and stays broken for 40 years. The one nice thing about it is that you never have to worry about damaging anything. . . . There's nothing to intimidate you because you can't ruin something that's already ruined."

If she was exaggerating for effect, she wasn't exaggerating

much. The place was, to put it kindly, run-down. Carpeting that had torn was repaired with black electrical tape; in some places, especially around elevators, where people tended to idle and congregate, it was worn down to the lining and left that way. Cheap light fixtures replaced any wall sconces or chandeliers that had broken. Ripped wallpaper was left in place, often sutured with adhesive tape. Plaster would sift down from ceilings, sometimes right on top of sleeping guests, and furniture broke, sometimes right out from under guests, as happened one regrettable afternoon to, of all people, Myrna Loy. The decay was everywhere. "The shower knob came off in my hand," David Mamet remembered, "and the shower bar fell down."

Writer Eve Babitz, so sharp in describing the hotel as it was in the sixties and seventies, quipped, "The only reason anything was off-white at the Chateau was because it had once been just plain white." That was meant as a note of affection; she felt comfortable in a place where she was among "the kind of people who *like* to spill things, things like wine, blood, whiskey, cocaine, ashes, and bodily fluids." But she recognized, too, that the condition of the place had become a flaw, not an amenity: "So little care had gone into maintaining it that even people who *liked* seedy hotels thought it was too much. Even people who *wanted* to feel depressed started staying away."

And the stuff that didn't break was, amazingly, *stolen.* Carmel Volti, the switchboard operator, recalled that "people would come in off the street at night in their stocking feet and steal things—antiques, pictures off the walls, whatever they could get their hands on." Lynley recalled a few years later that management had "started to chain the furniture to the floor," but even that wasn't enough: "One morning, we found the furniture gone, chains and all." And when it wasn't neighborhood junkies looking for something they could sell, it was staff members: One former employee helped himself to some of the best pieces in the building, decorating his home with his prizes until it looked like a copy of the hotel—or, rather, what the hotel had once been. (At around this time, Susan Sarandon, then shooting *The Front Page* for director Billy Wilder, had her luggage and personal belongings stolen from her suite *while she slept*.)

In 1973, the owners under which this decay had become chronic decided they'd had enough. They thought about razing the building—the site was valuable, even if the building, however sturdy in its bones, was decrepit. The state of the place was summed up in a *New York Times* travel story titled "It's Shabby-Genteel but the Stars Love It," in which a longtime resident was quoted as saying, "You start at the Montecito, then you move to the Marmont, the Sunset Towers, the Beverly Wilshire, and finally, if you really make it, you have a bungalow at the Beverly Hills Hotel. . . . I'm on my way down. Next week I'm moving into my tennis club."* The owners might've been justified in treating the place as a teardown, but they opted instead to seek a buyer. And in the spring of 1975, they found one.

Sarlot-Kantarjian was a construction and development firm co-owned by builder Raymond Sarlot and attorney Karl Kantarjian, and active in a number of high-end projects in the Los Angeles area, including, at the time it purchased Chateau Marmont, a multimillion-dollar condominium project in Bel Air. In 1973 and 1974, the firm sold an estimated $1.5 million and $4.5 million in new homes and condominiums, respectively, making it cash rich.† It acquired the Chateau for approximately $1 million in March 1975,‡ and thought of it, at least partly, as a potential

---

* The story was notable chiefly for an amazing error it contained. Author Victor S. Navasky contended that one Oscar night saw a quartet of Marmont guests come home with Oscars—Martin Balsam, Melvyn Douglas, Patricia Neal, and Sidney Poitier. Sharp-eyed *Times* readers out-fact-checked Navasky's editors, noting in letters that (1) there was never an Oscar night with *three male* winners in acting categories; (2) while Douglas, Neal, and Poitier won in 1964, Balsam won in 1966; and (3) Neal wasn't present to accept her Oscar but at home in England, very pregnant. In response to their corrections, the *Times* published a remarkably unapologetic note from Navasky: "Folklore is folklore—even Hollywood folklore."

† About $8.05 million and $21.49 million in 2019 terms, respectively.

‡ About $4.7 million in 2019 terms.

tax write-off. "The bank was ready to foreclose," remembered Sarlot. "Bills hadn't been paid in months, and the building was in total disrepair. . . . The place looked like a dungeon. Or worse. It was so bad I wouldn't have stayed free for a one-nighter." And in addition to its state of disrepair, its finances were being managed with indifference. "Occupancy had never been a problem," Sarlot said, but "it was losing some $2,000 a month. Rates were as low as $12 for a single room and $26 for a two-bedroom suite. Those were the *publicized* rates. From there, deals were made."*

But a funny thing happened to Ray Sarlot as he evaluated the property he had acquired. Wandering the halls and rooms in a state of worry and despair, according to his second wife and widow, Sally Rae Sarlot, "He fell in love with the place. It became almost like a mistress."

That was only a slight exaggeration. Sarlot was a big, bearish, affable man given to enthusiasms. He was a butcher's son from Chicago, born in 1924 and intent on studying engineering when World War II interfered and he found himself in the army serving as a mapmaker. After his discharge, he moved to Southern California and became a contractor, working his way up to a position from which he could build homes and, later, apartment complexes. When he bought the Chateau, Sarlot was heading toward divorce from the mother of his three children, and the hotel provided him with a place to live—a case not of bringing one's work home but of bringing one's home to work. He would live there for the next five years, during which time he not only stopped the flow of damage in the hotel but reversed it—enhancing what he found and expanding the property, inside and out, in something of a return to better days.

"When I came in here," Sarlot told the *Los Angeles Times*, "I was what you call shocked." The effort that went into restoring

* That loss would be $9,406 a month in 2019 terms, and those room rates would be $56 and $122, respectively.

the place was immense. There were physical changes to virtually every room and public space: carpeting, baseboards, lighting fixtures, wallpaper. There were structural changes: A sprinkler system was installed for fire safety; a breakfast nook was built off the main lobby; the pool was drained and restored with a new lining; the exterior of the main building was repainted; the grounds were torn up and replanted. Throughout, as well, there was a new emphasis on decor. Sarlot's soon-to-be ex-wife, Regina Bernstein, oversaw the purchase and placement of new furniture throughout the hotel—one-of-a-kind antiques and quality everyday pieces, much in the spirit of the "Marmont look" that Albert Smith and Ann Little had instituted more than forty years prior. The murals, woodwork, and windows in the lobby and lounge were restored by craftsmen. "We ended the reign of plastic garbage," Sarlot declared.

Not everyone appreciated the work. Tuesday Weld had lived at the hotel on and off through the late sixties and the seventies, going as far as renting multiple suites at a time when the 1970 fires in Malibu destroyed her beachside home. Wandering into the hotel after Sarlot's renovations, she groused to a reporter, "Well, they repainted this place. I liked it better the old way. It smelled homier then."

Her complaint aside, most guests appreciated the upgrades, and Sarlot recognized that he was uniquely suited to the job of reviving the Chateau. "Probably the only reason we could do what we did," Sarlot explained to a reporter, "is because I am a builder. I knew what I didn't have to do—I didn't waste money doing things different. It's an old hotel, and we kept it an old hotel." But he also confessed that he was in love with the place, and he doted on it accordingly. "I don't think it'll ever go into the black because it's kinda like a toy," he said, chuckling at himself. "You never stop. Craziness."

And Sarlot *didn't* stop. Within a few months of acquiring the hotel, he purchased the property immediately to the east at 8171 Sunset Boulevard, where a string of cottage apartments climbed the hill in a line behind a restaurant. Initially, he planned to raze those units and build an annex to the hotel, with plans calling for twenty luxury suites, a rooftop pool, a cocktail lounge, office space for hotel management, and eighty-five underground parking spaces. An architect was retained, and the cost of the expansion was reckoned to be in the neighborhood of $1.5 million.* But the renovations required in the main building were so extensive and costly, in both time and money, that Sarlot and Kantarjian scaled back their ambitions. Instead, as Albert Smith had with the units he added to the hotel nearly forty years earlier, they converted these newly acquired cottages into yet more bungalows, giving the hotel three distinct areas outside the main building: the poolside bungalows (the Smith units, which had been built before the pool), the modern bungalows built by Erwin Brettauer in the far northeast corner of the property, and these new units, referred to as the garden bungalows. With their purchase, the physical plan of Chateau Marmont reached completion, almost exactly fifty years after Fred Horowitz first beheld the site where he would build his castle.

Ray Sarlot had other enthusiasms—he was an avid booster of the Los Angeles Marathon (ironic since, according to his widow, her burly husband was "forever popping a button on his shirt"), and he served on the board of the Museum of Contemporary Art in downtown Los Angeles, a position that nicely dovetailed with the circle of painters who had become regular guests of his hotel, such as David Hockney, Robert Rauschenberg, Jasper Johns, Roy Lichtenstein, and Eduardo Paolozzi. But whatever else commanded his attention, the Chateau was his great love.

In a great coup to signal to the world that they had acquired a gem, Sarlot and Kantarjian managed in March 1976 to get the hotel declared a Historic-Cultural Monument (number 151, to be exact) by the Los Angeles Cultural Heritage board. This meant that their renovations and improvements would be subject

---

* Approximately $7 million in 2019.

to supervision and approval by a landmarks board, but it also gave their new acquisition some well-deserved cachet. They just missed out on placing an even bigger feather in their caps. At around the time the hotel became theirs, Sarlot and Kantarjian became aware of a new film that Warner Bros. was producing titled *Bogart Slept Here*. Written for the screen by Neil Simon, then arguably the most popular working playwright in the world, it was going to be directed by Mike Nichols, also a very big deal, and star Robert De Niro, who had won a Best Supporting Actor Oscar just that spring for *The Godfather: Part II*. De Niro was to play a New York Method actor who comes to Hollywood on the strength of an unexpected hit film and finds himself flailing against the trappings of good fortune as he makes his next picture. The title comes from the fact that the lead character is put up by the studio at Chateau Marmont in a suite that he is told was once occupied by famed tough-guy actor Humphrey Bogart (who, of course, never lived at the Chateau).*

De Niro had his own history with the hotel. The first time he visited, a few months earlier, he was literally snubbed and made to feel unwelcome. Approaching the front desk, he asked to see the penthouse, only to be shooed back into the night by the manager on duty. Another hotel employee, shocked to see a movie star rebuffed in such a way, asked, "Do you know who that is?" "A bum!" the manager replied. The owners called De Niro's agent the next day to apologize.

Now, making a film set at the hotel, De Niro no doubt felt as if his Method training *demanded* that he live in a suite there. He took one on the fourth floor, and he made himself at home, almost immediately beginning an affair with a woman he met in the elevator——Carole Mallory, a New York model, teacher,

---

* Simon had thought about calling the picture *Gable Slept Here*, which was closer to the truth—if, in fact, Gable had done any sleeping when he was visiting Jean Harlow there.

writer, and socialite who at the moment was engaged to the son of Pablo Picasso and would soon have a nine-year affair with Norman Mailer. (To even the score, De Niro was, himself, also engaged, technically, to the woman he would soon marry, actress and singer Diahnne Abbott.) Their connection barely lasted a week, but not necessarily because of their other relationships.

De Niro's stay in Hollywood was unexpectedly brief. He had arrived in Hollywood to work on *Bogart* only three days after completing shooting on *Taxi Driver*, a complex physical and emotional performance that clung to his body and nervous system for a considerable while. Finding himself in a fake hotel suite on a soundstage in Burbank, he strained to connect with the broad comic contours of Simon's script. De Niro's fanatical attention to detail had already been a matter of frustration and concern for the filmmakers; he had determined that his character should wear an earring, and he spent an entire day obsessively choosing just the right piece of jewelry from among hundreds provided by the prop master. When he got in front of the cameras, working opposite Simon's wife, Marsha Mason (who had performed at the actual Chateau Marmont in *Blume in Love* a few years earlier), De Niro was unable to bring Simon's bouncy, jokey dialogue to life. Simon's script, as Nichols and the Warner Bros. brass saw it, required verve and panache and a broad brush, and not only did De Niro seem incapable of providing it, but he actively argued against it, challenging Nichols repeatedly on their divergent approaches to his scenes.

After a week or so of torturous effort, Simon, Nichols, and the producers did the unthinkable: They decided to shut the film down, relieve De Niro of the role, recast the lead, and start up again. Parts one and two were swiftly—if not painlessly—accomplished. But they were unable to find the right actor to replace De Niro, and the production fell apart. Nichols went back to New York—he wouldn't direct another picture for eight years—and Simon continued his string of successful plays and

scripts. He didn't give up on *Bogart Slept Here*, though. He liked
one of the actors who auditioned to replace De Niro and rewrote
the script to suit him. That new version, directed by longtime
Simon collaborator Herbert Ross, was released in 1977 as *The
Goodbye Girl* and won an Oscar for Richard Dreyfuss, a far more
elastic comic actor than De Niro. And, alas, it was set in New
York, without any mention at all of Chateau Marmont.

2.

The Sunset Strip continued to draw nightclubbing crowds
into the early seventies, but there was a different tenor to the
scene. The street felt more like a thoroughfare than a destination. You didn't hang out there; you drove through it. In large
part that was because the sense that it was where the newest
music was happening had evaporated. The vital new acts of the
era weren't gigging six nights a week down the block from one
another; they were ensconced in their homes in Laurel Canyon or
Malibu, and they played in arenas, not discotheques; you didn't
go club hopping to see the Eagles or Fleetwood Mac or Jackson
Browne, to name just some of the big local acts of the day.

Yet oddly, just when pop musicians were becoming less physically present on the Strip, they were dominating it more than
ever before with their images. The Strip of the day was lined
with giant billboards advertising new albums and concert tours,
an outdoor art gallery celebrating hit-making bands and giving
the big PR push to up-and-comers. You could truly spend an evening driving back and forth on the Strip just appreciating the
pictures.

Yet even with those riches right there, just as in the days of the
Sahara showgirl, the billboard at the foot of Chateau Marmont
was arguably the most memorable of them all. In 1976, ten years
after the Sahara showgirl was taken down, the Philip Morris
agency placed a new billboard at the corner of Sunset and Mar-

mont, a depiction of a *different* Wild West icon that would occupy the space longer even than his pirouetting predecessor had. He was fifty feet tall, form cut, two-dimensional, a cowboy, complete with Stetson hat and duster overcoat, lighting up a smoke, with a single word emblazoned across his hips: "Marlboro."

The Marlboro Man stood long enough on the gateway to the Sunset Strip that he became a landmark. In 1991, an architecture critic in the *Los Angeles Times* declared him "a more enduring urban monument than almost any other building in Los Angeles." And just like the Sahara showgirl, he both upstaged and complemented Chateau Marmont. In a way that only made sense in Hollywood, the cowboy and the castle went together.

❊

Roman Polanski had been avoiding Chateau Marmont for years. Ever since he had moved out of the hotel in 1969 with his pregnant wife, Sharon Tate, mere months before she was slaughtered by Charles Manson's lunatic disciples, the place held nothing but painful memories for him. He mainly lived and worked in Europe, keeping his visits to Hollywood to a minimum until 1973, when he made a triumphant return to American filmmaking with the brilliant drama *Chinatown*. In the spring of 1977, he was back in Los Angeles to prepare work on a new film when another sensational incident buffeted his life, this one of his own devising.

In March of that year, while staying at the Beverly Wilshire, Polanski was arrested for the sexual assault of a thirteen-year-old girl at the home of Jack Nicholson, where he had taken the child to photograph her for a layout in *Vogue* magazine. He was released on bail, pending trial, and he moved into a friend's house in Coldwater Canyon. He was quickly discovered by the media there and unsparingly pursued. "My world was in ruins," he later complained. "I couldn't even go jogging any more for fear of being recognized and accosted." Besieged, he moved into Chateau Marmont, where he knew he could keep to himself, hopeful, perhaps, to recapture some of the warmth he remembered from his earlier days in the hotel.

He arrived in April, and he would stay there on and off as his case made its way through the legal system. He didn't like to use the grounds, even though he trusted the place. He would receive visitors in his suite, where guests would find him up late into the night "listen[ing] to some doleful jazz," sitting in a large chair that looked ready to "swallow him up," going on for hours-long monologues about the ins and outs of his case, about the American legal system, about "the people who won't rest until they get me." Staffers recalled that Polanski kept to himself, sneaking out after dark to get in a workout at a friend's ballet school on Melrose Avenue or to have a meal at the Hamburger Hamlet on Sunset Boulevard. Eventually, he became friendly with the parking valets in the Marmont garage, often coming downstairs to sit and chat with them, snacks and sodas in hand. Elsewhere in town he was a pariah, scratched off guest lists, spoken of in terms of villainy. "I'd crossed the fine line between decent folks and scum," he moaned.

Months of investigation, deposition, grand jury testimony, and legal maneuvers followed. Polanski was allowed to leave the country for brief visits to Europe. He even found a producer, Dino De Laurentiis, willing to hire him to direct a film, a remake of the 1937 disaster movie *Hurricane* to be shot on location in the South Pacific, and the court allowed Polanski to travel there to scout locations. He moved in and out of Chateau Marmont to make these trips, always with a sense of trepidation.

His lawyers arranged a deal in which Polanski would plead guilty to unlawful sexual intercourse with a minor and be remanded to a psychiatric evaluation at a prison in Chino, California. If the doctors there deemed him fit to return to society, he would be released after no more than ninety days and serve probation thereafter. Polanski reported to Chino, complied with the court orders that he submit to examination, and, after forty-two days, was released, just before Christmas, returning to Chateau Marmont and resuming work on *Hurricane.*

He was supposed to report to court for final sentencing in early 1978, expecting to be given probation as had been agreed to by his attorneys, attorneys for his victim, the district attorney, and the judge. But word began to get around that the judge was going to scuttle the deal for something more substantial; the press was publishing too many pictures of Polanski at liberty, and there were grumblings that the director had gotten preferential treatment because the judge was starstruck. The judge told the attorneys that he was unilaterally altering the terms of the plea agreement, planning to send Polanski back to prison for the remainder of the ninety-day period and then to give him a sentence of indeterminate length, perhaps in probation, perhaps also including a stipulation that he voluntarily deport himself from the United States. Polanski learned that the judge had put on an even tougher face in private, telling acquaintances over dinner at a country club that he was going to sentence the director to fifty years in prison. "I'll see this man never gets out of jail," he was heard saying.

Learning of this change in climate, Polanski felt cornered. He had escaped the Holocaust as a child by roaming the Polish countryside, pretending to be Catholic. He had avoided slaughter at the hands of the Manson family by sheer happenstance and paid the price of having his wife and unborn child murdered. Now, facing punishment for a crime of his own making, his instinct for survival kicked in. "The judge seemed determined to prevent me from ever again living and working in the United States," he remembered. "What had I to gain by staying?" In his suite at the Chateau, he packed a bag, then drove to De Laurentiis's offices. "I've made up my mind," he declared, "I'm getting out of here." With $1,000 cash that the producer thrust on him, he went to LAX, parked his car, and bought a ticket on the first flight to London, where he had an apartment. The following day, he went to France, where extradition regulations protected him from deportation back to the United States. He would never see Hollywood, or Chateau Marmont, again.

❆

Even though Ray Sarlot was struggling mightily to infuse the hotel with a veneer of respectability, there was a patina of old-time naughtiness to the place that couldn't easily be shaken off. The actress Faith Dane, best known for her portrayal of the burlesque artist known as Miss Mazeppa in the play and film *Gypsy,* was a regular, as was, fittingly enough, the drag queen known as Gypsy (born James Haake) and, for that matter, an actor and musician who became famous in drag, Tim Curry, who stayed at the Chateau while performing in the original Los Angeles production of *The Rocky Horror Show,* which was staged at the Roxy nightclub on the Sunset Strip and lasted a full nine months.

And the world of music could always be counted on to provide some hair-raising incidents. The soul-funk singer Rick James frequented the Chateau Marmont when his star was rising in the late seventies. "I moved into a bungalow at the Chateau Marmont," he remembered in his autobiography, "the hippest scene in decadent, dope-crazed Hollywood." Ensconced in his hideaway, James partied prodigiously and with a gallery of famous names. "Rod Stewart became my best friend," he said. "Timothy Hutton became my best friend. Robin Williams became my best friend. Elisabeth Shue became my girlfriend." That James would remember his days at the hotel at all was impressive, because members of his entourage would occasionally find him blue-skinned and nearly lifeless from all the drugs he had consumed and would have to revive him with cold showers and, sometimes, medical intervention. (Years after James's death, an associate claimed that this sort of near catastrophe happened not only at the Chateau but at the Sunset Marquis down the Strip, L'Ermitage in Beverly Hills, and the Plaza in New York.)

One of the people whom James saw frequently when he was staying at Chateau Marmont was Jan Gaye, the ex-wife of singer Marvin Gaye, with whom James was having an affair that, he said, made him think of marriage despite all the other women he was dallying with while dating her. Jan knew the hotel well, because her former husband used to stay there occasionally when he was seeking a place away from home to indulge in sex-and-drug escapades, which sometimes included his wife. Gaye was enough of a regular that he had run up a tab of $14,000 by the time of his death in 1984.* Ray Sarlot claimed that the hotel tried to collect before the singer was killed, but to no avail. "He stiffed us for thousands in unpaid room rent," he said. "We billed him but nothing happened. Later, we submitted a bill to his estate, but discovered there was nothing there. After that, what were we to do? Say we sued Marvin Gaye?"

If Sarlot was ambivalent about using the courts, not all of his guests were. In 1977, when her marriage to Rolling Stone Mick Jagger was sputtering toward divorce, Bianca Jagger, the Nicaragua-born socialite and activist, decided to have a go at a career in acting. She moved to Los Angeles and, as she said, "I stayed at the Chateau Marmont Hotel rather than one of the more fashionable places because I wanted people to realize that I was there looking for work." Such was the repute of the hotel that her posh friends were horrified to learn that she was there. "Ryan O'Neal was appalled when he found out," Jagger remembered. "'How can you stay in a place like that?' he said."

Just two years later, Jagger was back at the Chateau in a different frame of mind. This time, she was trying to establish residency in California to take advantage of the divorce laws there. During her stay, she was injured in a roller-skating accident and

* Around $34,000 in 2019.

sued her estranged husband for $2,500 in medical bills, $35,000 in legal fees, and, what the hell, $5,000 for her tab at the hotel. The judge was good with the first two claims, but he balked at the hotel bill.

※

Given all of this, it was no wonder that Sarlot and his staff thought so highly of one of their regular guests, a fellow who had been patronizing the hotel since he first started coming regularly to Hollywood to shoot a TV series in 1970. Tony Randall first checked into the Chateau when he began work on *The Odd Couple*, which ran for 114 episodes between 1970 and 1975, and he returned when he was in town to shoot *The Tony Randall Show* (1976–78) and *Love, Sidney* (1981–83). Randall and his wife, Florence, preferred the bungalows to the suites, partly because they liked the size of the kitchens. "We don't want to go out to dinner every night, or send down for dinner," he told a reporter. "We want to cook our dinners like Ma and Pa back home. Like Mr. and Mrs. Front Porch." But unlike that imaginary rustic couple, the Randalls also liked to sunbathe au naturel, and the extra privacy afforded by being well outside the main building and even the pool area made that luxury possible. Even when the unit next to theirs was engulfed in tempest, as happened during their final extended stay, they were isolated from the commotion.

But for all that comfort, Randall was never fully satisfied with his accommodations, not because of anything to do with the hotel, but, rather, because of the setting. Los Angeles, he complained to a friend in the press, wasn't a good town for pedestrians: "They don't walk out here. There's not one decent place to walk." When his schedule permitted, Randall would fly back to his Central Park West home just so he could enjoy a day or so of walking around Manhattan, his absolute favorite pastime. His newsman chum tried to get him to walk along the Sunset Strip, through Beverly Hills, or up and down the row of art galleries on

La Cienega. A good sport, Randall tried them all but found them wanting. "I'm a New Yorker," he said finally, as if that were the only explanation that anyone would require.

It was another New Yorker, with another set of habits, who would make a more permanent mark on the Chateau.

3.

When he checked in at the front desk on the night of February 28, 1982, John Belushi was a time bomb, a waste site, a mess.

Sweaty, flabby, edgy, pale, disheveled, worn to a stump at the age of thirty-three, he had called ahead to reserve his favorite bungalow, number 3, one of the ones Al Smith had purchased that stood close to the private entrance on Monteel Road. Like other members of the extended *Saturday Night Live* family, Belushi had been introduced to Chateau Marmont by the show's producer, Lorne Michaels, who stayed there when he was a comedy writer for a variety of TV shows and who liked to joke that he moved around the place as his fortunes in the business ebbed and flowed: "I lived all around in the hotel, moving from room to room. If I had the money, I moved to a larger suite. If not, I took a smaller one."

Belushi had been in residence at the hotel for more than a month earlier that winter, at first in a suite in the upper floors, number 69, only to abandon it when he and his neighbors found one another noisy: them complaining about Belushi's music and carousing, him being woken by their crying baby. He moved to a penthouse, number 54, and then, after a visit from his wife, Judy, who found the setting depressing—"Are you sure you want to stay here?" she had asked him, after finding a Quaalude on the floor of his room—he moved into the bungalow, with his script drafts, his research materials, a new stereo system, and the rest of his belongings. He was going to get a movie written. He was going to create a hit.

The film he wanted to make was *Noble Rot*, a romantic comedy about a robbery scheme set in the early days of the California wine industry. And in the days after his frazzled arrival at the front desk, he would take meetings with writers and development executives and ask any number of friends in and out of the business to give their impressions of the script.

But the work wasn't going well, and neither Belushi's manager, Bernie Brillstein, nor executives at Paramount Pictures were happy with his work. The studio had run out of patience and was willing to cut its losses and start anew; Michael Eisner, Paramount's production boss, even came around to the Chateau to pitch Belushi on a whole new idea, a spoofy adaptation of *The Joy of Sex* with Belushi playing a variety of characters representing the range of human sexual experience.

But it became clear to everyone dealing with the comedian that he was off, badly: His attention span was negligible; he took and made mysterious phone calls around the clock; he was frequently hours late or completely AWOL from meetings and appointments; his hotel room was a pigsty; his speech was scattershot and even incoherent; the clothes he wore were dirty and rumpled; he didn't seem to be bathing or shaving regularly; he was barely sleeping. When the filmmaker Al Reinert came across Belushi waiting for his car in the hotel garage, he noted the star's clearly disoriented manner: "He would pace around the valet area, muttering incomprehensible curses, his pupils as black and dilated as wide-open camera lenses."

Everyone assumed Belushi was using drugs, and the suspicions were absolutely correct. He had long been known to be an all-in sort, devouring food and booze and controlled substances with the same impressive gusto with which he dove into physical comedy. His superhuman capacity had always been a point of amazement, and he wasn't shy about boasting of it. Heedless hedonism was one of his great comic gifts, and he made great comedy of his appetites on-screen and off. But the state of him that winter wasn't a piece of acting. He had been drinking and smoking pot and, especially, using cocaine all day, every day, for a long time, and he'd begun to dabble in heroin, partly, he would tell people, as research for a movie he wanted to make about the punk rock scene.

Given that it was Hollywood and the early eighties, this sort of behavior, while extreme, was often tolerated: You generate income for entertainment conglomerates, they don't care too much what you do with your free time or to yourself. But Belushi was riding a poor streak. His two 1981 films, *Continental Divide* and *Neighbors*, were bombs, as was his 1979 film Steven Spielberg's *1941*. He had a modest success with 1980's *Blues Brothers*, which had a cult following but hadn't sold enough tickets to compensate for its out-of-control budget. His last true hit was *Animal House*, almost four years earlier, a lifetime in Hollywood. He was in danger of squandering his career, and his life choices were making that seem a likelier outcome than not, even to casual observers. During his stay at Chateau Marmont, he took a meeting at a Sunset Strip nightclub with a pair of studio executives who brought their wives along. After their parley, which was, as was becoming more common with Belushi, disjointed and unproductive, one of the women said to her husband that she was reminded of a classic Hollywood tale: Billy Wilder's *Sunset Boulevard*. But that was a movie about a forgotten star, he replied; everyone knew Belushi. "*Sunset Boulevard*," she repeated. "I'm telling you. We just saw it."

❈

While Belushi was trashing his bungalow and himself, people around him were scheming to get him back to New York, where his wife, Judy, and his partner and best friend, Dan Aykroyd, felt they could help him get clean from drugs and resume working productively. Aykroyd could always bring out the best in Belushi; when he visited the Chateau during Belushi's previous stay, the pair were seen on a lark, staging a mock sword fight in the lobby lounge, using two-foot-long candles as weapons. He was busily working on a script, titled *Ghostbusters*, for the two of them to make together with another *SNL* alumnus, Bill Murray. But even tracking Belushi down to have a chat was becoming impossible. He darted around erratically from nightclubs to people's homes to restaurants to guitar shops to his favorite bathhouse to assignations with drug dealers, sometimes abandoning limousines he hired and driving off with some new acquaintance. When he was in the bungalow, he was often too addled to talk or answer the phone, or he was surrounded by clutches of sycophants and drug world people and hangers-on and unable to have a serious conversation. He was a wreck, and he was spinning beyond the reach of anyone who could help him.

At Chateau Marmont, Belushi was occasionally seen in the company of Robert De Niro, who had returned to Los Angeles to look into some new film projects. The pair knew each other from lower Manhattan. De Niro had been a guest at Belushi's home, where a basement rec room was the scene of some wild late-night parties (at one, De Niro cut his hand so deeply that he had to go to the hospital for stitches). Since he had last visited the hotel to make the aborted *Bogart Slept Here*, De Niro had acquired the habit of keeping more or less on retainer an upper-floor penthouse at the Chateau, preferring to stay in the hotel after having some bad experiences with rental houses during recent working trips to Hollywood. His laundry was done by the hotel staff; his car was kept under a dustcover in the hotel garage; and he came and went unnoticed: a New York apartment dweller utterly at home in a place that felt like a Manhattan high-rise.

On this visit, De Niro had been joined for a time by his young son and adolescent daughter. One afternoon, he took them to a party where they encountered Belushi snorting such quantities of cocaine and heroin that he had to excuse himself to go find a place to vomit. That sordid spectacle didn't stop De Niro, who was using cocaine himself in those days, from seeking Belushi's company regularly after the kids went back east. De Niro would occasionally come down from his suite to Belushi's bungalow to hang around, laugh, and party, or the two would bump into each other in the VIP rooms of various Sunset Strip restaurants and nightclubs and set off together on some sort of spree.

On Thursday night, March 4, De Niro was bopping around town with actor Harry Dean Stanton, and the two kept phoning Belushi to get him to come out and join them, first at Dan Tana's, an Italian restaurant favored by movie people, and then at On the Rox, the exclusive nightclub on the Sunset Strip where famous folks could get up to just about anything. Failing to raise him, they drove over to the Chateau to see if they could coax him into a bit of play. Instead, they found him—and his bungalow—in an awful state. The living room was a shambles—not sloppy, but actually trashed, as if in a rage. And worse, a flinty, hard-eyed woman named Cathy was lounging amid the discarded pizza boxes and wine bottles and dirty laundry as if she had some claim to the place and to Belushi himself. De Niro didn't like the look of her at all—he called her "trashy" later—and he was happy to leave when Belushi suggested that he and Stanton go back to On the Rox and return to the bungalow after the club closed.

De Niro left, and when he returned to the Chateau a few hours later, it was to his own suite in the company of Stanton and a pair of women they'd met. There, he got a phone call from Robin Williams. The comedian had run into De Niro and Stanton at On the Rox, and they all agreed to meet up at Belushi's after Williams performed an unscheduled set at the Comedy Store, also right on the Sunset Strip (and, formerly, Ciro's). On the phone, De Niro told Williams that he was busy and that he should stop by Belushi's on his own. Williams did and, like De Niro, was creeped out by the scene, leaving after a few words and a little coke. After he left, De Niro, too, stopped in at the bungalow, entering through the sliding glass patio door. He had a few words and a few lines and then took some of the cocaine that was piled on the living room table and went back to his suite. It was some time past 3:00 a.m.

At 8:00 a.m., a room service waiter delivered wheat toast, jam, and a pot of coffee to Belushi's bungalow; Cathy Smith, the woman whom De Niro had shied away from, signed for the order, had her breakfast, cleaned up the room, especially the drug paraphernalia, checked in on Belushi, who was snoring loudly in bed, and left.

A little while later, the musical producer and manager Derek Power came knocking on the bungalow door while looking for Miles Copeland, manager of the rock trio the Police, who was himself staying in one of the hotel's bungalows. Power knocked several times without getting a response before realizing he was at the wrong door and moving along.

At around noon, a taut, spry man walked through the grounds of the hotel, past the swimming pool, with a typewriter in his hand. The sky was clear, the air was warm, and the few sunbathers and lap swimmers who had come out to enjoy the weather took no notice of him: People were often passing through the pool area with musical instruments, wardrobe cases, cameras, easels—the clumsy stuff that creative folks use to make art.

Maybe twenty minutes later, a second man came by, in a suit, rushing, but, again, nothing terribly odd, and, again, nobody paid much mind.

But presently there were paramedics, moving with purpose, and then policemen, snooping about, and within an hour, outside the hotel grounds but creating an unignorable hum, television camera trucks and packets of paparazzi.

Finally, one of the sunbathers wandered into the lobby, which was unusually active, and asked a hotel employee what was going on. He was told, in the understatement for which the Chateau had long been known, "There has been a slight disturbance." Presently, he learned that the truth was more than just "slight" and far bigger than a "disturbance."

John Belushi had been discovered in a state of unconsciousness by the man with the typewriter, his personal trainer and bodyguard, Bill Wallace. Wallace had performed CPR on the comedian but wasn't able to rouse him. Because it was Hollywood, and agents mattered more than cops, Wallace had phoned Bernie Brillstein, whose offices were just down Sunset Boulevard at 9200—ten blocks away.

"I'm having trouble waking John up," Wallace said, clearly agitated. Brillstein thought Belushi might be playing possum to avoid a meeting he was to have that day with Paramount executives, and he told Wallace that he'd send someone over. Wallace called again a few minutes later, in an even more stressed voice: "There's something really wrong with John!" Brillstein had his secretary call a doctor, who recommended calling for paramedics, which she did, and then he ordered his assistant, Joel Briskin, to get over to the hotel, and he was the second man on the scene, the man in the suit who'd rushed past the pool.

When he got inside the bungalow, Briskin found Wallace weeping, still trying to perform mouth-to-mouth resuscitation on Belushi. "Get out of here," Wallace hollered at him. *"John's dead!"* Almost immediately, an ambulance arrived and EMTs assessed the comedian's state. They didn't even try to defibrillate him; he was, as Wallace had declared, gone. They called for the medical examiner, but they saw the needle marks on Belushi's arms: They knew he had died of an overdose.

Brillstein, for his part, had left his office and driven to Cedars-Sinai Medical Center, where he assumed Belushi would be brought for treatment. He warned the staff that a major star had suffered an accident and was on his way and would require immediate care and, above all, privacy. And then he waited for news, which was painfully long in coming. He paced and smoked, his mind racing: He imagined that Belushi didn't need to come to the ER at all, or that he was taken to another hospital, or that it was the worst case possible and time wasn't of the essence, an outcome that he didn't want to believe.

And then the call came from his office with the horrible news.

He felt his body react with sweat and hollowness and a shudder that was "like a little stuttered giggle." He hung up and gathered himself sufficiently to act on next steps, a professional manager and problem solver in his bones. He called Dan Aykroyd and told him what had happened, point-blank, no sugar coating, instructing him to get to Belushi's house and tell his wife before the media got the story. And then he returned to his offices to deal with the aftermath of an unimaginable tragedy that almost everybody had seen coming and no one knew how to prevent.

❇

The hotel staff were busy improvising a response to an event that none of them had ever faced or prepared for. By chance, general manager Suzanne Jierjian wasn't at her usual post when the news came from Belushi's bungalow but at a medical appointment. When she returned, she was jolted by the spectacle of emergency vehicles on the street and a steady flow of reporters and cameras to the site. She was greeted by her assistant Tom Rafter, with word of what had happened, and even that was sketchy: Belushi had died, he told her, but nobody knew how or why. She was at a loss as to what to do when rescue came in the form of co-owner Ray Sarlot, who had been having lunch at the Friars Club in Beverly Hills when the news broke there. He had raced back to the hotel. "It was bedlam," he remembered, "swarming with outsiders, the switchboard was lit up."

Among the callers was Robert De Niro, who had been trying to reach Belushi throughout the late morning and wasn't getting through. Perhaps noticing the commotion in the streets below his suite, he called the front desk directly, only to find his inquiries rebuffed. He demanded, finally, to speak to Jierjian, who reluctantly took his call.

"Where's John?" he asked her.

"There is a problem," she said.

"What?"

"It's bad."

"Is he sick?"

"It's really bad."

De Niro suddenly understood. He dropped the phone, crying.

✤

Sarlot, meanwhile, leaped into action. He had every intention of cooperating with the authorities, whatever that meant in
such a situation, but he didn't care for the tumult being caused
by the droves of newspeople and gawkers who were descending
on Chateau Marmont. He had to protect his other guests, as well
as the reputation of his business. He stationed guards at all the
entrances to the hotel, directing anyone who wanted to come
inside to the garage, which was the easiest point of entry to control. The police set up a barricade at the foot of Marmont Lane,
allowing only hotel guests and residents of the streets above the
hotel through. "It was the first time in all the years I've stayed
there that I had to show my room key to get back into the hotel,"
recalled a guest.

Some in the media breached the cordon. One camera crew
made its way up to De Niro's suite, hoping to get a response
from the actor. They banged on his door repeatedly—on live
TV—until they finally heard a voice from within hollering, "*Go
away!*"* Another reporter found an uncharacteristically talkative
subject in one of the hotel's gardeners, who stated with great confidence that Belushi had died of a heart attack with his clothes
neatly folded beside him, "as though he had gone to bed for the

---

* The combination of Belushi's death and the intrusions on his privacy kept De
Niro away from the hotel for a few years. When he returned in November 1988,
he took a bungalow that was burgled *twice* in November 1988, once when he was
in bed asleep. That incident resulted in the burglar making off with his rented
Mercedes. Questioned by police after reporting the theft, De Niro admitted that
he had left the patio door to his bungalow ajar. "New York people like fresh air,"
he explained cryptically.

night. . . . It looked like he choked on his tongue and the phlegm in his mouth." (The next day, when his bosses saw his comments in the paper, the chatty greensman was sent away from the property and assigned to work on Sarlot's San Fernando Valley home before returning a few days later to his regular post.)

Sarlot and his team managed to keep a lid on the situation so that other guests of the hotel not only avoided intrusions into their lives but didn't even know that something so dreadful and sensational was going on right under their noses. Sarlot relished a particular example of how well his staff managed to deal with the awful scene. "What people don't realize about the night Belushi died," he confided to the *Los Angeles Times* a few years later, "is that the whole time all of that stuff was going on, Tony Randall was living right next door! Tony had no idea what was happening until he saw the coroner's wagon." ("Sarlot made Randall sound like an agent from the Vatican," noted *Times* reporter Chris Hodenfield.)

❦

Eventually, Belushi's body was strapped to a gurney and rolled out to a coroner's vehicle on Monteel Road. The street was lined with photographers, reporters, and curiosity seekers, as close to the bungalow as they had been able to get for hours. The reporters pushed toward the body, barking out questions, until Suzanne Jierjian stepped up and reproved them. The reporters, chastened, quieted and backed off. A police lieutenant watching the spectacle approached her and asked if she had any interest in working for the LAPD. "We need somebody like you who can handle the press," he said.

The following day, Bernie Brillstein and an assistant were permitted to enter the bungalow and retrieve Belushi's personal belongings. The police had already made a thorough sweep of the place, turning up some marijuana and residue of white powder in a dresser drawer and in some small folded paper envelopes of the sort commonly used to package cocaine and heroin. Brillstein couldn't believe the state of his client's rooms: "The scene was not only depressing, it was depraved. I couldn't believe John had lived there." There were half-drunk beers and bottles of wine and cups of coffee, plates of cold food, heaps of garbage and dirty laundry, and scattered papers, including piles of phone messages. Brillstein grabbed up a few documents that he thought looked personal and a jacket that he thought was appropriate to dress Belushi in, and he left for the mortuary, where he would help prepare the body to travel back east for a funeral, a trip on which he would accompany it.

Sarlot and his staff, meanwhile, cleaned the bungalow more thoroughly, throwing away most of what they found and identifying a few valuable-seeming items to put in the hotel safe in case the comedian's family claimed them later. They then set about completely remodeling the room, changing all of the furniture and decor. "It was no longer the same unit," Sarlot said. "We didn't want the place to become a cult symbol." The hotel kept a small but tight security cordon in place for about a month after the comedian's death, hoping to discourage the wrong type of attention.

But that wasn't to be, not entirely. For decades, even during the sixties heyday of the Sunset Strip, Chateau Marmont had enjoyed something of a privileged position amid the hurly-burly of Hollywood: It stood slightly apart from the commotion around it—compact, old-world, elegant, just off to the side of the circus, much as it sat just off Sunset Boulevard itself.

After Belushi, that changed. The Chateau became part of the show. A species of tourism sprang up in the eighties, a variant on the traditional tours of movie stars' homes dedicated, instead, to the locales where various notorious Hollywood incidents occurred. Invariably, these "ghoul tours" would slow down in front of Marmont Lane so that guides could point out the famous "naughty" hotel where John Belushi died. Looky-loos would occasionally enter the grounds trying to get a glimpse of the infamous bungalow, but they would either be turned away or simply leave in disappointment when they saw how staid and demure the setting was. (Among those who wanted a piece of the place was the New York painter Jean-Michel Basquiat, who came to Los Angeles soon after Belushi's death and insisted that his art dealer host put him up in the bungalow where the comedian had overdosed—a fate to which Basquiat himself would fall in 1988.)*

In 1984, Bob Woodward of *The Washington Post* and Watergate fame published *Wired: The Short Life and Fast Times of John Belushi,* a painstakingly thorough but often tone-deaf account of, in the main, the final years, days, and hours of the comedian's life, interviewing scores of Belushi's intimates including his widow; his brother Jim; Dan Aykroyd; Bill Wallace; Bernie Brillstein; even Cathy Smith, who in 1986 pleaded no contest to involuntary manslaughter for supplying Belushi with drugs and injecting him with his final fatal speedball doses of cocaine and heroin. The book was a best seller, but it was something that nobody wanted: a misdeed-by-misdeed account of a life gone wrong, a chronicle of addiction that indicted everyone, a book that uncovered everything about Hollywood, drugs, and Belushi and yet seemed to understand none of it.

Brillstein felt that Woodward had an agenda of his own by taking on a project outside his habitual milieu of politics, saying he "came to town and looked at the situation through the eyes of a guy who knew nothing about the times or the environment or the people. He didn't want to understand how Hollywood worked.

---

* Others would settle for dubious claims of almost having been there. The singer Billy Idol claimed that he spent a drugged, drunken night smashing everything in *his* Chateau Marmont bungalow that he could get his hands on, including the doors, windows, and TV. Passed out naked on the floor, he said, he was awakened by the sound of sirens. He assumed they were coming for him, and he stepped out his door—naked, he claimed, and covered in blood—only to find the cops rushing toward another bungalow to see about Belushi. The story, to be kind, has holes in it.

He just wanted to condemn it. I think he already had his mind made up." Aykroyd shared in the disappointment: "He painted a portrait of John that was really inaccurate. . . . This was my friend that was being besmirched. . . . It was all about the drugs and the excess, not about the quality of work and the background in theater and the preparation and the respect that John's friends had for him." And Jim Belushi held back nothing in his disdain for his brother's biographer: "Woodward—that cocksucker. That motherfucker! . . . I don't think Woodward's capable of understanding what love is, or compassion, or relationships. He is one cold fish."

Even from the vantage of Chateau Marmont, to which Belushi was technically no more than a guest who'd caused an unusual disruption, *Wired* was an affront. The owners of the hotel didn't mind what was said about the comedian. They objected, rather, to the first line of the dust jacket: "John Belushi was found dead of a drug overdose March 5, 1982, in a seedy hotel bungalow."

"Seedy"? Their $250-a-night bungalow?* That was a fighting word.

"He made it sound like some place near a downtown bus station where big drug deals are made," Ray Sarlot moaned. He and Karl Kantarjian filed an $18 million† defamation suit against the publisher, Simon & Schuster, demanding that the cover be removed from the books and/or recalled. "Ray had spent so much time and effort bringing the hotel up to respectable condition," remembered Sarlot's wife, Sally Rae. "It was a blow to him to hear someone call it seedy. He was defending its honor."

At first, Simon & Schuster pushed back: "It was the author's opinion that the bungalow was seedy on March 5, 1982." But they quickly realized it was best to put the squabble behind them. They settled with the hoteliers within weeks, changing the wording in subsequent printings of the book jacket and

* Approximately $655 in 2019.
† Approximately $43 million in 2019.

issuing a press release in which Woodward qualified that it was Belushi's *mess* that he was referring to and not the hotel itself. "The Chateau has a charming ambience," the author said, "and I would enjoy staying there myself."* (His first words had a lasting sting, though: The month after the hotel and Woodward worked out their conflict, a travel piece about the Chateau in the *Chicago Tribune* was published with the headline "If the Marmont's So 'Seedy,' Why Is It a Retreat for the Elite?")

Wired was a big enough hit to draw the attention of movie-makers, although many in Hollywood were loath to touch the material. Veteran producer Edward S. Feldman managed to get the film made, despite obstacles and even violence: Jim Belushi stormed into his office one day and trashed it, instructing a secretary to "tell Feldman who did this"; "I would," she replied, "but I don't know who you are, sir." The film premiered at 1989's Cannes Film Festival to a reception of walkouts, catcalls, and boos. Much of the film was set at Chateau Marmont, which was explicitly named and shown in exterior shots several times early on. A mock-up of a bungalow stood in for Belushi's rooms (for the record, it wasn't especially seedy); it was the primary set for the final third or so of the story. Woodward, who was written into the script as a kind of observer/hero, walking through Belushi's final days with him like an impartial guardian angel, told reporters that he found the film "exceptional. . . . It deals with the themes with utter clarity." But critics and audiences agreed with the Cannes crowd; the picture died, grossing barely $1 million.

More than three decades after Belushi's death, the tragedy was still synonymous with Chateau Marmont. Almost every article about the hotel would mention the connection, and even for many in the Hollywood community the comedian's overdose was considered a feature of the hotel and not a sad fact from its past.

---

* The hotel's lawyers weren't very close readers. The *whole hotel* was referred to as "seedy" on page 303 of *Wired*, and the description remained in place in later printings of the book.

Novelist Jay McInerney, who was a regular at the Chateau for a number of years and became a good friend of one of its owners, made his first trip to Hollywood as a guest of a production company that was interested in acquiring rights to his novel *Bright Lights, Big City*. "They told me they were putting me up at Chateau Marmont," he remembered, "and I said, 'Is that good?' And they said, 'Is it good? John Belushi died there!'"

4.

One afternoon in the early eighties, a journalist sat in the lobby lounge of the Chateau with coffee and a notepad, writing down impressions of the place for a long story that was growing out of his obsession with the hotel. The whole while, he was slightly rattled by a spectacle on a nearby couch: "a small, elderly man dressed in a herringbone suit and a brightly colored ascot. His hair was dyed bluish-grey, and he wore matching eyeshadow. He was sleeping—arms akimbo, mouth open—with all the abandon of a child." The dozer turned out to be Quentin Crisp, the eccentric English author and bon vivant, passing through Los Angeles on a book publicity tour and happily ensconced in the hotel with his publisher and co-author Donald Carroll. Crisp loved the Chateau and rhapsodized over it in a travel piece in *The New York Times*. "It is a place apart," he said, conjuring "a leisurely, almost rural past." He marveled at the lack of amenities, such as the overly solicitous bellmen who'd besieged him at the Beverly Hills and Beverly Wilshire hotels on previous visits: "I at last felt completely liberated from the fear of hotel staff by which my new life had so far been haunted. There didn't appear to be any. . . . No demands were made, no suggestions even were put forward. . . . It is possible to carry on exactly as though you are living at home."

Crisp wasn't a regular at the hotel, but in a mere three-night stay he captured its decaying charms perfectly, and the fact that his article appeared within weeks of John Belushi's overdose was a boon to the hotel, which was in danger of becoming notorious. The air of ill repute hovered over the place for several years afterward. In a 1985 article describing a film director's rebound from a career dip, the *Los Angeles Times* mentioned that he was staying in a bungalow at the Beverly Hills Hotel rather than "a back room at the Chateau Marmont." And Michael O'Donoghue, one of the very few among Belushi's *Saturday Night Live* chums who didn't abandon the hotel in the wake of the comedian's death, made a joke of the Chateau's lack of creature comforts, such as nighttime turndown service of guests' bedding and complimentary mints on the pillows; in 1987, he was staying at the hotel and played a prank on a friend who was also in residence, inviting him for a late-night drink and then, before the friend arrived, turning down his own sheets, placing a mint he himself bought on the pillow, and acting as if the hotel provided these little amenities for him each night. Such was the quality of service at the hotel that a guest could readily be convinced that his or her room was simply being overlooked by staff.

※

But not long after the death of John Belushi, the Chateau went from a hidden bohemian enclave to an open secret, taking on a patina of retro chic. Along with the Musso & Frank Grill and the Formosa Cafe, two other long-standing relics of the classic era of Hollywood, the Marmont was elevated into a status it had never enjoyed previously, with nostalgia for a heyday that had never quite existed, at least not in the tenor in which those celebrating it assumed. During this time, the hotel's name was bandied about in the press more than it ever had been. Virtually every newspaper or magazine interview with an actor or a director that took place on its grounds saw the hotel's name mentioned in it, at first with the obligatory "where John Belushi died" attached but after a few years with no need to explain what the Chateau was at all. It was fashionable, even though it was still, in the words of one frequent guest, *Washington Post* TV critic Tom Shales, "funky—not quite dumpy, but not luxurious either."

This was an era of regular media accounts of interviews at the Marmont with such auteurs as Jim Jarmusch, John Sayles, Agnès Varda, Spike Lee, Alejandro Jodorowsky, Jocelyn Moorhouse, Derek Jarman, Wim Wenders, Claudia Weill, Bruce Beresford, Claire Denis, Terry Gilliam, Jonathan Demme, Stephen Frears, Jim Sheridan, Shirley Clarke, Terence Davies, and Volker Schlöndorff. John Waters became a Chateau regular in these years in part because he considered it his lucky hotel: The one time he didn't stay there, he liked to complain, "I didn't get my deal and I caught the flu." Actors continued to pour into the place and sit for interviews—the likes of Carol Kane, Fernando Rey, Sonia Braga, Klaus Kinski, Judy Davis, William Hurt, Dominique Sanda, Annie Girardot, and that almost-vaudevillian pair Andre Gregory and Wallace Shawn. Musicians residing at the hotel were another interview mainstay, not only such longtime regulars as Betty Buckley and Tommy Tune, but Sting, Bono, Joe Strummer, A Flock of Seagulls, Duran Duran (one of whose members, Andy Taylor, was married at the hotel in 1982), and the Lemonheads. In the feature sections of American magazines and the Sunday arts sections of American newspapers, the phrase "Hollywood's legendary Chateau Marmont" became more and more common.

At the same time—and not necessarily in print—the eighties was when the era of Hollywood bad boys going wild at the Chateau began. The rascals of the Method acting insurrection were legitimate hell-raisers. But they were, by and large, still under the thumbs of movie studio publicity departments. The new lot seemed happy to let the whole world know what sorts of antics they were getting up to at the funky old hotel they were colonizing. The whole of the Brat Pack—as the young Hollywood of the moment was known—seemed to wander into its halls, sometimes at tender ages, always in some sort of rite of passage to do with excessive boozing, drugging, and sexing. It sometimes seemed as if the agents, managers, and studio executives running the town deliberately placed these young stars in an environment where they would get up to no good, perhaps in hopes of the stories leaking to the public—just the opposite of the strategy that Harry Cohn had employed with Glenn Ford and William Holden decades earlier.

"I remember arriving at 17," recalled John Cusack, "and I had been in one movie, and they put me up in the Chateau Marmont where Belushi had died not long before. And I saw Andre the Giant in the lobby with a satin jacket that said 'Hell,' and I thought, 'Rock on!'" Cusack was in town to make *Sixteen Candles,* and another member of that cast, an actor even more associated with the Brat Pack label and the antics that went along with it, Anthony Michael Hall, would also soon reside at the hotel. At age seventeen, he was living in a suite overlooking Sunset Boulevard where stood a giant billboard of . . . himself. Cusack didn't quite buy into the hedonistic world into which he had been thrust. "I was a teen star," he once said. "That's disgusting enough." But Hall had his head turned. "I was living by myself at the Chateau," he remembered, "and though the scene around me wasn't like an Elvis trip, there was a fair share of that. All of a sudden you've got girls whenever you want 'em, and the place was always full of people I hardly knew."

Robert Downey Jr., then beginning his struggles with substance abuse, was an occasional guest, and he made himself at home in the hotel in his own fashion. "My wife and I were sitting in the lobby one night having coffee," remembered the screenwriter L. M. Kit Carson, "and all of a sudden Robert Downey Jr. comes in, wrecked and surveying and scanning the room. He looked like he was thinking, 'I'm supposed to be having a meeting but I don't have a clue with who. . . .' So he comes over and sits down beside us and says, 'Hey, how about having a meeting? I know I'm supposed to be having a meeting. Can we have a meeting? Let's just start having a meeting.'" They chatted for a while and Downey left, satisfied that he had done his agent's bidding.

Other stars merely cavorted, prankishly, boyishly, and if they were chemically altered in the moment it didn't seem to affect them. English actor Rupert Everett recalled a Christmas when he and a pair of acting chums, Eric Stoltz and John Philbin, alleviated boredom by climbing around the fire escapes and seeing what they could see. When they found a suite that was fully decorated for Christmas—tree, wrapped gifts—but apparently unoccupied, they began an elaborate practical joke, replacing the packages under the tree with wrapped gifts of their own devising: a box of sex toys with a gift card reading, "Happy holidays from everyone at the William Morris Agency"; a kitchen knife with a card declaring, "To stab yourself in the back—we can't be bothered to do it. From all your friends at Paramount."

Ethan Hawke, another semi-regular of the era, had a more sober and reflective attitude toward the hotel. "If someone spun you around in Manhattan and then dropped you down anywhere, you'd immediately know where you are," he said. "Los Angeles is not like that. I'm not a huge fan of it, but the Chateau makes me feel like I know where I am. It's a tad reminiscent of New York to me. There's so little history in L.A. and something so attractive about a place that has a past."

Among the other young actors of the era who stayed at the Chateau were Matt Dillon, James Spader, Winona Ryder, Sarah Jessica Parker, and a pair who made their homes in Hollywood but kept returning to the hotel for staycations—Johnny Depp and Keanu Reeves, the latter of whom actually lived in a suite for several years between periods of owning his own house in the area.

The granddaddy of all of this excess was, arguably, Dr. Hunter S. Thompson, the famed gonzo journalist and lifestyle experimentalist who became a semi-regular at the hotel during the seventies and eighties. His visits occasioned the appearance of odd characters of his acquaintance at all hours, not to mention the various actors, writers, and filmmakers who chased around after him trying to secure rights to his books—even his life—

for new movies. He was such a large character that his influence over the hotel persisted even when he wasn't there; the actress Jennifer Beals recalled reaching for the bedside table Bible in her room one night to solve a question that had arisen during a day's work on a film set, only to find a piece of Chateau Marmont stationery tucked inside with the inscription "I hope you enjoy reading this as much as I do" and Thompson's signature below.

※

As much as he might have loved the hotel, Ray Sarlot had a steeply uphill job on his hands making a true success of it. For one thing, he had a clientele who, however enviable their celebrity status might make them to other hoteliers, actually preferred the Marmont to be low-key, slightly less than luxurious, and, most of all, *cheap.* Carol Lynley, for one, complained in the mid-eighties that Sarlot's price increases drove her to seek less costly accommodations. Lauren Hutton, speaking with affection but calling attention to the low-fi character of the hotel, called it "my dorm for 15 years. I would never stay anywhere else." And Jill Clayburgh, spotted by a reporter while she was having coffee in the lobby, actively *discouraged* him from praising the Chateau in print: "Oh, don't mention the hotel! Then all the tourists will come. If you must say something about this place, say it's terrible. Please say it's terrible!"

As if a cadre of regular customers resistant to change weren't obstacle enough, the neighborhood around the Chateau had grown increasingly seedy and unappealing throughout the years after the "riots" on the Sunset Strip had driven the music scene away. There were still some music clubs, and there was always nightlife of *some* sort, but the tenor of things had changed. The strip clubs outnumbered the coffeehouses, there was hardly any street life of the sort that characterized the sixties, and the businesses—especially the entertainment businesses—that had flocked to the Strip in its heyday had begun to move away: Playboy Enterprises, Warner/Chappell Music, and United Talent Agency had all found new homes in less seamy environs.

There were some signs of resurgent life, though: In 1972, the entrepreneur Mitzi Shore acquired the lease to the onetime Ciro's and turned it into the Comedy Store, which launched the careers of generations of superstar comedians and helped create a comedy club boom in the eighties. And in 1982, the visionary Austrian chef Wolfgang Puck opened Spago, a restaurant that had some of the glamorous cachet of the old movie star haunts of decades past, drawing young and old Hollywood alike and helping define modern California cuisine for the rest of the world. But no matter how influential the two places were, neither seemed to define the Sunset Strip the way the coffee shops of the fifties or the music clubs of the sixties had.

And the music venues that still thrived, the spots where so much classic rock talent emerged in the sixties, had given way to a new sound and culture, a scene that combined elements of glam style and thrashing, guitar-dominated music that was supported, again, by kids from the L.A. suburbs but didn't have the same allure or sense of cultural self-declaration that the scene of a prior generation had borne. Rather, it was a time of screaming guitars, peroxide blond hair, ferocious partying—think Mötley Crüe, Van Halen, Ratt, and their ilk. Outside the fervent adherents of the style, there was, up and down the Strip, a sense that the golden age had passed—again—and that the new crowd represented a cultural and social falloff. "This ain't rock 'n' roll," said Llana Lloyd, a veteran of the Strip scene. "This is genocide. These people are vegged out. I think the era is dead."

It was a tough time, in short, to be in the business of restoring a genteel hotel.

Unless, that is, you were a visionary in the vein of Fred Horowitz, able to see riches where others saw a wasteland.

Part Six

A GOLDEN AGE (1990-2019)

Hollywood dream, from *Somewhere*. *Photofest*

When Ray Sarlot and Karl Kantarjian cashed in on their investment in Chateau Marmont after fifteen years of development, they reckoned they'd done pretty well for themselves and for the hotel. It was dilapidated— hemorrhaging—when they took it over. They stanched the bleeding, modernized much of the infrastructure, added some crucial elements to the layout and design, and generally rescued the place from a decade-plus of neglect.

But they didn't have the showmanship or savvy to imagine the next phase in the evolution of the property they had saved from ruin, much less to realize it. That set of skills came in the form of a slick East Coaster, a man who, unique among the owners of the Chateau, self-identified as a hotelier, with connections in movies, fashion, publishing, and finance that preceded his arrival at Marmont Lane.

He saw things in the hotel that no one had previously: a golden era that hadn't really ever existed, even though everyone *thought* it had; a gem of a building in a prime location (down at the heels at the moment, which made it a bargain); a launching pad for a new era of Hollywood swank and polish; and the keystone jewel of a chain of trendy, luxurious hotels that would sparkle all the more brightly for being siblings to the "legendary" Chateau Marmont.

Never mind that a lot of this was smoke and mirrors. Like a movie producer, he knew that the show itself was often what people wanted to see. As it happened, he added substance: a thorough restoration on top of Sarlot's work, new amenities to bring the hotel into a new century, and a level of cachet, exclusivity, and sophistication that not even Fred Horowitz had dreamed of. In his hands, for the first time in its six-plus-decade history, Chateau Marmont became famous *for*—not *despite*—its physical condition and the things that went on inside its walls. Not even a scandal involving the owner himself could tarnish what the hotel had become.

I.

On Oscar night 2018, the most influential couple in the entertainment world, Beyoncé and Jay-Z, hosted an after-after party, an ultrasecret little wingding for 150 or so of their dearest chums on Hollywood's night of nights.

How secret?

"They wanted to mind-fuck everyone," said an insider.

And they succeeded.

Guests not only needed invitations to get in; they were asked to keep from sharing even a hint about the party's very existence, and they didn't learn the location until the day of the event; workers at the site were told only that the party was being thrown by a "host and hostess"; the paparazzi, who knew that the shindig was happening, never conned to the when-and-where; and the people who'd paid thousands of dollars that day to use the host building for its ordinary functions were told by letters slipped under their doors that the front entrance and the driveway would be closed as of 3:00 p.m. and were given instructions on alternative routes in and out of the place—and, of course, apologies for the inconvenience.

Word that the party was happening *at all* started to spread at other post-Oscar galas (keeping a secret in Hollywood is like keeping one in a high school).

But by then, if you weren't on the list, well . . .

Those blessed with golden tickets were instructed to drive *past* the venue's front door and parking valets and go to the service entrance around the back, where no photographers or journalists or red carpets awaited them. (Partiers who showed up with bodyguards were barred from bringing them in; some actually left rather than take any chances.) From there, they were guided through a kitchen to an elevator that took them not *up* to one of the building's famed penthouses, with their incomparable views, but, rather, *down* a flight, where an unlikely space—low ceilinged, windowless, with a number of bulky structural columns and a slightly mechanical aroma—had been turned into a pop-up nightclub with a Monte Carlo casino theme: red and gold drapes, crystal chandeliers, potted palms, roulette wheels, an ornate bar.

Guests drank champagne and ate pizza and danced to the music of the host and hostess—the invitations expressly stated, "No sitting, only dancing"—and gossiped and joked and took selfies well into the predawn hours.

The gala brought together a number of stars from across the arts and even the generations: the party's honoree, Mary J. Blige, who'd been nominated that night as Best Supporting Actress *and* as writer of Best Original Song (she'd won neither); Stevie Wonder; Chadwick Boseman; Whoopi Goldberg; Best Actor nominee Daniel Kaluuya; Jamie Foxx; Rihanna; Drake; Shonda Rhimes; Anthony Anderson; Tiffany Haddish; Angela Bassett; Dave Chappelle; Mindy Kaling; and two freshly minted Oscar winners, screenwriter Jordan Peele and animated short producer (and basketball star) Kobe Bryant.

"It was all of black Hollywood," said a guest.

(Plus Leonardo DiCaprio and Tobey Maguire, because it was a party on the Sunset Strip and those two were apparently obliged by law to attend such things.)

And the venue for this über-exclusive party, the year's most enviable ticket, the biggest conclave of the hottest personalities on the starriest night of Hollywood's calendar year was . . . the garage of Chateau Marmont.

Beyoncé and Jay-Z had invited the biggest names in show business to party in a place where they normally parked their cars (or, more likely, had them parked for them).

That was odd enough. But even more curious was the ques-

tion of how it came to be that *anyone* would want to throw a gala
in a place so deservedly renowned for its gloomy, airless, laby-
rinthine atmosphere. There wasn't a hotel or restaurant in Hollywood (nay, the world) that wouldn't have wanted to host this
party. But never mind the garage: How in the world did this deal
wind up at Chateau Marmont *at all*, a place that had managed to
sit in the middle of Hollywood for nearly ninety years without
ever being the hottest destination on even its own street?

The answer lay in the transformation wrought on the Chateau by the man who bought it from Ray Sarlot and Karl Kantarjian in 1990 and turned it into one of the most exclusive, chic, and
famous of all Hollywood hangouts.

André Balazs was his name, and as proven by his tenure as
owner of the Marmont, he was as much a magician as he was a
hotelier.

※

Among the owners through whose hands Chateau Marmont
would pass, few would leave much trace on the world outside
the grounds of the hotel. Fred Horowitz had his legal career,
which had some headline-worthy highlights. Albert Smith had
his legacy as a cinematic pioneer, which included an honorary
Oscar and the publication of a 1952 autobiography, *Two Reels and
a Crank* (which, by the way, didn't mention his tenure as owner
of the Chateau). Erwin Brettauer vanished into the fog of history,
his name misspelled, the stories about him and his family half-
true. And Ray Sarlot was well liked but little noted outside Los
Angeles building circles and the pages of a history of the hotel
that he himself co-authored. The others were all businessmen,
more or less, often running the hotel through a series of corporate screens, never making names for themselves save for their
roles in acquiring and then passing on a singular possession.

That changed with André Balazs, the New York investor,
club owner, hotelier, and squire of famous beauties who remade

the hotel into something it had never been before: a glamorous hot spot known for fine dining, a buzzy bar scene, swank showbiz parties, and a global reputation for exclusivity, naughtiness, and scandal—the sort of place that turned people away at first glance if they were deemed to have fallen short of its aesthetic ideals. Balazs rebuilt the Chateau both as a building and as an idea, renovating and redecorating the rooms, expanding the facilities available to guests, and creating an aura around the hotel partly built of a new level of luxury and service and partly of a fantasy of a swank heyday that, truly, the place had never enjoyed. Under Balazs's reign, the longest of any of its owners, the Chateau became more fashionable, stylish, and upscale than it had ever been. And, ironically, the most infamous behavior associated with it turned out to be not that of a celebrity guest but that of the owner himself, who was accused of sexual misconduct in the storm of the Time's Up and Me Too movements of the late years of the second decade of the twenty-first century.

At the time of those accusations, Balazs's name was already familiar to consumers of gossip news. His hotel empire included Chateau Marmont, the Mercer in New York, the Sunset Beach on New York's Shelter Island, and the Chiltern Firehouse in London, and he owned major pieces of real estate in New York City. He had been a founder of the Standard hotel chain, which began on the Sunset Strip, just down the road from the Chateau, and eventually expanded to downtown Los Angeles, Miami Beach, and Manhattan.* He had been married for almost twenty years to an important fashion world figure with whom he had two children. After that union dissolved, he spent more than a decade being serially attached to such celebrated partners as Chelsea Handler, Courtney Love, Cameron Diaz, and, especially, Uma Thurman, to whom he was engaged for a time and then, after a hiatus, for a second go-round. He served on the boards of directors of major

---

* Balazs sold his interest in the Standard chain and left the board in early 2017.

cultural institutions, including the New York Public Theater, and was known equally well in Hollywood, New York, Miami, and London for his slender, tanned form, his flirtatious manner, his affection for the limelight, his instincts for trends and innovations, and his demanding—sometimes tyrannical—stewardship of his properties. In 2017, at age sixty, in the wake of a water-skiing accident, he was slowing down in some ways but not in others. That year, when he became a father for the third time, he told newspapers that he would help raise the baby, though he was "not attached" to the mother, Cosima Vesey, daughter of an Irish peer, the Viscount de Vesci and, at age twenty-nine, three decades Balazs's junior.

This quasi-public figure—among the best-known hoteliers in the business—seemed perfectly suited to Chateau Marmont. He was finicky about details; solicitous of the custom and company of celebrities and in maintaining their privacy; discerning in aesthetic choices; forgiving of the excesses of famous guests; and equally unforgiving of staff members and noncelebrities who failed to live up to the standards to which he dedicated his establishments. He went so far as to institute a coded system for his most famous guests, who were dubbed not VIPs but PPs—for *personne privée*—with a ranking system: PPX1, PPX2, and so on. But, as it turned out, he himself would shine a darker light on his empire than any wayward guest or employee ever did.

⁂

Balazs became owner-operator of Chateau Marmont because he was interested in entering the world of hotel hospitality at more or less the same time that Ray Sarlot and Karl Kantarjian were interested in exiting it. Sarlot and Kantarjian had come into possession of the Chateau in 1975 strictly with the intention of making money on their investment—even if only as a tax write-off. The two of them—especially Sarlot—began to feel a bond with the place that went beyond sheer financial opportunity. They were custodians of a trust, keepers of a flame, guardians of a treasure; their hotel was unique in all the world, and the affection that its most loyal guests harbored for it became theirs as well.

Over the years, various suitors sought to buy the Chateau from them and forge their own bonds, economic and otherwise, with it. In the mid-seventies, Francis Ford Coppola, seeking to expand his Zoetrope empire of filmmaking, publishing, and artistic patronage, was said to be considering buying the hotel and turning it into an artist colony of some sort—a kind of Yaddo or MacDowell on the Sunset Strip. But his financial managers, accustomed to putting out fires that their profligate client started without much in the way of analysis or forethought, dissuaded him from pursuing the purchase in earnest. And Sarlot and Kantarjian weren't thinking of selling.

By 1990, though, that had changed. For one thing, it had been some fifteen years since the pair had acquired the hotel—longer, perhaps, than they had intended to hold on to it. For another, relations between the partners had taken a downward turn, with rumors circulating among hotel staffers of unfriendly interpersonal encounters between the two. And perhaps most important, one of their initial intentions—to turn a profit on their investment—was being realized. A buyer emerged who was prepared to pay them $12 million for Chateau Marmont,* a massive sum that more than tripled what Sarlot and Kantarjian paid, even with their 1975 dollars adjusted for inflation.

That buyer was Balazs, a New Yorker who, like Sarlot and Kantarjian, had never owned a hotel before. Hardly anyone had ever heard of him in New York, much less L.A., and little in his background indicated that he would reinvent the Chateau or launch a string of similarly successful hotels on the strength of that feat.

---

* Approximately $23.35 million in 2019.

❋

André Tomes Balazs was born in Massachusetts in 1957 to Eva and Endre Balazs, Hungarian immigrants who had left their homeland after World War II for Sweden, where Endre, a biomedical researcher, worked at finding applications for hyaluronic acid, a collagen-like lubricant that occurs naturally in the eyes of cows and the combs of roosters and was proving useful in combating such ailments in humans as burns, arthritis, and cataracts. The couple moved to the United States in the early fifties, when Endre was asked to establish Harvard Medical School's Retina Foundation. Soon, Eva received a Ph.D. in psychology and began teaching and practicing family therapy.

They raised their children, André and Marianne, in the Spy Pond neighborhood of Arlington, Massachusetts, just west of Cambridge, where the kids learned to swim, boat, water-ski, ice-skate, cross-country ski, forage for mushrooms and crab apples, and tap maple trees for syrup. Eva became involved in community activities such as land conservation, wrote columns for a local newspaper (later collecting them in a book), and learned how to play jazz piano, which became a lifetime pursuit. In the late sixties, Endre founded a company named Biotrics and sought patents on some of the medical applications of his work. A few years later, when his marriage dissolved, he moved to New York to take a post at Columbia University and the Columbia-Presbyterian College of Physicians and Surgeons.

Despite having a passion for outdoor sports, André didn't care much for life in the suburbs of Boston. "It's surprisingly close-minded," he recalled. "It's scared. There's a fearfulness there." He attended the elite, all-male Browne & Nichols School* in Cambridge, then Cornell University, where he majored in English, memorably enrolling in a short fiction writing class taught by the author Harold Brodkey, who remained a long-term

---

* Since renamed Buckingham Browne & Nichols School.

friend and mentor. He also worked on the college newspaper and started a for-profit magazine that listed local events of interest to young people such as rock concerts. Upon graduating, he moved to New York to attend Columbia University's School of Journalism, studying for a degree in journalism and business. "For my thesis," he remembered, "I checked into the Bowery Mission. I lived there for a week, as though I were homeless." He got his master's, but he never worked in journalism. "I couldn't write fast enough," he admitted. Instead, he took a job with political consultant David Garth and worked as a press aide to Bess Myerson, the former Miss America and New York City commissioner of consumer affairs who took a run at a U.S. Senate seat in 1980. Myerson lost, but Balazs derived an interesting lesson from the experience, namely "how much control one had—you can almost force-feed stories to political journalists."

In 1981, after his foray into politics, André joined his father in a new business venture—Biomatrix, a pharmaceutical firm that Endre was launching with his second wife. (Previously, André had spent time away from college helping Endre with his research, including one summer vacation during which he was assigned to acquire umbilical cords.) This new company turned out to be a spectacular success, with significant patents on products that became therapeutic standards throughout the world, earning it many millions. The young Balazs began to look for new opportunities and horizons. "There was a big dichotomy between the life I was leading in New Jersey and everything I was interested in," he later said. "I had a desire to merge the work and the private life." And when Biomatrix proved such a huge moneymaker (it sold to a larger competitor in 2000 for $738 million*), he would have his chance.

Compact, fit, active, with chiseled good looks, dark wavy hair, and Continental fashion sense, Balazs became a man-about-town in New York's go-go eighties, moving into the up-and-coming

* Approximately $1.08 billion in 2019.

SoHo neighborhood, where he began purchasing and developing real estate. In 1985, he married Mary Katherine Ford (known as Katie), the daughter of Eileen and Jerry Ford, founders of the famed Ford Modeling Agency, which Katie had joined as an executive in 1980. The two had met as graduate students at Columbia, and they suited each other—both comely, educated, and rich. But in the opinion of observers, he had made the better match. "The fact he is Hungarian is the only exotic thing about him," a socially conscious English friend of Balazs's told a journalist. "His family are middle-class academics."

Balazs and Ford were an It Couple of the moment, seen at the best restaurants, clubs, and parties of the late eighties (their children wouldn't be born until 1991 and 1994). Balazs spent some of his Biomatrix money on successful real estate investments in Manhattan. His ability to sense the energy and vibe of the era extended into businesses that had nothing to do with the sources of his fortune. In the late eighties, he took note of the frenzy of the international art market and mounted a show in Tokyo that consisted entirely of avowedly fake works in the styles of such masters as Miró, van Gogh, Mondrian, and Schiele; touted by a manifesto claiming that the show was a critique of commercialism, the paintings—priced between $5,000 and $10,000—sold out quickly.

A few years later, Balazs's friend Eric Goode enticed him into putting money into MK, a new downtown supper club he was developing along with the designer and impresario Serge Becker, whose wild artistic inspirations helped turn the Tribeca nightclub Area into a legend. MK had a golden reputation, but it lasted only two years, and its demise left some tension in the air, as evidenced by Becker's insistence that Balazs, whom Becker claimed as a friend, was a "master of taking credit for M.K. . . . He said he was an owner, but he wasn't. He was an investor, and his wife was an investor. There were about 10 investors in M.K."

Whatever his actual role in MK, Balazs had acquired a taste for the club business. In 1989, he and Goode went west with some other investors to open b.c., a semiprivate supper club along a nondescript stretch of Sunset Boulevard in Hollywood. It was a hit from the start; Madonna and George Michael were there on opening night, and other scene makers started showing up in droves, choking a previously quiet neighborhood with parking problems and late-night noise. Almost inadvertently, what was meant to be a dining club had become a chic dancing spot. "We never really wanted to be a discotheque," Balazs said. "It just sort of happened, and it became so popular so fast that things got out of control." Fracases with Los Angeles authorities ensued, with the club's owners eventually being cited for operating a dance hall illegally. Those infractions hobbled their ability to acquire a liquor license, and what with legal pressures and neighborhood protest looming constantly, the club didn't last even a year.

That brief foray into managing high-wattage nightlife would serve Balazs well in the new line of business he was stepping into back east. In his own SoHo neighborhood, he was working to transform an abandoned six-story building into an eighty-one-room hotel with a restaurant and retail spaces on the ground floor. On the corner of Prince and Mercer Streets, it would be known as the Mercer, and it would cost \$33 million,* which Balazs and a partner, the designer and architect Campion Platt, had on hand. As it turned out, it would take the better part of a decade for the Mercer to pass through all of the hurdles that Manhattan real estate development poses. But the project got Balazs interested in the hotel business, and in 1990 he assembled a team of investors to buy Chateau Marmont.

❖

On the first day that he visited the Chateau as its owner, André Balazs drove up to his new property and felt a rush of horror: A large crane was removing a chunk of the hotel roof. It turned out

---

* Around \$65 million in 2019.

that it wasn't the *actual* roof being removed but rather a prop version of it that was built by Oliver Stone and the production crew of *The Doors* so that they could re-create Jim Morrison's famed antics on the site (more or less) where they'd occurred. For Balazs, the scare turned out to be a good story about his especially apt welcome to the make-believe kingdom of Hollywood, but it was a joke that included a great deal of uncomfortable truth. Ray Sarlot and his team had worked hard to keep Chateau Marmont hale and vital, but the place was nonetheless always in a state of near dilapidation. "It felt like a very neglected, abandoned soul," Balazs said. The state of the place was depressing business, he acknowledged: "A lot of people hated having insulating tape on the carpet. Occupancies were down." If he was truly going to turn Chateau Marmont into something elegant and chic, he had a lot of work to do.

And it would be very *particular* work. Balazs might have been a newcomer to Hollywood and the hospitality business, but he recognized that he had a delicate job on his hands if he was going to renovate a classic cult hotel in a way that retained its traditional identity. "The full weight of what I had inherited came upon me when people suddenly discovered that I had bought it," he said. "Longtime guests would come up to me and say, 'Please don't change it,' but in the same breath admitting the inconveniences of its decayed state—missing shower heads, tattered curtains. I decided they meant 'Don't violate the spirit of the place.' "

But what was that spirit? The hotel had been built in the twenties, flourished in the forties and fifties, gone to seed in the sixties and seventies, and only became truly famous and iconic in the eighties when John Belushi died there. If you were going to give the place a face-lift, which of its faces would you choose to restore? And how could you do that without alienating longtime guests such as Helmut Newton, John Waters, and Wallace Shawn, among many others, whose love for the hotel had kept it afloat and given it its enviable cultural currency?

Balazs understood the problem and took it to heart. "It was

not initially clear to anyone how you could upgrade the place and bring it into the modern world without losing its sense of history," he said several years after buying the hotel. "I now realize that the key is to match the reality of what we are doing with the fantasy that people have had in their minds. The old Chateau had a lot of problems that nobody liked, but they were willing to overlook them as they walked around with an image of what the hotel should have been. For me, it has become a matter of bringing the reality up to the point where it matches the fantasy."

The renovation would take years, and it involved a lot of conceptualizing and a lot of trial and error. The hotel that Balazs acquired was a hodgepodge both visually and functionally. "Things from different eras had been mixed together, and there was no sense of cohesive style, no sense of magic," he said. "The de facto main entrance was down by the garage, yet there was no sense that you had arrived at a hotel. The grounds reflected what they had been—a series of acquisitions—and were unlandscaped. The main lobby was not properly thought out as a real living room. You had a vast hall with only one seating area. That meant that if two parties of people sat down, they would have to sit next to each other."

Slowly, he began to change all of that, first by finding the right look and feel for the place. "We scoured archives," he said. "We wanted to stay away from 'design.'" He was very clear on that last idea, that a powerful "design," such as he had seen imposed on other trendy hotels, would suffocate what was best about Chateau Marmont. "It was important not to be that monolithic," he explained. "I felt the guests here are very sophisticated people, they know their own style, they might want to experience that design intensity once but they are hardly likely to come back. . . . They don't want to check their personalities at the door and buy into someone else's fantasy."

And so the process began, with a number of decorators and designers—some, naturally, from the worlds of film and theater—taking a crack at renovating a room to see if they could realize Balazs's admittedly inchoate vision. Some rooms were redone multiple times, because Balazs kept insisting that the designers had gotten it wrong. Predictably, some of the designers he commissioned felt that their work wasn't properly appreciated. "I don't think he has a particularly strong vision himself," said Alison Spear, one of those whose proposed rooms were rejected. "He gets his taste from everywhere." But Balazs did have an idea, as he told an interviewer. "We put ourselves into the minds of designers from the '20s through the '50s," Balazs said. "For the lobby, we went with the '20s, but for the suites we went with the '40s and '50s—the height, I think, of what people perceive as Hollywood's glamorous heyday." As he later explained, "It's not a real past. . . . The past is really not that interesting."

Eventually, the job of restoring the place went to Fernando Santangelo, an Uruguayan designer who had created some memorable installations at the New York nightclubs that Balazs frequented and had invested in, and Shawn Hausman, another designer associated with the New York nightclub scene (and, incidentally, the son of actress Diane Varsi and producer Michael Hausman). Gradually, a new version of the old hotel began to emerge. The dining area was at once expanded and made more secluded, with an eye toward someday turning it into a restaurant; a gym was installed in an attic space where there used to be offices; proper outdoor seating areas were designed; the landscaping was coherently unified. And rooms were remade one by one, in such a slow and deliberate and careful way that it wasn't obvious, even to old Chateau Marmont hands, that the place had changed.

"To me, the greatest sign of our success was when Helmut Newton came back and stayed in one of the new rooms," Balazs said. "He liked it so much that now he wants to stay only in the new rooms. Helmut's response was a validation that we had done something right." It wasn't only Newton. "So little has been changed that even Wally Shawn didn't know the hotel had been sold," Balazs bragged, "and he, you know, is the type to worry."

Another longtime guest, director John Waters, agreed. "I can't tell you what is and isn't fixed up," he admitted.

Even Eve Babitz, who relished the Chateau's decrepitude, came around. "If the romantic depressiveness of the hotel is lost, I have to rise above my nostalgic despair and be glad," she said. "Except for not wanting to kill myself when I walk into the room, the Chateau feeling is the same as ever. Only cleaner. It's as though the Chateau had died and gone to heaven."* Learning of Babitz's joke that she could no longer imagine wanting to commit suicide in one of his hotel's rooms, Balazs replied, in mock horror, "Oh no! I've lost a major market!" But, in truth, he was sensitive to the longtime clientele who preferred things as they were, at least superficially, and the hotel kept a supply of the old furniture to move into suites when one of the veteran guests who liked the aura of decay was in residence; when the room was vacated once again, the new pieces would be moved back in.

❦

Along with the decor of the hotel, Balazs and his staff went about redefining its image, its use, and even its physical structure.

They began advertising the hotel in a way that seemed to sell not specific rooms or amenities but a state of mind. In glossy East Coast magazines like *Spy* and *Interview,* full-page images began to appear: black-and-white or sepia-toned shots of nude or barely dressed women cavorting or performing gymnastics in

---

* Babitz knew something about recycling/repurposing/renovating. A story in her 1993 collection, *Black Swans,* repeated an episode from her 1974 book, *Eve's Hollywood,* involving Chateau Marmont. In the first, the semi-fictional Eve misses the Watts riots of 1965 because she's shacked up in the Chateau with a lover. In the second, the narrator of the story "Expensive Regrets" misses the 1992 Rodney King riots because . . . she's shacked up in the Chateau with a lover. Renzo is the name of the new guy, a writer from New York, and he is deeply ashamed to have been oblivious to such a huge news story while visiting the town in which it happened. " 'Nobody's going to believe I missed this and I was here,' he said. 'I'm usually more abreast of current events.' "

some unidentifiable Arcadian idyll with only three words—and a phone number—accompanying them:

CHATEAU MARMONT
hollywood [*sic*]
(213) 656–1010

Balazs was delighted with the sparse, allusive, provocative feeling the ads created. "When they first ran four years ago in *Spy* magazine," he said, "the editor received a letter from a reader who wanted to know what the hell was being advertised. Was it a woman? Was it a brothel?"

Balazs also began to think of new ways to draw Hollywood into the hotel if not for overnight stays, then for notable events. The first years of his ownership coincided with a fascination among movie people with literary and spoken word events—poetry readings, staged readings of plays, book launch parties. Various venues throughout Los Angeles held regular nights dedicated to this brand of cultural enrichment. Balazs, the former short story writer, immediately saw the charm of these sorts of events ("He admires artists," a friend said. "He loves the idea that creativity is happening under his auspices"), and Chateau Marmont became one of the premier destinations for them. For several years, the Poetry Society of America curated a series of readings at the hotel where some of the nation's best-known poets—James Merrill, Carol Muske, Mark Strand, Tess Gallagher, Galway Kinnell, Sharon Olds, and James Tate among them—shared their work alongside well-known actors (including Tim Curry, Alfre Woodard, Helen Shaver, John Lithgow, Ally Sheedy, and Michael Ontkean), who recited work by still other noted poets. It was an unlikely marriage of verse and screen, and it was very successful. The poets, naturally, knew that the crowds that turned out to see them were drawn more by the movie stars than by the words, but they were appreciative of the opportunity to reach new audiences, and they were admiring of the venue, both for its intrepid choice of programming and for its physical grandeur. "I think a lot of people will be curious about the setting," said poet Amy Gerstler. "It's very highbrow."

In addition to the many poetry readings, Balazs's Chateau began to host a variety of events that were facilitated by Balazs's connections in the worlds of fashion, hospitality, and show business: wine tastings (some of Southern California's first unbottlings of Francis Coppola's Napa Valley wines were held there), fashion shows (featuring models from the Ford Agency), art shows and sales, and, as the hotel became trendier and trendier, parties marking film premieres, awards shows, and other staples of the publicity side of the movie industry. These events drew photographers and reporters, limousines and sports cars, and, increasingly, a youthful segment of Hollywood that came to see the Chateau as one of its principal hangouts and oases.

2.

One day not long after André Balazs purchased the Chateau, the journalist and bon vivant Anthony Haden-Guest was returning to his room at the hotel, only to find the place evacuated, the residents out in the street. Haden-Guest suspected an earthquake might have struck, but he was set straight by a staff member who told him that there had been a bomb threat. Broadway composer Jerry Herman, among the displaced guests milling about, overheard the explanation and responded, "Ridiculous! People come here to write bombs, or direct them, or act in them, not plant them!"

A joke, yes, but not without truth. Without a doubt, there were masterpieces imagined, written, and created by artists who were resident at the Chateau at the time and, at least in part, influenced by their surroundings: *Rebel Without a Cause* chief among them, but also *Sunset Boulevard,* "You've Lost That Lovin' Feelin'," and works by such writers as Ben Hecht, Lillian Hellman, S. J. Perelman, Elaine Dundy, Carole Eastman, and Menno

Meyjes. Curiously, a number of screen adaptations could claim to have been born at the Chateau, including Meredith Willson's of his stage musical *The Music Man*, Leonard Gardner's of his novel *Fat City*, Robert Stone's of *his* novel *A Hall of Mirrors* (retitled *WUSA* for the screen), Waldo Salt's of Nathanael West's novel *The Day of the Locust*, and Gore Vidal's of Lew Wallace's *Ben-Hur*. And then there was the sort of creation that actress-director Lee Grant reveled in when she spoke of the hotel: "I lived, worked, and conceived a daughter in this baroque shelter. I love it here."

In the early nineties, novelist and screenwriter Bruce Wagner became another of those who tried to create something great during a stay at the hotel. Wagner had grown up in Los Angeles and knew the Chateau, if only vaguely, as a landmark glimpsed from the backseat on family drives. "The grand, mysterious house on the hill," he recalled. "For a long while, I didn't know what it was (an apartment house?) but it soothed me. I suppose what I'm saying is that it always had a dreamy quality for me."

When he became a limousine driver based at the Beverly Hills Hotel, he entered the Chateau for the first time and was gripped by the experience. "The high ceilings and cool, sepulchral quiet reminded of a monastery" humbled him. "It had an otherworldly vibe, and my conventional head struggled to fill in the blanks. I grew up surrounded by great wealth and the clichéd venues that money could buy; knowing those with money might choose to stay in that place opened my eyes. The cognitive dissonance was way sexy."

A few years later, commissioned to adapt his own magazine comic series, *Wild Palms*, into a script for a TV miniseries, "[I] mentioned to my agent that I needed an office. I may have suggested the Chateau in jest, but he jumped on it. I moved right in. I don't think I'd actually ever been inside one of the larger rooms and it was essentially an apartment. There was a kitchen and that fairly shocked me. I rarely left the room; why would I?" The show, produced by Oliver Stone and directed by Kathryn Bigelow, Keith Gordon, and Phil Joanou, aired in 1993, an acid, dystopian, and visionary take on Hollywood, power, cult religions, and technology run amok. It was a TV event of the sort that would likely have been received with more fanfare in the era of binge watching, which it all but predicted, and it remained one of the finer projects that could truly trace its genesis to the Chateau.*

A year or two after Wagner's stay, Balazs saw fit to allow a feature film to shoot extensively at the hotel, and while there were no negative episodes associated with the production, the movie that resulted didn't make anyone particularly glad they'd made it. *Dangerous Game* (which shot under the title *Snake Eyes*) was written and directed by the New York indie filmmaker Abel Ferrara, whose three previous movies—*Bad Lieutenant, King of New York,* and *Body Snatchers*—had created enthusiasm among critics and garnered some decent box-office receipts. On the strength of that string, Ferrara had a $10 million budget for his new picture, the story of a New York director (Harvey Keitel) living at Chateau Marmont while making a movie with an actress (Madonna) whom he is falling for, even as she is involved with the leading man (James Russo). There is a strong connection between the manipulation of the actress by the director and the film they are shooting (which is titled, in case you didn't otherwise get what was going on, *Mother of Mirrors*). And, for that matter, we are asked to at least consider that there's a connection between Keitel's character and Ferrara himself, because the actress playing the former's wife is, in real life, the *latter's* wife, among other such "coincidences."

A good portion of *Dangerous Game* is set inside the filmmaker's suite in the main building of the Chateau—as well as the lead actor's bedroom in one of the Chateau's bungalows. Neither room had yet enjoyed the upgrades in decor, furnishing, and ameni-

---

* Wagner returned to the Chateau, at least on the page, in another dark satire on Hollywood, the 2014 feature film *Maps to the Stars,* directed by David Cronenberg and featuring at least one memorable scene at the hotel in which Carrie Fisher wanders by with her dog and changes the life path of one of the lead characters.

ties that would characterize Balazs's ownership of the place. As a result, the atmosphere was heavy, cramped, tacky, and decidedly not chic or glamorous. (A few years later, writer-director Paul Schrader was staying at the hotel when he came across the film on TV, and he had a startling experience: "Harvey was in bed with Madonna in the very room I was in, and the camera was exactly where the TV was. So it was like a reflection. I was looking at the room in the reflection, only I wasn't in it; they were in it. And I thought, 'Wow, they haven't even changed the decor. The only thing that's changed are the people in the bed.'") As in *Blume in Love* and a few other films in which the Chateau played itself, the specific name of the place was never given; you had to know what you were looking at to know how apt a choice it was.

Not that anyone saw the thing. *Dangerous Game,* which was the first film released by Madonna's briefly lived Maverick Picture Company, premiered at the Venice Film Festival to wildly mixed reviews, then played one week each in New York and Los Angeles, grossing a paltry $23,671 before finding its almost inevitable home on late-night cable. From the point of view of the Chateau, unless a guest happened to catch it (and him- or herself) on TV while channel surfing, it was like it never happened.

�֎

The Chateau of the thirties, a place where high society held its teas and Hollywood types kept very quietly to themselves, had its ideal chronicler in Pauline Payne, who never had anything scandalous or off-putting to say about any of her neighbors.

The Chateau of André Balazs called for a different sort of scribe——garrulous, gimlet-eyed, partisan, arch, and bitchy. And that voice belonged to a man who had first glimpsed the hotel as a nine-year-old boy from Connecticut touring Hollywood with his aunt, a former nun, and was dazzled by the castle across the street from the soda fountain at Schwab's.

Dominick Dunne had long connections to the Chateau's history; he regularly visited his friends Camilla and Earl McGrath there during the sixties, when he was a successful television producer. But he was most intimate with the place in the nineties and the first decade of the twenty-first century, when he spent months at a time living at the hotel and filing stories for *Vanity Fair* and other publications about the trials of O. J. Simpson, Phil Spector, Robert Blake, and Erik and Lyle Menendez. He might have first become aware of the hotel as a starstruck lad, but the Dunne of those later years was another species of creature altogether: an avenger bent on blaring out injustice, a jaded elder unwilling to let crimes and horrors pass unremarked, an acid gossip keen to spill all the beans if doing so could help bring criminals to heel.

He had begun writing about crime in the most painful way possible: recounting the experience of losing his daughter, Dominique, to murder, and then watching helplessly as the justice system seemed to demonstrate more sympathy for the killer than for the victim. Outrage built in him, and he channeled it into writing. He wrote about the ordeal for *Vanity Fair,* which then assigned him to cover the trials of Claus von Bülow and William Kennedy Smith and, finally, that string of sensational murder cases in Los Angeles. Just as his juicy novels about the moral lapses of the rich and famous became international best sellers, his fierce magazine journalism helped shine a harsh spotlight on criminals whom he feared would be exonerated because of their wealth and their connections.

During those latter trials, which kept him in Hollywood for years, Dunne preferred to occupy a suite on a lower floor of Chateau Marmont, with windows facing west or south, which, he felt, was the quieter side of the place. He particularly relished the spectacle, out his window, of a nearby mansion, a pink neo-Georgian monstrosity built on spec in the eighties and never sold but still carefully maintained, with the sprinklers going on each night and lights inside and out turning on and off "as if a wonderful party was going on."

But fond as he was of his quiet, Dunne was hardly monkish or isolate. He was one of the hotel's presiding spirits, seemingly always on hand, taking gossipy lunches, chatting with hotel staff, and mixing incongruously among the other famous guests, his Savile Row suits and Turnbull & Asser ties contrasting with their more bohemian appearances. "One of my earliest memories of the hotel," recalled Philip Pavel, who managed the Chateau through several of Dunne's stays, "was seeing Iggy Pop walking around the lobby with no shirt, barefoot, with leather pants . . . and Dominick Dunne walking around in the middle of that." (Dunne wasn't overly fond of that lobby, though, comparing it to "Norma Desmond's living room"—a reference to the sepulchral mansion in Billy Wilder's *Sunset Boulevard*, which wasn't meant as a compliment.) He was such a fixture of the hotel that the painter Sacha Newley (son of Joan Collins and Anthony Newley) had him sit for a formal portrait there, scribbling away in a green notebook, an image that was unveiled to acclaim in 1997 at a cocktail reception and art show held—where else?—at Chateau Marmont.

�֍

It was a chance meeting with André Balazs that drew Dunne to the hotel for his first extended stay, to cover the Menendez trial. They were both at a party in New York when Balazs introduced himself, saying that he adored Dunne's novel *An Inconvenient Woman* and adding, "If you ever come to Los Angeles again, please stay with us." Dunne obliged. He took the suite that he eventually came to think of as his and turned it into a press room, with files and papers piled on the floor and in cupboards, notes to himself taped to walls and mirrors, and photographs, videocassettes, and envelopes stuffed with research strewn about willy-nilly. "It was just overwhelmed by books," recalled a visitor, "snowdrifts of papers going up the walls, the fax was spewing new information." Dunne was absolutely at home amid the clutter. He woke daily before sunrise, read the Los Angeles newspapers and stories from the New York press that had been faxed to him, tuned in to the morning talk shows, and made his way to the courthouse. In the afternoon, he repaired to his suite to write, filing a story to his editor, Tina Brown, every four weeks.

That visit, which ended when the Menendez jury couldn't reach a verdict, lasted seven months. Dunne was, once again, infuriated that justice had failed to triumph, but his mood changed when he showed up at the front desk to check out of the hotel and return to New York. "I was spirited into a back office where Philip Truelove, the manager, had assembled all of the employees whom I had come to know," he said, "and they toasted me with orange juice in champagne glasses, in honor, I suppose, of my long years of sobriety. I was so touched, I cried."

That wasn't the only time he was moved during his stay. A few weeks prior at 4:30 in the morning of January 17, 1994, the Northridge earthquake struck, a massive 6.7 tremor that killed fifty-seven people, collapsed freeways and apartment buildings, and caused widespread devastation around Southern California. Almost predictably, the jolt left Chateau Marmont merely shaken and stirred, just as Fred Horowitz and his architects had planned, with no structural damage. Even still, like almost everyone else in the region, Dunne was asleep when the earth rumbled, and he was just as fearful and rattled and unable to think clearly as millions of others:

I did not do that smart thing that you are supposed to do—hop up and get under a table. I just lay there and thought, "Well, this is the end of the line." I collected myself, said my little prayer and watched my television set fly out onto the floor. I was extremely calm. When it stopped, I began to think of what I wanted to have with me, and I began to collect my things—my glasses, my wallet, my watch. It was pitch dark. And I took the latest draft of my article and stuck it in my back pocket, and made my way down the stairwells.

All the guests gathered out on the lawn in front of the hotel, and then we realized there was a surreal light above us. It was coming from the huge Marlboro sign in front of the hotel, there on Sunset Boulevard. Somehow, the Marlboro man was the only thing left shining in the whole city. That was truly strange—something I will never forget. Finally, the sun came up, I returned to my room, and I started working.*

Dunne's next visit, to cover the O. J. Simpson murder case, ended in another episode of outrage at justice avoided and another episode—seriocomic this time—of being caught unprepared. He had taken the same suite as previously, this time for more than a year, and had once again become part of the hotel family. Again a rat's nest of papers and materials grew in his suite; again he observed a daily routine of taking in the morning news and then showing up immaculately attired at court. By then, Dunne was part of the show; Judge Lance Ito gave him a choice seat in the front row of the spectators' section (to the consternation of professional court reporters who called him "Judith Krantz in pants"). This time Dunne was, in his own estimation, "the toast of the town. I went out every night." He loved the fact that everyone he met knew who he was and what he was up to. "I was walking out of my room to go to dinner," he said of one such encounter at the Chateau, "and Keanu [Reeves] came out at the same time. We each headed for the elevator, and after the door closed, he said to me, 'How's the trial?'" He even wrote an entire novel featuring a semiautobiographical character—Gus Bailey, who had appeared in an earlier novel, *People Like Us*—who lived in New York and stayed at Chateau Marmont while he covered the Simpson trial. But no matter how much he enjoyed his fame, he always made

---

* All in all, he fared better than Tommy Tune, the dancer and choreographer who was staying at the Chateau the previous spring, when a smaller earthquake hit. Tune was walking down the stairs when the temblor struck, and he stumbled, breaking his foot and disrupting his performance schedule.

time to fully digest the daily happenings in the case and get home early enough to be well rested before another day in court.

It was during this period that Dunne agreed to sit for his portrait by Sacha Newley, who recalled the fraught circumstances of the day, which was, propitiously, the day of the Simpson verdict. "Dominick was very appalled and angry," he said. "He was an absolute sweetheart most of the time, but when you got him on a subject he felt passionately about, the animus would kick in, and he'd flame. That day at the front desk at the Chateau, I think he received death threats."

In the wake of Simpson's acquittal—Dunne's slack-jawed reaction to the verdict from his front-row perch was one of the most memorable images that the courtroom cameras broadcast on that surreal day—the writer was flying back to New York when he realized, to his horror, that he had left something behind in his suite. He phoned the hotel as soon as his plane landed and spoke with an assistant manager. "Something terribly embarrassing has happened, and I need your help," Dunne told him. "I'm afraid I've left a pornographic video of a very low-rent nature in the VCR. Do you think you could remove it before Maria the maid finds it? We've become very good friends in the last two years, and I don't want to go down in her estimation." Fortunately, he noted, "nothing shocks at the Chateau." Not only did the manager volunteer to fetch the incriminating item immediately; he offered to send it to New York. "Good God, no!" Dunne replied.

There would follow other trials—Blake and Spector—and other visits to Chateau Marmont. And then Dunne laid down his pen and stopped covering crime stories and stayed back east, in his homes in Manhattan and Connecticut, until his death in August 2009. A memorial was held at the Chateau a couple of months later, the sort of party that he would have loved as much as any thrown by his old friends the McGraths: Movie people, entertainment journalists, crime reporters, and even courtroom personnel mingled with his son Griffin, former Los Angeles district attorney Ira Reiner, and others from the varied circles of his life. They gathered in one of the hotel's penthouses—Griffin reminisced about his firecracker tossing during the Sunset Strip "riots"—and toasted and eulogized him in a town that, the title of his 1997 novel, *Another City, Not My Own*, notwithstanding, was truly one of his homes. He loved the setting, the people, the hotel, and he would've been warmed to realize all that love was returned.

3.

More than even the owner of the Chateau, André Balazs was its glossy-magazine face, a status he seemed to strive for, accommodating requests for photo shoots and lengthy profiles filled with casually dropped boldfaced names.

But he wasn't an Angelino. He was a jet-setter with an increasingly large collection of hotels in his portfolio, and he made his home principally in New York, where his wife ran her business, his children went to school, and the family maintained homes in Manhattan and on Long Island. So, perhaps even more than any of the hotel's previous owners, he needed someone on the grounds and behind the desk to serve as the day-to-day face of the hotel—as well as its eyes, ears, and operational brain.

In 1996, he found just the fellow, someone who would stay with the Chateau for more than twenty years, longer than any other general manager in the hotel's history. Philip Pavel was born in 1969 in an outlying neighborhood of Chicago's South Side, where his dad was a gas meter reader. Or, rather, Philip Pawelczyk was born then and there. Philip—sometimes Philippe—Pavel was born in 1991, when Pawelczyk, a theater major fresh out of Northwestern University, came to Los Angeles to find his fortune in acting. Without any experience, he sought table-waiting jobs and found himself hired—"cast," as he put it—as maître d' at a high-scale restaurant in Century City; with his dark hair and eyes and trim six-foot-two frame, management thought he looked French, and so he took on the part, as it were, of a French waiter. But a French waiter, he insisted, with midwestern scruples: "If you made a reservation, and you were nice to me at the maître d' stand, you got a better table than the TV actor who would actually yell, 'I'm famous, doesn't that mean anything?' I kind of saw myself as Robin Hood."

He spent a few years at La Chaumiere in Century City and then a few more at Barney Greengrass in Beverly Hills, where he continued to parry off the tempers of Hollywoodians who thought that their time and status excused them from simple human decency ("agents were the worst"). When the folks who'd hired him left the restaurant business and moved into the Chateau, where they were advising Balazs on starting up a new food-and-beverage service, they rang him up and asked him to join them and run the room service operation. "It's only sixty-three rooms, they have a new no-party policy, . . . and there's about five tables in the lobby," they assured him.

Ha.

Pavel discovered chaos, even if only on a relatively small scale, when he took the job. The small room service menu basically amounted to home cooking by whichever waiter happened to be on duty when a guest rang down for food. There were no set menus or recipes, no strictly kept hours for service (this indifference toward food service was long-standing: Twenty years earlier, a journalist writing about the hotel claimed that he learned about the Continental breakfast that his room entitled him to only when he was checking out; when he asked about the oversight, a desk clerk replied, "Oh, we don't tell anybody anything unless they ask"). Pavel imposed some order on the mess, and Balazs, impressed with his initiative and vision, promoted him to general manager.

As ringmaster at one of the greatest shows on earth, Pavel was utterly in his element. "As a child," he recalled, "I would fantasize about being at a glamorous party. I envisioned my adult life to be something like the party scene in *Breakfast at Tiffany's*."

His new job gave him the opportunity to live that life, every day, in a fabulous setting, on someone else's dime, with a full-time staff of house cleaners, bellmen, and, in time, cooks and waitstaff to make it happen.

He was truly born to the job. He had a fantastic memory for guests' habits, tastes, and needs: which rooms they liked, which magazines, which chocolates. He understood creative people; even with a full-time job, he continued to go out on auditions as an actor, and occasionally got parts, as in such films as *Scream 2, The Wedding Planner,* and *13 Going on 30* (he even sometimes played himself, or someone very like himself, in films with scenes shot at the hotel or, in inside jokes, he might appear as a room service waiter or bartender). He schmoozed with visitors who seemed to want somebody to talk to. But mainly he ran things: He hired employees (he favored candidates, he said, "who are unfazed by certain behavior");* he greeted residents, famous or not, upon their arrival; he solved crises; he made the place feel like a harbor. Sometimes this meant adding little personal touches to their rooms or services to their stays to make them comfortable. Sometimes it meant doing homework. "I work hard to keep up on the art world and the London social scene," he said, "because those things are important to André Balazs. Since the hotel has this bohemian vibe, I have to cast my net a bit wider than just old-school Hollywood." And sometimes it meant dealing with heavier issues. "Let's just say," he once revealed, "when I studied Shakespeare, Ibsen, Chekhov, and Shaw I never thought I'd become so good at transitioning people into rehab."

After he'd been at the job for a while, Pavel came to embody the hotel's demeanor toward its guests and their quirks. "People

---

* Among Pavel's hires was a young guy banging at the doors of a career in film and making ends meet by working as a bartender, Mark Ruffalo. "Working here was a blast," he told a journalist years later when he was doing a publicity interview at the hotel. "But I wanted to stay here instead of work here."

do things here that they wouldn't dare think of doing at the Peninsula or the Four Seasons, and we think that's a good thing," he said. "I'm like the parent: I am both facilitating the level of rambunctious fun but also policing it. It's about allowing people to embrace it but also making sure no one overdoses. Oh, that sounds bad."

He was one of those people whose love for his work translated into a feeling of goodwill and ease on the part of the folks with whom he interacted. Staff and guests responded with affection to him. (He was thanked in the acknowledgments of Michael Chabon's novel *The Yiddish Policemen's Union,* which the author said was inspired in part by his stay at the hotel; the hat tip, Pavel said, "was like winning an Academy Award.") And even more than Balazs, whose high-veneer life might feel alien to even some of the Hollywood crowd, he seemed to embody the traditional spirit of the hotel.

Perhaps literally. Pavel had an interest in spirituality and mysticism, and he was delighted when "three different psychics" revealed that the Chateau "was built on an energy vortex." That, he said, helped him to understand why he felt so immediately comfortable in the hotel as soon as he arrived. He might even, he half joked, have been drawn to the place by unseen forces. "The first manager, Ann Little, was this old character actress," he said. "I wonder if I'm Ann Little reincarnated!" Little, of course, had been the quintessential manager of the hotel, and she had been succeeded by the likes of Meemi Ferguson in the fifties, Tor Olsen in the sixties, Urs Schwank in the seventies, Suzanne Jierjian in the late seventies and early eighties, and Philip Truelove in the eighties and early nineties, all of whom steered the Chateau through any number of obstacles and episodes. But Pavel, who was fortunate enough to preside over the hotel during the historic height of its fame, luxury, and cachet, had, it could be argued, the greatest job of all of them.

�֍

The Marlboro Man stood in front of Chateau Marmont for almost twenty-four years—not the same man for all that time, but whatever the Marlboro Man of the moment looked like. By the mid-nineties, having him on that highly visible spot cost Philip Morris $25,000 a month,* and they seemed perfectly happy to keep paying it.

But a few years later, the Food and Drug Administration declared war on outdoor advertising for cigarettes, and the Marlboro Man's doom was writ. He came down in March 1999, unceremoniously. Within weeks he was replaced by an imitation—another gigantic cowboy, looking very nearly like his predecessor, holding a cigarette that dangled flaccidly from his hand above a warning that read, "Smoking causes impotence."

Almost predictably, it was *this* cowboy, not the one with the cigarettes, who ruffled feathers at Chateau Marmont.

"The old Marlboro Man was a symbol of the Marmont's way of life," said Michael Banks, then working as reservations manager. "The new sign is in bad taste. We have an awful lot of people who smoke here." A visiting photographer complained, "He's gone from being a doorman to a policeman." But André Balazs took the change in stride. "The message is appropriately perverted, given its proximity to the hotel," he said. Then, apparently remembering that Philip Morris owned Kraft Foods, he saw a glimmer of light: "I mean, what if it had been a cream cheese ad instead?"

❋

Balazs had a right to laugh about the changes on the Strip. They had been favorable, by and large, in his years of ownership, and his concept for the hotel bled out into other establishments along the street, in spirit if not always in aesthetics. He both sparked changes and watched them happen with a canny eye.

---

* Around $42,000 in 2019.

At the start of his tenure, the Strip didn't carry the glamorous aura it had once enjoyed. "When I bought the Chateau in 1990," he recalled some years after the fact, "I couldn't walk down Sunset. I have a friend who is a designer from New York. Back then she decided to walk from the Chateau to Sunset Plaza, and two times during her walk, drivers pulled up to proposition her. Their attitude was, Why the hell are you walking if you're not a prostitute?"

That might have sounded like a jaded New Yorker's joke about car-crazy Los Angeles, but it was built on an undeniable truth: The Sunset Strip outside the Chateau Marmont had been in steady decline for many years. Locals saw it just as they saw Hollywood Boulevard: a tourist trap and a mart for the sex and drug trades with nothing like its former cachet. And neither local business interests nor West Hollywood city officials had any idea how to turn it around.

Balazs had a vision for his hotel that would restore (or, indeed, *instill*) some glory to it, but his plan, like the Chateau, stood apart from the Strip, above it but not quite of it. He was engaged in a project to transform a hotel, not a street. Any renaissance that Chateau Marmont would enjoy would be its own business. But the investment he and his partners made was inevitably noticed by others. The Sunset Strip of the early nineties might have been, like Times Square, better appreciated for the glitter of the past than the grime of the present, but it was still one of the most famous stretches of road in the world, and a few of its clubs and restaurants still imparted a legitimate glow. The physical thing might have been in disrepair, but the legend—the *really* valuable thing—needed no burnishing.

In fact, to some eyes the decay of the Strip imparted a certain allure. In 1993, Chateau Marmont regular Johnny Depp and a group of partners took over the lease of a failing nightclub called the Central and renamed it the Viper Room, attracting a young Hollywood crowd from the get-go. The following year, a coalition of investors including comedian Dan Aykroyd and a co-founder of the Hard Rock Cafe chain opened the House of Blues, the biggest live performance space the Sunset Strip had ever seen. In 1996, Ian Schrager, André Balazs's rival in the boutique hotel game, bought and remodeled the old Le Mondrian hotel at Sunset and Olive, gussying it up and rechristening it the Mondrian, complete with a nightclub space called Skybar. A new vibe started to be felt up and down the Strip—bohemian chic, sometimes sleek, sometimes grungy, but always with a lot of money to throw around. Chateau Marmont was in the midst of it.

In late 1995, Balazs and Sean MacPherson, who operated several high-end bars and clubs around Los Angeles, capitalized on the growing cult of the Chateau to open a new business, Bar Marmont, the first watering hole officially associated with the hotel (whose guests had always been reckoned to be half in the bag even without a bar on the premises). Bar Marmont stood on Sunset Boulevard proper, just downhill and to the east from the Chateau. For a few years it had been the French restaurant La Toque; back in the sixties, it was a nightclub called the Scene. Balazs and MacPherson hired Shawn Hausman, who had taken part in the redesign of the hotel, to create the look and feel of the place, and he concocted a vaguely noirish tropical cave, decorated with bamboo, artificial butterflies and peacocks, and a live parrot.

The very idea that Chateau Marmont—which hadn't even had a full liquor license until 1992—would open its own almost-on-premises bar was news. When Balazs and MacPherson held auditions—there was no other word for their hiring process—for new staff, *The New Yorker* covered it in a "Talk of the Town" piece. Bar Marmont opened in November 1995, with a stunning coup: Leonardo DiCaprio's twenty-first birthday party, which the *Los Angeles Times* remembered as "the night even movie stars got turned away." The turning away was done by Connie, a.k.a. Constance, a bald-headed drag queen who came from New York at Balazs's behest to serve as hostess and held sway for the better part of a decade, negotiating pushy patrons, famous faces, and barroom randomnesses with aplomb.

Bar Marmont, Skybar, and the Viper Room transformed the Sunset Strip. What had been a dingy thoroughfare, roamed by drug dealers and prostitutes, blossomed once again into a center of nightlife, chic and flashy and laced with a naughty air that was a considerable part of its charm. "I would be embarrassed if the Body Shop closed down," Balazs said of the strip joint across Sunset from Chateau Marmont. "With those nude figures outside, it has become Sunset Boulevard's Statue of Liberty."

Conversations about the future of the Sunset Strip had once borne the tone of a planning session for a funeral. Now, with nightclubs so hot that even celebrities could be denied admission, the Strip was experiencing another golden age.

In the midst of this ascent, West Hollywood authorities got busy branding their stretch of Sunset, deciding which businesses could legitimately say they were on Sunset Strip and which were not (controversially, Chateau Marmont did not make the cut because part of it sat on a lot that was, technically, outside West Hollywood city limits). They had big plans to turn the Strip into an even bigger tourist mecca, with perhaps a Disney facility of some sort to draw families and a coherent overall plan to integrate all the new development under a single vision.

Balazs, who was remodeling a second Sunset Strip building, the Golden Crest retirement home, into what would open in 1999 as the first of his chain of Standard hotels, was hopeful but dubious about the effort. Rhapsodizing about "this organic chaos that is the Sunset Strip," he opined, "A place's sense of past, its quirkiness and history, is what makes a place rich."

❧

Pavel was fully in charge of things when, in 2003, Balazs launched the final—and in some ways most important—

addition he would make to the hotel. For the first time in its history, Chateau Marmont would have a restaurant. Ray Sarlot had been against the idea. "I don't want to have people sitting around staring at the guests," he explained. But André Balazs understood that there were advantages in that very thing. And so he found a way to make it happen.

The restaurant, which didn't, technically, have a name, wasn't a big, stand-alone place, and it lacked a lot of the conveniences that would have made it more of a destination: You still had to find a way to park your car, and there was no place to wait around for your table. There were two dining spaces—a dark, delicately moody interior that, per the *Los Angeles Times,* recalled "one of the little rooms at Caffe Florian in Venice" and an outdoor garden area, which was where the action was, especially during the many months when it was comfortable enough to dine outside. The first chef, Mohammad Islam, most recently of the Mercer Kitchen in New York (the restaurant was Jean-Georges Vongerichten's, but the hotel in which it sat belonged to André Balazs), was noted for simple, elegant, fresh cooking that suited the atmosphere, making diners feel, per the *Times,* more like they were dining "at a rather grand country house than at a proper restaurant."

The restaurant was immediately a hit, and not only with Chateau guests, who could order off the menu, which was available in the restaurant or in their rooms 24/7 and ranged from breakfast to late-night dining. The real innovation was that there was now a destination *inside* the hotel—a gathering spot for locals or out-of-towners staying elsewhere. Almost immediately, Hollywood, especially young Hollywood, began to gravitate toward the place, and the Chateau became a true hot spot in a way it never had before. Which led to a new kind of problem. In more than seventy years of operation, there had almost never been cause for hotel management to deal with the sort of social geography common to Hollywood restaurants: which were the most desirable tables; who preferred to be seen (or not); which boldfaced names were feuding and needed to be seated as far apart as possible. Now, with the scene-making likes of Paris Hilton and the Kardashian clan starting to turn up regularly, as well as legitimate stars and paying hotel guests, the Chateau had call for a maître d' and general manager well versed in the art of juggling personalities and egos. Hell, they even felt comfortable turning people *away:* a situation previous iterations of management never imagined.

※

Fortunately, Philip Pavel was born to the hospitality business and had been battle tested in Beverly Hills restaurants, so he knew very well how to do the job facing him. But there were limits, even at Chateau Marmont. One night in 2007, pop star Britney Spears, in the throes of a prolonged and public episode of substance dependency and apparent mental breakdown, made a spectacle of smearing food across her face in the restaurant. Other diners present, among them fellow pop diva Victoria Beckham, mentioned to the staff that Spears was "acting weird." When she started to play dress up with her dinner, she was escorted from her table and informed that she was no longer welcome on the hotel grounds. The restriction was lifted after Spears cleaned herself up, and she was back in the restaurant two years later celebrating her twenty-eighth birthday.

Her sin wasn't the behavior itself, not entirely, but rather the public and, worse, unapologetic nature of it. The secret, apparently, to not only indulging in eyebrow-raising doings at Chateau Marmont but getting away with them was to keep mum about your antics entirely and then, if caught, be playfully vague or obviously exaggerate your account of whatever it was you were supposed to have done. Johnny Depp, who was introduced to the Chateau by his friend and mentor Hunter S. Thompson and who was fond of spending nights there, even though he owned a home nearby, epitomized the attitude perfectly: He liked to brag that he and his onetime girlfriend model Kate Moss made love in every room in the hotel—presumably not all in one stay but over the four years of their relationship. Whatever Depp did there, and whomever with, was hidden behind the smoke screen of a titillating—if dubious—tall tale.

That sort of thing *burnished* the hotel's reputation, as did the story that circulated around Hollywood and beyond late on Oscar night 2004. That evening, Benicio Del Toro was nominated for Best Supporting Actor for *21 Grams,* just three years after winning the same prize, on his first nomination, for *Traffic.* Among the award presenters on the show was Scarlett Johansson. Somewhere amid the after parties, the two stars cozied up together, and she invited him back to the Chateau, where she had been renting a suite since selling her nearby house, which she had found too big and lonely to live in by herself. Johansson made a home at the Chateau, moving in with her Chihuahua, Maggie, a Japanese fighting fish named Cassius (dead, alas, and buried by her in the hotel garden surreptitiously under cover of night), and her own furniture, including a red coffee table designed by Diana Vreeland. No doubt the chance to see that Vreeland was what enticed Del Toro to accept the invitation to her suite.

Whatever happened between them happened fast. On the way up to Johansson's place, they *might have* kissed. And however the rest of the evening went, that bit of it—the two stars enmeshed in the elevator—became famous. In part, Johansson joked to a magazine, that was because they *weren't alone:* "Apparently there was somebody with us in an elevator, and we were making out or having sex or something—which I think is very unsanitary." So, for the record: no actual sex. Probably. At least not in the lift.

Once word of their tryst got out, the pair did nothing to deny or explain it. Del Toro (then thirty-seven years old, some eighteen years her senior) even encouraged the possibility that the rumors were true. "Did I ever have sex in an elevator with Scarlett Johansson after an awards show," he was quoted as asking rhetorically in 2005. "I kind of like . . . you know . . . I . . . well . . . I don't know. Let's leave that to somebody's imagination. Let's not promote it. I'm sure it has happened before. It might not be the last time, either." Thinking about the logistics a little further, he continued, "But the Chateau Marmont only has eight floors. I would still be struggling out of my leather jacket by the second floor and wouldn't have my shirt off by the seventh."*

※

As a privately owned business, Chateau Marmont was always able to keep details of its finances out of the public record. But in 2003, at least a glimpse of the hotel's financial state was revealed in the course of a federal legal proceeding against the hotel's one-time controller, who was prosecuted on two counts of felony wire fraud having to do with his embezzlement of nearly $14 million from the Chateau and its sister hotel, the Hollywood Standard.

Kelly Timothy Ebert had been hired to run the accounting at the Marmont in 1993 and had been put in charge of the books at the Standard when it opened five years later, earning a salary, at its maximum, of $113,000 per year. He didn't live as if that were his only source of income, though. He owned a $2-million-plus home in Sherman Oaks, belonged to an exclusive country club, drove a Toyota Land Cruiser SUV *and* a Mercedes sedan, and collected high-end memorabilia to do with Elvis Presley and Lucille Ball.

He accumulated the means to acquire all of that by, it would seem, stealing from the hotels. His scheme involved siphoning

---

* In the spirit of "we report; you decide," it must be noted that Johansson eventually denied that the incident ever occurred and took responsibility for starting the rumor: "I went home alone that night to my mom's house, but nobody cares about that. It was so embarrassing. I felt horrible about the way that portrayed Benicio Del Toro." She needn't have. Like Nicholas Ray when he realized that rumors of him sleeping with Marilyn Monroe were a *good* thing, Del Toro would smilingly entertain questions about the incident for years.

credit card payments from the hotels' legitimate accounts into an account that he could make withdrawals from without anyone else's countersignature. He kept the ruse afloat by ordering his subordinates to watch the mail for certain bank statements and then take them to his car on a route that wouldn't be seen by the hotel's surveillance cameras. (Fearing detection, he also destroyed so many incriminating documents that he broke his paper-shredding machine.)

Ebert's theft lasted six years and was first noticed in late 2001, when he failed to make a payment on the Hollywood Standard's mortgage. He missed another payment the following spring for the Chateau's mortgage, causing management to incur a $100,000 penalty fee. At that time he was fired, and his successors discovered irregularities in the hotel's books, eventually calling in authorities. Caught dead to rights, Ebert entered a guilty plea in June 2003 and was sentenced later that year to fifty-one months in a federal penitentiary—the maximum sentence allowed—and ordered to make financial restitution for what he'd stolen.

In the entire colorful history of Chateau Marmont, Ebert's would be the only criminal conviction associated with the hotel on the public record. For all the scandalous behavior that had gone on inside its walls, Chateau Marmont had always managed to keep misdeeds out of the newspapers, save, notably, John Belushi's death. That, in fact, was one of its most important guarantees as a hotel for celebrities: What happens here stays here. You literally had to either rob the place blind or die there for word to get out.

�֍

The aura of naughtiness associated with the Chateau never dissipated, even if it was given a veneer of exclusivity and luster during the Balazs era. During Sarlot's reign, the bad boy (and girl) -ism at the hotel was the stuff of whispered legend, making it out into the world sometimes years after the fact, often in gilded form to make it more enticing and scandalous. Balazs, on the other hand, owned the hotel in the age of *TMZ*, smart phones, and social media, when everyone was a paparazzo and plenty of the hotel's guests didn't care what sort of impression they made on the larger world and even courted it.

For some guests, this wasn't value added but value lost. The fashion designer and photographer Hedi Slimane, who was a regular before acquiring a permanent home in Los Angeles, spoke for those who found the hotel less inviting than it had once been. "I used to stay for months at the Chateau Marmont, which typically was a really different place then, very private, filled with young actors or directors living there all year long. No social media at the time—it was private and had the authentic feel and dusty glamour of old Hollywood."

For others, the new vibe of the hotel made it homier than ever. Take Courtney Love, the unfiltered rock star and sometime actress who had an on-again, off-again relationship with the hotel (and, it was said, Balazs himself) that resulted, at least for a time, in her being labeled persona non grata. She managed to get her ban reversed and continued to frequent the place on and off for years. Director Gus Van Sant, who knew her during their days as unknowns in Portland, ran into her there one morning. "I was meeting with my DP, Harris Savides, and Courtney just flopped at our table and started to monopolize the conversation," he recalled. "She had been at the first screening of my first film, and she was carrying on about that. And they used to serve cappuccino in those big bowls, like in France, and she made the wrong move with it, and it wound up in her lap, all over her dress, and she just kept talking."

Other celebrities loved to push the edge at the Chateau: Alan Cumming bragged about having sex on the piano in his suite and delighting when, the following day, he could see smears on the shiny black surface of the instrument while receiving business guests; Michael Madsen, who lived in a bungalow for a few years with a pair of Rottweilers, liked to hang around the pool in biker's leathers—jacket and pants—even in midday, the better to creep out the gawpers; James Franco wrote and published poems, likely tongue in cheek, about over-the-top sexual antics at the hotel; old goat Jack Nicholson chased the young supermodel Bridget Hall around the pool, only half in jest; and Hunter S. Thompson, in some ways the spiritual goddaddy of hedonistic young Hollywood, continued to visit the hotel almost until his death in 2005, throwing around $100 tips and screaming out of the parking garage in his rented convertibles with a cocktail balanced in one hand.

These sorts of escapades added to the Chateau's image as a noirish playground for the naughtiest of celebrities—an enclave for debauchery and hedonism. Anthony Bourdain, the chef, TV travel show host, and boulevardier, rather epitomized this aspect of the Marmont's image. "I stay on campus at the Chateau a lot, you know, that way I don't have to stumble far," he explained. "I love driving here. The fact is, if I get overserved, now I've got a car problem. If I'm getting seriously in the alcohol, chances are I'm staying on campus."

On the other hand, some people still tried to keep their doings out of the limelight, such as actor Josh Hartnett, who called EMTs to his Marmont suite in 2009 because he was severely stricken by a gastrointestinal ailment that he'd picked up while doing humanitarian work in a Third World country and needed to be taken to a hospital by ambulance; such were the times that a recording of his call for emergency help for an episode of diarrhea and vomiting was available online within days. For years afterward, he was taunted by paparazzi about the phone call whenever he showed his face near the hotel.

But some of what was gotten up to was actually rather sweet. Actor Sam Rockwell, who would one day meet his future life partner, Leslie Bibb, at the Chateau, once spent an awards season giving away everything that had shown up in his swag bags to hotel staffers and anyone who came to visit him in his suite. French director Luc Besson met *his* future wife (his third, actually) and star Milla Jovovich at the pool when he was casting *The Fifth Element*, in which she played her breakout role. Actor Ben Mendelsohn married writer Emma Forrest there in 2012 (it didn't last). And Jeff Goldblum, notorious for his tomcat-about-town lifestyle, married his third wife, Emilie Livingston, at the hotel in November 2014; the couple went on to have two children, making Goldblum a father for the first time in his life at age sixty-two.

4.

As might be surmised from acquaintance with his work, the man knew how to make an entrance.

"There was this very recalcitrant elevator," remembered a Chateau regular, screenwriter and director Menno Meyjes. "One day it broke down. We were all standing there going, 'There's someone in the elevator!' . . . [T]hey had to open the door with a crowbar and the doors just sort of fell away, and [he] was leaning against the elevator wall with a lit cigarette in his mouth and a leather jacket slung over his shoulder—the very picture of insouciance. He barely glanced down at the people who had freed him, walked on to his convertible, and drove out."

And he also made a sensational exit.

At about noon on January 23, 2004, a silver Cadillac SRX came careering out of the garage of Chateau Marmont and, instead of turning left and downhill toward Sunset Boulevard or right and uphill toward Monteel Road, gunned straight across Marmont Lane. There were some people walking along the street, one of whom, a photographer named Ann Johansson, was brushed by the speeding SUV. Before she could holler at the driver, the car smashed into a retaining wall and some shrubs across the narrow street, crushing the entire front end. Johansson and other passersby rushed to the vehicle and found a white-haired, stylishly dressed man slumped over the wheel. The air bags hadn't deployed, and the passenger compartment of the car was intact, the engine area having absorbed the brunt of the collision. But the driver was clearly in peril. An ambulance was summoned, and the driver was extricated from the car and taken to Cedars-Sinai Medical Center, where he was soon declared dead, not from injuries resulting from the crash, but from a heart attack, which was apparently what *caused* him to lose control of the car.

The next day, headlines around the world announced the death of Helmut Newton, the eighty-three-year-old enfant terrible of fashion photography. The so-called King of Kink, who infused his work with an erotic daring and who had spent winters at Chateau Marmont for nearly a quarter century, had died in an accident as attention grabbing as any of his photo shoots.

Since the early eighties, Newton and his wife, June (who was a photographer in her own right under the *nom de caméra* Alice Springs), would arrive at the Chateau during Christmas week and stay until March or so, at which point they would decamp to their permanent residence in Monte Carlo. In the fall, they'd leave the Riviera for Paris, and then start the cycle all over again as the Yuletide approached. "I have this fascination for familiar surroundings," Newton once said. "My favorite photos are often those which evoke a strong feeling of 'I have been here before.'"

It was an ironically homey sentiment from a man known for the iconoclastic sexuality of his work, which agitated the world of fashion photography with graphic and, to some eyes, exploitative and degrading imagery. In Newton's work, designer clothing, the ostensible reason for the photos in the first place, was less emphasized than the highly erotic and fantastical atmospheres in which Newton displayed it. His work was haunting, electrifying, polarizing, and deeply influential. There was the famous image of a model shoving another girl's head into a toilet; a billboard in Times Square showing a woman lying facedown wearing only stockings; a series depicting nudes in orthopedic body braces; images of two women kissing, one of them in handcuffs; naked women, often accompanied by vaguely sinister men, in laundromats, limousines, stately homes, often shot in and around Chateau Marmont.

"His photographs had more of a signature than any photographer I can think of," said his longtime *Vogue* editor Anna Wintour. "Fashion would change, but Helmut's vision didn't." He delighted in provocation and the fallout from it: He bragged about the time that more than a thousand *Vogue* readers canceled their subscriptions after the magazine ran an image he'd shot of two women, a man, and two dogs in a suggestive pose. According to Wintour, he relished the furious responses of those whom he'd agitated: "Helmut would say, 'Send me the letters.' If there were none he'd be terribly disappointed."

Newton wasn't the only photographer who made a studio out of the Chateau—Annie Leibovitz's sensational 1992 image of Demi Moore with a man's suit painted, trompe l'oeil–style, on her naked body was one of many famous photos taken in the hotel, and such photographers as George Hurrell, Herb Ritts, Mario Testino, and Bruce Weber often rented suites for photo shoots. But Newton returned to the Chateau again and again and shot scores of photos there over his many years of residency. There were images of nude women in the hotel laundry room, of Dennis Hopper (his head shaved bald) and Christopher Walken sitting side by side and staring with gazes of indeterminate menace, of Hurrell himself setting up Michelle Pfeiffer for a portrait session in an unmade hotel bed. In a sense, Newton was the hotel's ideal guest, availing himself of its singular identity as long-term residence and bohemian escape while at the same time helping to shape its identity as a sinful but discreet adult playground, and becoming a fixture of the place in life *and* in death.

Newton's very arrival at the Chateau each winter seemed to alter the place. Rupert Everett remembered feeling miserably alone in his very first stay at the hotel, which coincided with the Christmas holidays. And then, a miracle. "One afternoon," he recalled, "Helmut and his wife, June, surged into the hotel surrounded by luggage" and an entourage that included fashion editor Michael Roberts, a friend of Everett's. The young actor was able to attach himself to the group, joining them in their freewheeling days: lunches, cocktail parties, and the ritual of dining out. "Most nights our group met in the hotel foyer and clattered down to the basement parking lot, where we bundled into Helmut's car. . . . I sat in the back with Michael, giggling and nudging (*la vie en* Newton was eccentric, to say the least) while Helmut—shrieking at the wheel—negotiated the blind corner from the car park onto the street. He was driving over his own grave."

⚜

Newton was born in Berlin in 1920 as Helmut Neustädter, the son of a prosperous button manufacturer. Raised in bourgeois comfort, he attended private schools and enjoyed family vacations at spa hotels where he preciously noticed that "a gigolo and a gigolette sat at separate tables away from the customers." His sharp eye drew him to photography at an early age; he acquired his first camera at age twelve and at sixteen started work as an assistant to the celebrated photographer Yva, a Berliner who specialized in both fashion shoots and experimental images.

In 1938, just after *Kristallnacht*, the Neustädters fled Germany. "It was very sad for my father," Newton recalled. "He believed nothing would happen to him because he was a German." While his parents went off to South America, Newton made his way to Trieste and boarded a boat headed to China with a special passport issued by the Nazi government. "My Jew passport," he called it, "stamped with a J on every page!" He got as far as Singapore, where he fell in with an older French woman who kept him as her boy toy, dressing him in fine clothes and paying his way at the best restaurants and hotels.

When Germany invaded France in 1940, Newton's German citizenship made him an "enemy alien," and he was sent to an internment camp in Australia. In 1942, he was allowed to leave and enlisted in the Australian military, for which he drove trucks. At war's end, he became a British subject, set up shop in Melbourne, and changed his name formally to Newton. "It was like having a new identity," he said. In 1946, an actress named June Browne came in for head shots. They married two years later and remained together for more than fifty years.

Newton steadily built his client list and reputation as both a commercial photographer and a fine artist, and he was offered a yearlong contract by the British edition of *Vogue* in 1956. He traveled between Europe and Australia, finally settling in Paris in 1961. Two years later, he joined the staff of French *Vogue* and began to make an even bigger name for himself.

Not everyone was enamored of Newton's work. Diana Vreeland, the famed editor of the American *Vogue*, was among those unimpressed, and as a result he didn't get his foot in the door of that publication until she left in 1971. At around that time, Newton suffered a heart attack, and the combination of a new platform and his health scare changed the man and his work. As his wife said, the moment "opened up something in him. He started doing work that was tremendously influenced by his bourgeois background." He put it more bluntly: "I wasn't so interested any more in making money. I wanted to do exactly what I wanted to do." Specifically, that meant images of models lounging nude or nearly so in opulent environments, often spiced with elements of S&M or mystery: dark alleys, shadowy lurkers, hints of a story that the viewer could only surmise. He was a provocateur, but, he insisted, he was showing exactly how people lived in the rarefied corners of Berlin, Singapore, Paris, and the French Riviera that he knew so well. He staged these images, yes, but he took them, he claimed, from reality. "I'm a frustrated paparazzi," he liked to joke.

In 1981, the Newtons bought an apartment in Monte Carlo that became their permanent home base, and they started frequenting Chateau Marmont regularly, allowing Helmut to work with American clients and movie people and chum around with such Hollywood pals as Billy Wilder, Robert Evans, and Jack Nicholson, as well as other Angelinos such as Tina and Michael Chow and Timothy and Barbara Leary. He was fond of the American West, frequenting roadside diners and shopping for clothes at Nudie's, the famed North Hollywood shop that outfitted so many rhinestone cowboys. "He was used to much darker European cities," recalled photographer Mark Arbeit, one of his Los Angeles assistants, "and he really loved the light here."

As evinced by Rupert Everett's recollection of the Newtons' arrival at the Chateau, the couple were a movable feast. According to Joan Juliet Buck, a *Vogue* editor who worked with him and partied with him at the hotel, the Newtons "taught everyone how to live. [They] were gregarious and had a large group of friends. Their enthusiasm and social life didn't diminish with age." Another friend, producer Jan Sharp, remembered that the arrival of the Newtons at the Chateau each winter was a festive event in and of itself: "Every year [they] would come and throw a party. We used to call it The Feast of Helmut and June. Men wore black tie, and we all got dressed up as if it were a Paris party."

Even at an advanced age, Newton was able to keep up a vigorous professional and social schedule through a dedicated exercise regimen. While staying at the Chateau, he swam or went to the gym most days; the addition of an exercise room was a boon to him. (About other updates that André Balazs made to the hotel, Newton was agnostic but generally accepting.) Another secret of his vitality, Newton explained, was that he and June lived sparsely and freely—even from one another. He would occasionally travel to Berlin for extended trips without her, she would go off on photo shoots without him, and they kept no office staff or studios in any of the cities they called home. Even their immediate surroundings were minimalist; as Newton explained in 1987, "I don't want to own anything anymore. I just want to take photographs."

Up to his final days, Newton exuded energy, positivity, magnetism. Novelist and screenwriter Bruce Wagner remembered sharing a milestone meal with him:

> I have the feeling there are lots of people who lay claim to having had dinner with Helmut Newton on his last night on earth, and I'm one of them. André Balazs invited me and my wife, so we joined him and Uma Thurman, and Helmut and his wife, June.... Helmut liked my wife because she looked like June when she was young. I told Helmut one of my favorite jokes, that goes something like, "I want to die in my sleep like my father did; not screaming, like everyone else in the car."

On the following, fatal morning, in the elevator, Newton ran into Sofia Coppola, another Chateau regular and one who would draw inspiration as a filmmaker from Newton's work. "He was coming home from the gym in his sweatsuit," she remembered, "and I thanked him for a photo that he had given me. A few hours later I came back and his car had crashed. There was the car with flowers all around it." The image would stick with her.

※

The gloss with which André Balazs managed to paint the Chateau meant that it became a mainstay of popular culture. Consumers of gossip news—in print, on TV, on the internet, or in social media—knew of the hotel not as a repository of old Hollywood or the place where John Belushi died but as a swank hot spot where young actors, musicians, and media personalities mingled and got up to naughtiness.

In part this was because the hotel truly filled that role—in 2006, Heath Ledger was famously filmed there on somebody's cell-phone camera indulging in what looked *a lot* like cocaine, and the carryings-on of such stars as Lindsay Lohan, James

Franco, Britney Spears, Keanu Reeves, Colin Farrell, Taylor Swift, and many others of their generation, if not their accomplishment or standing (Paris Hilton and various Kardashians), were religiously reported in gossip pages and websites even when there wasn't photographic evidence of them.

In part, too, this was because under Balazs the hotel became a hot spot for movie premiere celebrations, luxury brand product launches, and, during the weeks running up to the Oscar, Grammy, and Emmy awards, parties in honor of various nominees or suites leased by fashion brands, hairstylists, and sundry image-enhancing services who needed a dedicated, centrally located space where they could dress, tweeze, trim, and otherwise perfect their clients for the red carpet.

As a result of all this high-wattage energy, not only were the hotel's rooms almost always booked, often well in advance, but you couldn't simply drop into the restaurant, the lobby, or the bar. After more than seven decades of being mysterious, secretive, hidden in plain sight, Chateau Marmont had become something more: an icon, a catchphrase, a signifier, a brand; it was *hot*.

Ironically, this meant that the long-term residences of writers, artists, composers, and other creative types, a hallmark of the hotel for decades, were less common than ever; to be blunt, the hotel was no longer a bargain. In fact, it was *expensive:* An overnight stay in 2019 could cost anywhere from $500 for the tiniest room in the main building to $2,000 and up for a penthouse or bungalow—way higher than past prices, even when adjusted for inflation. The hotel was once an enclave of bohemians; after Balazs sprinkled his gold dust on it, it was more likely to be filled with a wealthy mix of celebrities, showbiz and fashion executives, and a jet-setting international crowd seeking to rub up against some old-fashioned Hollywood sinfulness. As Eve Babitz put it in 2018, "It's another fancy L.A. hotel; it's great, but it's not mine anymore!"

This trendy new version of the Chateau began to show up in popular culture in telling ways. In 1996, Balazs himself published a limited-edition volume, *Chateau Marmont Hollywood Handbook*, a scrapbook, to be exact, comprising a variety of previously published reminiscences of the Chateau and a lot of photos and writings about Hollywood history. There were two coffee-table-type photo books to do with the place: *About Glamour* (1997) by Len Prince and *Asleep at the Chateau* (2012) by photographer Jork Weismann. In the graphic novel *The Private Eye* by Brian K. Vaughan, Marcos Martín, and Muntsa Vicente, set in the not-too-distant future, the title character has his office in the Chateau, which is no longer a hotel but a commercial building and which gets destroyed in a bombing intended to kill him. In novels by Lauren Weisberger (*Last Night at Chateau Marmont*, 2010), Michael Connelly (*The Drop*, 2011), and Aris Janigian (*Waiting for Lipchitz at Chateau Marmont*, 2016), the hotel is an emblem of Hollywood opulence, indulgence, and cupidity. In films about the music world such as *Rock Star* (2001), *Laurel Canyon* (2002), and *Danny Collins* (2015), it simply appears, its very presence meant to tell us something about the characters and the events. The singer-songwriter Lana Del Rey, who had the words "Chateau Marmont" tattooed on her left forearm, shot a video on the grounds for one of her songs, and the singer-songwriter Jarvis Cocker, along with his collaborator Chilly Gonzales, released an entire album, *Room 29*, inspired by the vibe and legend of the hotel.* And in the Hollywood satire *BoJack Horseman*, the Chateau achieved something even rarer: It looks just like itself, but its famous neon shield sign reads *Chateau Marmoset*, entering the surreal world of the animated series as a parody of itself, much in the way the Warner Bros. cartoons of the forties once winkingly referenced such old-time Hollywood haunts as the Brown Derby, the Trocadero, and Mocambo.

---

* The album was well received critically but didn't exactly conquer the world, making it something of a very small consolation prize for the Chateau's *not* being the subject of the Eagles' 1976 smash hit "Hotel California," which was almost certainly inspired by the Beverly Hills Hotel and turned out to be one of the biggest-selling records of all time.

�֍

The epitome of all this attention came in the spring of 2009, when the entire fifth floor of the Chateau was rented out for three weeks by a single person—not a reclusive billionaire or a Saudi prince or a hedonistic superstar musician or a world-famous actor but rather Sofia Coppola, a daughter of Hollywood who had a personal history with the hotel, yes, but for the purposes of this unusual arrangement an Oscar-winning filmmaker at work on a new movie.

Somewhere, as the film was known, centers on a bad boy actor named Johnny Marco who passes time listlessly in a suite at Chateau Marmont until his routine is turned upside down by the arrival of his eleven-year-old daughter, Cleo. The girl normally lives with her mother, but Mom needs some me-time and Johnny, nursing a broken arm, is between pictures, so it's an opportune moment for some father-daughter bonding—or it would be if Johnny weren't in such a drifting fog.

Coppola wrote the script in France, where she had made her previous feature, *Marie Antoinette,* and shared a home with the musician Thomas Mars, the father of her two daughters. "I was living in Paris, and I was homesick," she remembered. She began to think about modern Los Angeles and noted that there wasn't a film that showed the city's current way of life. All there was, she recalled, was the cartoon version of the city she saw on television. "This fun, party lifestyle. . . . But what would that really be like? What's it like the next morning? It's like the flip side of *Entourage.*"

As she began visualizing her protagonist and his way of life, she knew one thing for dead certain about him: He would make his home not at the beach or in the hills but at the Chateau. "That's where that kind of guy would live," she said. "It's sort of a rite of passage for an actor to live at the Chateau Marmont. It means you've made it, but you're still 'down-to-earth.' "

❦

Coppola and the Chateau went way back. When she was just a kid, her father, Francis Ford Coppola, toyed with the idea of buying the place and turning it into a kind of artist colony. Her family stayed in the hotel occasionally, and she remembered Romulo Laki, the famed singing waiter, serenading her in the lobby on his guitar with Elvis Presley's "Teddy Bear." When she was a student at the California Institute of the Arts in Valencia, not far north of L.A., the Chateau was one of the regular stops she and her squad made on their circuit of partying. "Me and my friends would go there to hang out. The parking guy, who's been there for 20 years, would open the gates so we could use the swimming pool."

In 1993, she celebrated her twenty-second birthday there—a bash covered by newspapers and populated with the likes of Coppola's then beau, Donovan Leitch (son of the music star Donovan), actors Peter Gallagher and Ethan Hawke, members of the Beastie Boys and Red Hot Chili Peppers, restaurateur/club owner Brian McNally, *Vogue* editor Marina Rust, and a contingent of young New York fashionistas including Kelly Klein, Tatiana von Fürstenberg, and a clutch of Ford Agency models.

The bohemian vibe of the Chateau suited Coppola in those days, she later admitted—"There was a year I did nothing but go out. I was pretty flaky." But when she came back to the hotel in 2009, she was neither a child who would swoon to a song about a teddy bear nor a party kid looking for distraction. She had transformed herself into a bona fide auteur, having written and directed three feature films—*The Virgin Suicides* (1999), *Lost in Translation* (2003), and *Marie Antoinette* (2006)—the second of which saw her awarded the Oscar for Best Original Screenplay. That film, like *Somewhere*, was set in a hotel (as, in a sense, was *Marie Antoinette*, with its opulent Versailles, and, for that matter, "Life Without Zoe," a short film Coppola wrote with her father and that he directed as part of 1989's *New York Stories* anthology). The idea of living in in-between places was a core part of her life story and her artist-mind, and it ran richly through her new screenplay, which followed its protagonist to such make-believe places as an auto race track, an ice rink, a special effects studio, a hotel hosting a junket in Beverly Hills, a hotel in Milan with an in-suite swimming pool, and a hotel-casino in Las Vegas. The archetypal New Hollywood actor, Johnny Marco was almost too rootless even to inhabit a hotel room. But in her vision, that room, if it existed at all, would, for sure, be at Chateau Marmont.

Which presented her with a number of problems, starting with access. "The Chateau doesn't allow a lot of filming," said Coppola's producer G. Mac Brown. "If and when they do, they can charge a very high location fee, and it probably has to be done in the middle of the night." Philip Pavel concurred. "People ask all the time," he said, indicating the fruitlessness of those requests. But Coppola had advantages that other filmmakers couldn't match, and she made a personal appeal to management. "She's been a member of the Chateau family as long as I've been here," Pavel explained. "When she approached André Balazs, the owner, there was an innate sense of trust that the project would have integrity and reflect the true nature of the hotel."

Given Balazs's blessing, Coppola's production was granted permissions beyond those ever before afforded a filmmaker working at the hotel: the right to rent and use an entire floor-plus of rooms; the ability to shoot at all hours; access to all public areas, including the lobby, the pool, the restaurant, the elevators, the corridors, and the garage; and even certain members of the hotel staff appearing as themselves, including Pavel, Romulo Laki, and various waiters and parking valets. On the fifth floor, the crew set up separate rooms and suites to house various departments—camera, grip/electric, production offices, art and decor, hair and makeup—and they established the principal set for Johnny Marco's apartment: room 59.

The aesthetic of the film—both in its narrative and in its

look and feel—was meant to be minimalistic and almost documentarian, revealing Marco's days as if silently spying on them, anatomizing his behavior and habits. But production designer Anne Ross realized that she would, ironically, have to tinker with the suite and other locations to make them look as if they *weren't* tinkered with.

"The goal," she explained, "was to maintain the iconic feeling of the Chateau, so that no one would know that we did anything [in the way of adjustments to the interiors], they would say, 'They just went in and shot.'" Marco's suite was, she continued, where most of these subtle changes had to be made:

> When you're in a hotel room, you want a big TV, but on film, you need something a little smaller or it will eat up the frame. We had to change all of the art in Johnny's suite because none [of the existing pieces] is cleared. We picked ones that were in the spirit of the artwork. We also reupholstered some of the furniture with fabric that's reminiscent of the lobby. We wanted to bring some of the beautiful, lush look of the lobby in there because the rooms at the Chateau are often stark and sparse; they're painted all white, and I love that, but that can be too harsh for filming in such an intimate space.

On the other hand, she said, the public spaces used by the film were perfect as she found them: "We didn't change a thing in the lobby."

Just as Balazs and Pavel worried that a film production might inconvenience their guests, Coppola and her crew worried that the ordinary ruckus of a functioning hotel might make filming more difficult—the noise of elevators, doors opening and closing, carousers in other suites, and Sunset Boulevard and its traffic just below. But, said location manager Stephenson Crossley, Chateau Marmont lived up to its reputation as serene and isolated, even in the midst of chaos. "It's amazingly quiet for being so close to the

Sunset Strip," he said. "Even room to room, it's quiet; with the thick floors and ceilings, we wouldn't hear each other. It's a little island unto itself. We always felt protected."

For the role of Marco, Coppola and company pulled off a similar trick of transforming a found object into the fictional one they required with minimal adjustments. Stephen Dorff was thirty-five during the production, and he had already established himself as a bit of a Hollywood bad boy: scruffy, never married, with a reputation for indulgence. A native of Georgia, he'd been working in film and television since his teens, with a résumé that included as many misses as hits: from the vampire movie *Blade* and the Beatles biopic *Backbeat* to films by the likes of Michael Mann and John Waters to direct-to-disc and direct-to-cable pictures and a fair bit of work in videogame voice-overs, commercials, and forgotten TV series. During his nearly twenty years in Hollywood, he'd enjoyed wild days and nights at Chateau Marmont, celebrating his twenty-first birthday there and attending many functions, from Ford Modeling Agency galas to the premiere parties for his own films. He even lived in the hotel for a spell. As he recalled, "I had some money, and I didn't have a place to live. So I said, 'You know what? I'm checking into the Chateau.' It got to the point where my business manager called and said, 'Stephen, you need to take a movie or get a job, 'cause you're out of money.' And I said, 'O.K., I guess I'm moving out.'"

Cast as Johnny Marco, he found himself living in the hotel once again—in suite 69, right upstairs from his character's room, meaning that the floor plans of his real-life and fictional abodes were almost identical. He found the experience both nostalgic and strange. "It was kind of a trip to be back staying at the Chateau, not going back to my own home every night," he said. "I experienced a lot of what Johnny would have. Every night I would wonder, 'Do I go out to dinner, should I play piano, should I go downstairs, go out to a movie?' Many times I would think, 'Oh, I don't want to see anybody; I'm going to order room service.'" He availed himself of his unique position to help Coppola shape some scenes: "I was able to give some gossip to Sofia in the mornings. She always wanted to know what happened that night after we shot, and I would give her some stories and sometimes she'd really like them and we'd include some stuff." And he used one of the hotel's traditional amenities—personalized stationery for guests—to stay immersed in his role. "I got my own Johnny Marco/Chateau Marmont stationery, since Johnny is in residence there," he said. "So I started sending notes to people and I got mail at the hotel—as Johnny."

Cinematographer Harris Savides took advantage of the relatively close quarters and tiny crew to use natural light whenever possible, giving a subdued and intimate feel to the palette of the film. The crew was kept deliberately small, explained Roman Coppola, the director's brother and a producer on the film: "The vibe of Sofia's movie was one of being really intimate, and so we didn't want all that stuff, all the extra people and all the extra tools. If a guy had to ash his cigarette, he would just use the ashtray that was there, and if not he would just use the glass from the kitchen cupboard, and if not he'd just ash out the window. That was the attitude: Naturalistic, authentic to that place."

�֎

Somewhere debuted at the Venice Film Festival in late summer 2010, and it took the Golden Lion, the top prize, amid some grumbling that Coppola had an advantage in that she had once dated the president of the festival jury, Quentin Tarantino (a fact that she said, only partly joking, felt to her more like a handicap than an asset). It was released in December of that year in the United States, where its moody, plain aesthetic was appreciated, if not overly enthusiastically, by critics, and its depiction of a father-daughter relationship was deemed notable, particularly for Elle Fanning's performance as Cleo. But the audience was limited: The film grossed under $2 million domestically against its $7 million budget.

Those viewers who knew Chateau Marmont were no doubt amused by the inclusion of little details of life there, such as the old sinks and blue tiles in Marco's kitchen, the push-button light switches in the walls, the casual nudity on the terraces, the hidden outdoor Ping-Pong table, the spontaneous parties and sexual encounters, the piano in the lobby, the room service that will fetch groceries.

There were coy nods to some of the hotel's most infamous incidents: At one point, Marco boards an elevator to find himself standing with Benicio Del Toro, who, of course, was rumored to have hooked up with Scarlett Johansson in that very conveyance. ("What room you in?" Del Toro asks him. "Fifty-nine," Marco answers. To which, after a pause, Del Toro responds, "I met Bono in 59." "Cool," Marco replies.) In another scene, Marco exits the garage in his sports car and encounters an accident out on Marmont Lane, where a car has crashed into a retaining wall just as Helmut Newton's had in 2004, not long after Sofia Coppola herself had bumped into him in the lobby.

Perhaps most intimately, the film revealed just how fluid a relationship so many of its famous guests have with the Chateau. In the final moments, with Cleo off to summer camp and no work in sight, Marco decides to leave the hotel and fetches his car one last time from Ray Garcia, one of the hotel's actual parking valets, playing himself. As the movie star prepares to light out for an unknown destination, Garcia asks him, "Shall we put your things in storage?" For Johnny Marco, as for so many of its residents, Chateau Marmont is a home that one never truly leaves, even after one has checked out and paid the bill.

5.

On July 4, 2012, Lindsay Lohan threw a little birthday-slash–Independence Day party at the Chateau, where she had been living on and off for several months. The revelers spent several hours in the garden restaurant ordering food and drinks, and several more hours in Lohan's suite—number 33—calling room service to send up yet more goodies. Not content with the fireworks they could see from Lohan's perch, they ordered up a pay-per-view movie and lit one of those candles with which posh hotels decorate rooms on a you-light-it-you-pay-for-it basis.

After the last guest departed, the bills for all that Lohan and company had consumed added up to $2,649.60. Throw in another $710.33 for rental of the suite (the corporate rate, by the way) and $75.00 for rental of a laptop from the hotel, and taxes and whatnot, and the actress's total bill came to $3,563.67.

For *one day*.

That wasn't a lot in Hollywood money. Lohan was staying at the Chateau while she was playing the role of Elizabeth Taylor in the TV movie *Liz & Dick*, for which she was being paid a minimum of $300,000. And as far as she was concerned, her hotel bill didn't matter, because, as she believed, the producers of her film, or the network that would air it, would be paying it.

Except they wouldn't be.

Lohan had a history at the Chateau. The garden restaurant was one of her favorite places to party, but that didn't always mean happy times. In the spring of 2010, she got into a shouting match there with singer Avril Lavigne that ended when Lohan, rebuffed by security guards in her pleas to get Lavigne ejected, stormed out of the place. This time around, Lohan had arrived at the hotel in February, when she gave up a town house in the bohemian beachside community of Venice and moved into a suite that a friend had been renting but not living in. She only began running her own tab on June 5, living at first in a small suite and then a bigger one, and living in it *fully*.

Over the next fifty-seven days, during which time she wasn't always actually at the hotel but merely renting a room there, she spent $3,000-plus each on room service, hotel restaurant bills, and minibar charges, in addition to more than $700 on cigarettes,

$600-plus on laundry, nearly $400 on pay-per-view movies, and more than $100 on magazines and iPhone chargers from the hotel gift shop—plus, the room rate and the taxes and the parking charges and other miscellaneous fees.

In all, she accumulated a bill of $46,350.04 in less than two months, and she kept insisting to hotel management, which was understandably inquiring after payment, that she wasn't responsible for it—which was true on many levels.

On July 31, general manager Philip Pavel presented Lohan with a sixteen-page itemized bill for her stay, along with a note basically ordering her to vacate the premises as of noon the next day. "I regret to inform you," he wrote, "that we will no longer be able to extend any further credit for you to remain in the hotel." The letter didn't say so, but the word was that she was effectively banned from the premises—hotel, restaurant, bar: all of it.

※

It was only the latest misadventure of an actress who had only a few years earlier seemed destined for real superstardom. In 2005, on the strength of such hit films as *The Parent Trap, Freaky Friday,* and *Mean Girls,* she was one of the top stars in Hollywood, commanding a salary of $7.5 million for such films as *Just My Luck, Georgia Rule,* and *Herbie Fully Loaded,* all made before she turned twenty. She had hit records and a clothing line and was a massive presence in print, electronic, and digital media. She was also deeply troubled, having been raised in a turbulent household and been thrust into the limelight since she was barely twelve years old. In the years before her spree at Chateau Marmont, she had been cited twice for driving under the influence and for violating the terms of the probation stemming from those charges. She was in and out of rehab. The studio boss financing one of her highest-paying jobs wrote her an angry letter about how her lifestyle was detrimental to the production, calling her "discourteous, irresponsible, and unprofessional . . .

a spoiled child [who has] alienated many of your co-workers and endangered the quality of this picture." Like so many of her poor choices, the diatribe went public.

There was always hope she could rebound; her exorbitant birthday party at the Chateau was only her twenty-sixth. But even as she was celebrating it, she was under a particularly sordid cloud, being named as a person of interest by the Los Angeles County district attorney in the alleged theft of $100,000 in designer watches and sunglasses from the home of an acquaintance, a suspicion of which she was eventually cleared. And as her hotel bills showed, she was still living at a torrid pace and burning bridges in the process.

�֎

The news of Lohan's staggering debt to Chateau Marmont surfaced about a month after she received her notice of eviction, when the entire hotel bill and Pavel's letter were published on the *TMZ* gossip website. For Lohan, this was yet another awkward bit of negative publicity, but for Chateau Marmont it was a potential disaster. Fearful of scaring away other celebrity guests who might avoid the place if they thought that details of *their* activity at the hotel would emerge, the Chateau immediately issued an exculpatory statement: "Chateau Marmont places guest privacy as a core value and upholds this privacy with paramount importance. After investigation, it appears that a private correspondence between Chateau Marmont's general manager and Miss Lohan was leaked by a member of her entourage. We are as horrified, disappointed and troubled by this occurrence as Miss Lohan surely is." Lohan's publicist was mum: "We are not commenting on anything to do with Chateau Marmont." The Lifetime network, which would air *Liz & Dick*, washed its hands of the whole situation, offering no comment other than to tell journalists that it wasn't responsible for Lohan's bills.

From the hotel's vantage, the situation called for a fine

hand—and so, in stepped the owner himself. André Balazs was said to have relationships with both Lohan and her mother, Dina, and working with them, he managed to find a way to settle the actress's debt. Before very long, she was seen at Chateau Marmont again as well as at other of Balazs's hotel properties in the United States and London, though never for so long a stay again, and probably not throwing herself any parties. (In an amusing coda, Lohan would go on to sue the makers of the *Grand Theft Auto* video games because the fifth edition of their franchise included a character that she claimed was based on her, down to the fact that the fictitious movie star once had a scandalous stay at Chateau Marmont.)

⚙

Lohan was famous, and it was almost a positive thing for the hotel if word got around that there was some celebrity naughtiness afoot under its roof. But there were limits to that sort of notoriety as well. It was one thing for the staff to have to see after big stars who were clearly out of order; it was another if those same famous people had news of their activities leak out into the world. Management, especially under Balazs, was extremely strict in ensuring the security of its guests. "We've brought criminal charges against employees who have in any way violated the privacy of the guests," he assured the press. Employment contracts included nondisclosure clauses limiting hirees from sharing stories or images of goings-on at the hotel, the restaurant, or Bar Marmont in either print or digital media, even after they no longer worked there. Guests, too, were monitored for any leaks of information, especially during the age of social media. The response to any trespass on this secrecy policy was usually swift and often severe.

In 2011, reality TV personality Jenn Hoffman found herself banned from the hotel for a year for sending out a single tweet that made mention of the eccentric behavior of a supermodel who was carrying on in plain view of everyone at the restaurant. When a journalist from *Adweek* inquired about the ban, Philip Pavel wrote back to explain that it wasn't the use of social media per se that offended but the content of the tweet: "The Chateau Marmont has built its success on creating an environment where the privacy of our guests is paramount. . . . [T]he decision to not allow certain guests in our hotel is based solely on this concept, and has nothing to do with whether one uses Twitter."

In 2013, journalist A. J. Daulerio wrote a blog post about a bird invading his Chateau bungalow, and in the course of it he mentioned that he was planning to live blog his dinner at the restaurant that night. That afternoon, he received a letter from Pavel apologizing for the avian intrusion, explaining that the hotel had left a complimentary bottle of vintage wine in the bungalow to make up for the ruckus, and informing him, gently, that the hotel's policies forbade his intended social media event. "Our hotel's success has been about doing everything we can to protect the privacy of our guests," the letter read, "so we ask that you please respect our rule forbidding unauthorized photography, video, or internet posts about our guests while in house. The best part about my job is that this hotel attracts clever and fun people like yourself—I would hate to have to ask you to leave as a result of this policy being crossed."

The irony of this was that the hotel was forced to insist on strict measures to guard guests and patrons because Balazs had succeeded *too well* in turning it into a magnet for celebrities. As Jay McInerney once put it, "André tends to know the kind of people in New York and L.A. who make for a happening scene. Certainly any of the beautiful people who weren't already staying at the Chateau have probably switched allegiance." With the cachet of all those famous faces, with all those red-carpet parties and swaggy award-season suites, came a plague that had previously been unknown at the hotel—paparazzi—and then, in the age of the smart phone, the stolen-moment photo or video of a celebrity that could seep out into the world before the subject captured in it even knew it had been taken. For decades, Chateau Marmont was a sanctum sanctorum; in the twenty-first century, it was a place to be seen, to dress up for, to queue to get into, to share images of with absent chums to make them feel jealous they weren't there. It had once been a hideaway; it had become center stage.

✻

The question of privacy became extremely acute on Thursday, November 9, 2017, when the *New York Times* Style section featured a story about Balazs on its front page. This wasn't the first time he had been seen and name-dropped prominently in that outlet; his 1985 wedding to Katie Ford was announced in its pages, and he'd been profiled and promoted in several front-page Style features during his rise as a hotelier and man-about-town. But in this instance he, his family, his publicist, his lawyer, and his business partners were likely not sharing the article with any glee or relish. In the rising tide of the Me Too and Time's Up movements—sex abuse allegations against politicians, publishers, and, especially, show business figures, including the *Times*'s own exposé of movie mogul Harvey Weinstein—Balazs was accused of four acts of sexual assault, one against the actress Amanda Anka,* one against an unnamed Manhattan media executive, one against a former Chateau Marmont front desk employee identified only as "Sarah," and one against another former Chateau employee, who was unnamed.

The act against Anka was the most specifically described. In November 2014, the actress was in London with her husband, actor Jason Bateman, to attend the premiere of his film *Horrible*

---

* Daughter of singer Paul Anka.

Bosses 2. A party was held after the screening at Balazs's Chiltern Firehouse hotel, and Balazs offered to give the guests a tour. He invited the partiers to climb a ladder to a spot that afforded a notable view of central London. Anka, who was wearing a short leather skirt, suggested that it would be risky to do so given the way she was attired. Balazs encouraged her and, as she climbed, according to several witnesses, "slipped a hand under her skirt and grabbed her crotch." Anka immediately told all present what happened and a fracas ensued, with Bateman confronting Balazs so angrily that he spit a wad of chewing gum into the hotelier's face. Bateman and Anka soon left the party, managing to put on happy—or at least blank—faces for the paparazzi outside the hotel. Actress Mary Elizabeth Ellis was among those on the scene, and she told the *Times,* "I witnessed behavior by André Balazs that was inappropriate and offensive." A spokesman for Anka confirmed that "the account of André Balazs's outrageous and vile behavior on that night in London is factual. His actions were dealt with at the time."

The assault described by "Sarah" evinced a similar behavior: a quick, surprise move on an unsuspecting woman in a semipublic setting. In 1991, according to the *Times,* Balazs was in Los Angeles to oversee work at Chateau Marmont and asked her out to dinner. After a quick meal, they went to a mud-wrestling club where, she said, "he grabbed her arm, pinned her against a wall and covered her mouth with his mouth. He put his hand down the front of her pants and pushed his fingers in her vagina." Her story was supported by a roommate with whom she shared it at the time. The Manhattan PR executive told yet another story of an attack with a similar modus operandi: A short while after being greeted by him at a New York Fashion Week party in 2013, the woman was walking to the bathroom when she "felt a presence behind her. She said she felt a hand reach between her legs from behind and grab her crotch. . . . She turned and saw Mr. Balazs." Again, her account was corroborated to the *Times* by a friend whom she told about the incident on the day it happened. Only one of the four stories in the article concerned a woman who escaped Balazs's touch, a former Chateau Marmont employee who said that her boss one time pinned her against an elevator wall and tried to kiss her but that she evaded him.

The *Times* reached out to Balazs and his publicist Pierre Rougier to no avail. But the revelations were damaging. The story was repeated in the pages and on the websites of newspapers and magazines in New York, London, and Los Angeles, as well as in Hollywood trade publications, and it spread throughout social media. From Miami, a reporter put out a query asking people to contact him if they had similar stories about Balazs's behavior in that city, and the model and actress Carolina Parsons claimed publicly that Balazs had grabbed her "by the waist very tight" when she was an eighteen-year-old guest of the hotelier and his then wife at a ballet performance. Calls started for boycotts of the properties that Balazs still owned, including Chateau Marmont, and for several days every innocuous story about some innocuous red-carpet event or celebrity sighting at the hotel made mention of the allegations against its owner.

It was a very delicate moment for Balazs and his empire. Chateau Marmont might not have been the largest or even the most profitable of his properties, but it was universally recognized as the most important. "He needs that hotel," said one observer. "Not because of the income but because of the cachet. It allows him to do good hotels elsewhere."

For a while, it seemed as though the storm would pass; official denials were issued, no further stories emerged, and Balazs was invisible to the press. And then, in January 2018, the hotel was explicitly cited in another *Times* story about sexual assault, this time involving the celebrated fashion photographer Mario Testino, one of the many famous photographers who regularly used Chateau Marmont as a setting for shoots or for socializing with clients and models. In a carefully documented story, the *Times* reported that Testino forced himself on many of the young men whom he photographed in ad campaigns for Gucci, *Vogue,* and other world-renowned brands and media outlets. "If you wanted to work with Mario," said the former model Jason Fedele, "you needed to do a nude shoot at the Chateau Marmont. All the agents knew that this was the thing to excel or advance your career." Fedele went on to describe Testino's clumsy efforts to grope him or pull off his towel during a photo session, and his story matched those of other models and assistants who claimed that Testino behaved in a similarly predatory manner with them in hotel rooms. The charges—a rarer case of sexual assault against men to surface during the Me Too movement—led to *Vogue* and other magazines published by Condé Nast announcing they would no longer be commissioning work from Testino or photographer Bruce Weber, whose predatory behavior was also cited at length in the *Times* article.

⚜

In March 2017, after more than twenty swanky, celebrity-kissed years, Bar Marmont shut its doors, a sign of yet another turn of the page in the history of the Sunset Strip. Two years earlier, the House of Blues had closed, bulldozed to make way for a high-rise hotel, condos, and shopping space. Other Strip lots were similarly being bought up and transformed, with tall, opulent, pricey new buildings planned for their locations. The renaissance of the street, heralded in no small part by André Balazs's purchase and rejuvenation of Chateau Marmont, was entering a big-buildings, big-money, big-ballyhoo phase notable even among the most gilded eras of the Strip's brazen history.

Across Sunset Boulevard from the Chateau, where the Garden of Allah once stood, developers were proposing a five-building, 330,000-square-foot complex designed by architect Frank Gehry in his signature wavy-metal style that would include approximately 250 units of housing and 60,000 square feet of retail space. In April 2017, their plans were put on hold, however, for the most ironic of reasons: The previous year, the Lytton Savings building, which stood on the grounds that had once housed the Garden of Allah, was declared a Historic-Cultural Monument by the Los Angeles Office of Historic Resources. A building that had itself wiped away a significant slice of Hollywood history without so much as a by-your-leave was declared a work of art, "constructed in a distinctive Mid-Century Modern style that melds Googie and New Formalist stylistic influences." The builders would have to find a way to incorporate the Lytton building into their design or reconfigure the project altogether. A year later, the decree preserving the bank was reversed by courts, and demolition was once again likely.

Balazs, for his part, had no intention of razing Bar Marmont. Plans were made to introduce a new food-and-drink concept in the building it occupied.* In the meantime it continued to serve as a party space for occasional special events. And, as the use of its garage for an Oscar after party hosted by Beyoncé and Jay-Z in 2018 showed, there was no lack of interest, among the highest-flying names in showbiz, in gathering in and around Chateau Marmont. The Strip might continue to evolve, to the sound of bulldozers, pile drivers, and cement mixers, but the Chateau would stay, more than ever, an oasis of tradition, gentility, and calm.

6.

It was ironic. When Fred Horowitz first drove out of Los Angeles proper to the wilderness of West Hollywood, there was virtually nothing standing between him and the Beverly Hills city line, where the resumption of the paved road was declared

---

* In 2018, with almost no advance fanfare, the hotel opened Chateau Hanare, a high-end Japanese restaurant, in an unused bungalow on the property.

with the city's familiar coat of arms, a brown-and-gold shield. Staking an audacious claim to the eastern end of the dirt road connecting the two cities, he saw a day when the rutted thoroughfare would be paved, populated, maybe even celebrated. He had envisioned his castle, his Xanadu, as if in a dream, and unlike Kublai Khan and Charles Foster Kane he actually saw it through to completion, even if he didn't, finally, oversee its fullest fruition.

It was left to his successors Albert Smith and Erwin Brettauer to convert the building into its optimal function—as a hotel—and to deck it out with bungalows, a swimming pool, and a shield of its own: a red, blue, and yellow neon sign modestly identifying it as a hotel. During their thirty-plus combined years of ownership, the Chateau took on the identity it maintains today: a haven for celebrities, a lockbox of secrets, a place where people whose lives are lived outside the ordinary lines of propriety or the dominant culture can be safe, welcome, and, yes, pampered.

A series of indifferent owners threatened that status; the Chateau became "funky" if not a downright dive. But Ray Sarlot and Karl Kantarjian rescued it from potential wreckage, and Sarlot, especially, kept it vital with the builder's equivalent of mouth-to-mouth resuscitation. And then André Balazs came in, polishing what Sarlot had salvaged and sprinkling it so thoroughly with stardust that not even an appalling scandal involving its owner could threaten its station in the Hollywood firmament.

At age ninety, the Chateau is more youthful, polished, famous, and chic than it has ever been. It has credibly been cast by its current keepers into a repository of a past that didn't seem so grand when it was happening but has taken on the sheen and glow of gold through the remove of time. And it presides over the Sunset Strip with a stateliness that has always seemed slightly incongruous and now, in the age of social media and instantly self-destructing cultural moments, seems positively medieval.

But then, that was what Fred Horowitz was hoping to build:

a castle, a fortress, a keep, a place that would at once suggest an enduring history while looking forward to a buzzing future that he couldn't have imagined.

In an onion field on a dirt road, he envisioned something grand and permanent and alluring—and, though he might not have seen it that way, completely incongruous.

And he built it, and it all happened more or less as he imagined, not under his aegis, not right away, not without hiccups and diversions, but ultimately and surely.

In its way, Chateau Marmont has been essential and inevitable, its impact on its neighborhood and the business of show inestimable, its legend both unlikely and undeniable.

You can't fully tell the history of Hollywood movies or the Sunset Strip without making reference to it; it sits inside a pair of stories in which, technically, as an inanimate edifice of concrete, steel, wood, and glass, it has taken no part. Stately, steady, solid, redoubtable, it presides over its setting—literal and figurative—with an air of patient boredom. All the sensations that have transpired within and without it, all the zealots and visionaries and schemers and charlatans who've inhabited it, all the deals—of all sorts—that have been sparked or completed or scuttled within its confines: It's a saga of weight and drama and impact befitting an entity of far longer and more storied history.

Chateau Marmont isn't as old as Hollywood or as large or as influential. It doesn't define the Sunset Strip or symbolize it or embody its greatest legends. But it is intrinsic to the stories of both those institutions.

It is the castle that Hollywood and the Sunset Strip have always needed, a place outside time, indifferent, dependable, immutable, permanent, a man-made thing that couldn't be more ordinary and, at the same time, a thing of dreams and ambitions and aspirations that couldn't possibly be real, providing a grounding materiality to a business and a street that often seem apt to waft off into the ether out of sheer weightlessness and evanescence. It anchors Hollywood, figuratively, just as it anchors the Strip, literally, and it gives visible shape and tactile permanence to both.

It hasn't always been there, the castle on the Strip, and yet it has.

ACKNOWLEDGMENTS

Considering how much time one spends alone in writing a book, it's always remarkable to realize how many people contribute to it.

In this case, I start with the idea itself, which came to me from my editor, Yaniv Soha, who put a seed in my head that blossomed instantly into a vision of an entire book. The finished project may not be as perfect as the one I saw in that astonishing moment, but that diminishes by not one watt the brilliance of Yaniv's idea.

As ever, I worked at and with a number of hallowed institutions: the Multnomah County Library (the Central and Hillsdale branches and the indispensable interlibrary loan department); the Central Library of the Los Angeles Public Library; the Pasadena Public Library; the Billy Rose Theatre Division of the New York Public Library; the Margaret Herrick Library of the Academy of Motion Picture Arts and Sciences; and, though not technically libraries, Photofest in New York and Movie Madness and Powell's City of Books in Portland. I'm indebted to staff and management at all of them.

I was also afforded the kindness of individuals who shared memories, pointed to resources, offered insights, and generally supported me and my work in spirit and deed: Tim Appelo, Karin and Margo Brettauer, Mickey Cottrell, David Cress, Jennifer and Jason Freeland, Allan Glaser, Ari Gold, Herbert Gold, Tab Hunter, Alejandro Jodorowsky, John Krasinski, Harley Lond, Kim Morgan, Dewey Nicks, Danna Schaefer, Paul Schrader, Jeffrey Schwartz, Allyson Seeger, Tom Shales, Missy Stewart, Gus Van Sant, Willy Vlautin, Bruce Wagner, Marc Wanamaker, and Carrie White, as well as several others who expressed a desire to stay nameless.

At Doubleday, I thank, of course, Yaniv, as well as Cara Reilly and Bill Thomas, who first took a chance on me in 1992 and whose faith and enthusiasm I've never forgotten. And I am grateful to Ingrid Sterner for a lifesaving (and face-saving) job of copyediting.

At InkWell Management, I thank Eliza Rothstein and, perennially, Richard Pine, who has been with me since very nearly the outset of this unlikely career. Thanks—or, in this case, a dedication—don't begin to pay my debt.

At home Paula, Anthony, and Vincent Levy provide all the reasons for all the things.

And Shannon Brazil has been pretty dang much everything I could want, need, or ask for in a partner. Thank you so much, baby.

NOTES

INTRODUCTION

1   "The Chateau is a fluke": Scott Busby, "Tales of the Chateau Marmont," *L.A. Weekly,* April 8–14, 1983, 13.

2   "You can have": Chris Hodenfield, "Tales of the Chateau," *Los Angeles Times Magazine,* Sept. 14, 1986.

2   "Just check in": Anthony Haden-Guest, "Castle Kitsch," *Los Angeles Times West Magazine,* Sept. 12, 1971, 20.

7   "The Chateau is the only cheap": Ibid., 21.

PART ONE. THE DREAM (1927–1932)

21   "an architect may supervise": "Court Favors Architect," *Architect and Engineer,* Oct. 1930, 111.

23   "Never before in the history": Myrna Nye, "Social Affair Makes History," *Los Angeles Times,* Jan. 8, 1929.

23   "gentlemen judges and their wives": Alma Whitaker, "Sugar and Spice," *Los Angeles Times,* Jan. 20, 1929.

24   "The place had more doors": Sarlot and Basten, *Life at the Marmont,* 66.

24   "There were rooms, cubbyholes": Sam Wasson, "Chateau Marmont Celebrates 85 Years," *Los Angeles Confidential,* Feb. 3, 2014.

PART TWO. A SECOND BIRTH (1932–1942)

35   "During the past weeks": "Apartments Justify Faith," *Los Angeles Times,* May 1, 1932.

36   "was why the hotel became": Hodenfield, "Tales of the Chateau."

37   "I heard the other girls": *Ohio Statesman Journal,* undated clipping, New York Public Library.

37   "I could find my way": Gardner Bradford, "When Ann Little Got to the Peak . . . She Stepped Up!," *Los Angeles Times,* March 5, 1933, 5.

38   "I enjoy feats of horsemanship": "Some Preferences of Ann Little, Actress," *Los Angeles Times,* Aug. 18, 1918.

39   "I do not like sentences": Ibid.

39   "The tough tenants": Bradford, "When Ann Little Got to the Peak," 20.

40   "Everyone was high class": Sarlot and Basten, *Life at the Marmont*, 66.

40   "I had just come downstairs": Ibid., 34.

41   "My picture experience": Bradford, "When Ann Little Got to the Peak," 20.

41   "What are you doing here?": Sarlot and Basten, *Life at the Marmont*, 37.

41   "fingering the keys": Ibid., 239.

42   "that nice German": Alma Whitaker, "Sugar and Spice," *Los Angeles Times*, Dec. 11, 1932.

46   "Rachmaninoff has the next": William Overend, "From Poinsettias to Punk: A History of the Sunset Strip," *Los Angeles Times*, Nov. 26, 1981.

49   "It tells people where we are": Bob Bishop, "Where WeHo's Streets Got Their Names: Part 2," www.wehoville.com, July 6, 2016.

50   "The Trocadero was probably": Overend, "From Poinsettias to Punk."

52   "It was like a duty": Hodenfield, "Tales of the Chateau."

52   "I'd take over mostly sandwiches": Graham, *Garden of Allah*, 84.

57   "Oh heavens no!": Tia Gindick, "Reaping Memories of a Heyday," *Los Angeles Times*, Oct. 23, 1977.

59   "I know it's trite": Stenn, *Bombshell*, 138.

62   "She was like a little white rose": Barbara Wilkins, "Chateau—Last Elegance on the Strip," *Los Angeles Times*, Jan. 8, 1967.

67   "call[ing] him harsh names": "Bacon Files Divorce Action," *Los Angeles Examiner*, Oct. 30, 1935.

68   "break every bone": "Ruby Bacon Divorced," *Los Angeles Examiner*, Dec. 19, 1935.

69   "Harry really worried": Sarlot and Basten, *Life at the Marmont*, 71.

70   "It was so very private": Ibid., 74.

70   "only two friends": Ibid., 72.

71   "She was Lady Maud": Sperber and Lax, *Bogart*, 96.

71   "She died as she had lived": Ibid., 138.

72   "They were such nice people": Sarlot and Basten, *Life at the Marmont*, 31.

72   "There will be nets": Joe Bullmore, "No Rest for the Wicket: Hollywood Cricket Club," *Rake*, Jan. 2017.

75   "He stayed in his room": Sarlot and Basten, *Life at the Marmont*, 53.

76   "I forgot to notify": Lally, *Wilder Times*, 68.

77   "I could not sleep": Zolotow, *Billy Wilder in Hollywood*, 60.

80   "une idée poetique": Jacobs, *Christmas in July*, 179.

80   "the center of the Hollywood Resistance": Ibid., 245.

81   "I am very much afraid": Ibid., 391.

84   "fully improved estate": "Chateau Marmont in Hollywood Sold," *Los Angeles Times*, July 3, 1942.

PART THREE. AN IDENTITY EMERGES (1942–1963)

93   "It seemed cold": Karin and Margo Brettauer, author interview.

102   "a navel filled with sweat": Vidal, *Palimpsest*, 278.

102   "My father always made us": Karin and Margo Brettauer, author interview.

107   "They must have meant": Babitz, *Slow Days, Fast Company*, 139.

109   "So they pick up the phone": Sam Wasson, "Hotel California," *Angeleno*, Jan. 2011.

112   "Arnaz was a semipermanent resident": Sanders and Gilbert, *Desilu*, 182.

114   "It was very important in those days": Paul Hendrickson, "The Newmans: Fast Eddie and Eve in Paradise," *Washington Post*, Dec. 6, 1992.

117   "The Chateau is where all New Yorkers stay": Haden-Guest, "Castle Kitsch," 19.

118   "I was sure my place": Charles Champlin, "Jack Lemmon: It Should Happen to You," *Los Angeles Times*, July 31, 1984.

121   "If there had been an Olympic sex team": Winters, *Shelley II*, 103.

122   "I started to scream": Ibid., 192.

123   "For the rest of the filming": Ibid., 193.

126   "I didn't like her very much": Ray, *I Was Interrupted*, 173.

128   "He liked the Marmont": Eisenschitz, *Nicholas Ray*, 236.

129   "They had this big write-up": Ibid., 277.

129   "I want to make a film that I love": McGilligan, *Nicholas Ray*, 263.

130   "I drove up to Nick's": Eisenschitz, *Nicholas Ray*, 257.

131   "Are you middle-aged?": Ray, *I Was Interrupted*, 109.

133   "Oh, for God's sake, Dennis!": Folsom, *Hopper*, 39.

133   "Jimmy was peculiarly silent": Ray, *I Was Interrupted*, 110.

134   "enthroned," as Stern remembered: McGilligan, *Nicholas Ray*, 276.

135   "I'd like to fuck you": Winkler, *Dennis Hopper*, 26.

136   "I just kept repeating the number": Lambert, *Natalie Wood*, 90.

136   "They called me a goddamn juvenile delinquent": Winkler, *Dennis Hopper*, 30.

136   "I went to Nick Ray's hotel": Eisenschitz, *Nicholas Ray*, 242.

137   "rather openly having an affair": Vidal, *Palimpsest*, 278.

138   "See, that's your problem": Winkler, *Dennis Hopper*, 32.

139   "We had one rehearsal": Eisenschitz, *Nicholas Ray*, 260.

141   remembered bringing many "tricks": Bowers, *Full Service*, 218.

142   "That was the center of the universe": Winecoff, *Split Image*, 103.

143   "Who've you got who's different?": Bowers, *Full Service*, 217.

144   "I'd go take a dip": Hunter, author interview.

145   "Despite its prominence": Hunter, *Tab Hunter Confidential*, 130.

145   "tall and skinny": Ibid.

145   "But I love him!": Winecoff, *Split Image*, 124.

145   "Nothing," Hunter recalled: Hunter, *Tab Hunter Confidential*, 131.

145   "And the New York actors": Hunter, author interview.

146   "He was very circumspect": Winecoff, *Split Image*, 117.

146   "eating ice cream": Hedda Hopper, "Hudson Takes on Another Comedy," *Los Angeles Times*, March 11, 1964.

148   "I introduced him": Parini, *Empire of Self*, 120.

148   "Life at the Chateau Marmont": Kaplan, *Gore Vidal*, 394.

148   "We would meet Paul and Joanne": Parini, *Empire of Self*, 119–20.

148   "Gore liked clean-cut guys": Ibid., 120.

149   "One significant thing": Vidal, *Snapshots in History's Glare*, 152.

149   "He sees what he thinks": Kaplan, *Gore Vidal*, 412.

150   "a beautiful boy": Tim Teeman, "How Gay Was Gore Vidal?," *Daily Beast*, July 31, 2013.

153   "the outsize floozie": Brooks Atkinson, "Critic at Large: In Hollywood the Best and Worst Coexist Without Being Aware of Each Other," *New York Times*, Feb. 14, 1964.

154   "It's the whore Hollywood!": Sarlot and Basten, *Life at the Marmont*, 188.

154   "He pointed to the window": Rhonda Koenig, "Checking In to Limbo," *Independent* (London), Nov. 25, 2004.

154   "There he was," he said: Wasson, "Hotel California."

154   "She has not lost any of her fingers": Atkinson, "Critic at Large: In Hollywood the Best and Worst Coexist Without Being Aware of Each Other."

155   "She revolves slowly": Cheever, *Stories of John Cheever*, 583.

155   "Oh, God," he remembered: Peabody and Ebersole, *Conversations with Gore Vidal*, 71.

156   "to brighten my hotel rooms": Sarlot and Basten, *Life at the Marmont*, 198.

158   "My heart lurched": Brad Darrach, "My Romance with Marilyn Monroe," *People*, July 2, 1984.

159   "Had not someone in a nearby room": Stine, *Mother Goddamn*, 284.

159   "[She] said she'd never be back": Wilkins, "Chateau—Last Elegance on the Strip."

160   "Go to the elevator": Sarlot and Basten, *Life at the Marmont*, 214.

162   "He'd get up late": Miller, *Martin Ritt*, 170.

163   "Duke concocted his arrangement": Irvine Townsend, liner notes, *Swinging Suites*, 1961.

163   "I just imagine that I'm the ball": Gottlieb, *Reading Jazz*, 425.

163   "in a swell-elegant hotel": A. S. Young, "The Big Beat," *Los Angeles Sentinel*, June 20, 1960.

164   "She isn't here, motherfucker": Szwed, *So What*, 243.

164   "I speak about this with pain": Murray Schumach, "Poitier Says Bias Exists on Coast," *New York Times*, Aug. 19, 1960.

165   "we both lost": Poitier, *This Life*, 228.

167   "There was definitely a feeling": Priore, *Riot on Sunset Strip*, 37.

168   "Wine and beer bottles": Gilmore, *Laid Bare*, 154–55.

169   "I made several trips": Medina, *Laid Back in Hollywood*, 93.

169   "to be clever around men": Babitz, *Eve's Hollywood*, 99.

169   "You can't tear down places": Babitz, *Slow Days, Fast Company*, 140.

170   "In the end it took refuge": Ibid., 161.

170   "I don't think he had too many": Karin and Margo Brettauer, author interview.

PART FOUR. TUMULT AND DECAY (1963–1975)

174   "completely neglectful of his family": "Wife Granted Divorce and Eventual $600,175," *Los Angeles Times*, April 14, 1965.

175   "We added some touches": Sarlot and Basten, *Life at the Marmont*, 211.

178   "The value of the homes above the Strip": Overend, "From Poinsettias to Punk."

178   "It was almost impossible to travel": William Overend, "When the Sun Set on the Strip," *Los Angeles Times*, Nov. 27, 1981.

183   "I once stayed next door": Anthony Haden-Guest, "Heartbreak Hotel," *Mode*, Oct./Nov. 1994.

183   "We'd all sit around the edge of the bed": Kubernik, *Canyon of Dreams*, 209.

183   "if they had, out they'd have gone": Sarlot and Basten, *Life at the Marmont*, 220.

183   "For some reason": Gary Baum and Michael Walker, "Sunset Marquis: Secrets of Rock-n-Roll's Wild Hotel," *Hollywood Reporter*, Feb. 8, 2013.

184   "The Chateau Marmont was cool": Ibid.

184   "I had to move here": Dan Knapp, "Morrison's Last Days in L.A.: Hope for the Future," *Los Angeles Times*, July 25, 1971.

185   "got up on the roof": Ibid.

186   "He never used to get hurt": Densmore, *Riders on the Storm*, 258.

186   "He looked very bizarre": Wilkins, "Chateau—Last Elegance on the Strip."

189   "It's not a pleasant thing": Ken Reich, "Teen-Agers and Crime Ply the Sunset Strip," *Los Angeles Times*, Jan. 16, 1966.

192   " 'Riot' is a ridiculous name": Cecilia Rasmussen, "Closing of Club Ignited the 'Sunset Strip Riots,' " *Los Angeles Times*, Aug. 5, 2007.

193   "The peasants are revolting": Sarlot and Basten, *Life at the Marmont*, 266.

194   "It was nice spending the Riots in a penthouse": Babitz, *Eve's Hollywood*, 144.

196   "I think they want to win": Dave Felton, "Hippies Pout, Politicians Cheer as Pandora's Box Is Wrecked," *Los Angeles Times*, Aug. 4, 1967.

196   "This is a sad town": Haden-Guest, "Castle Kitsch," 19.

197   "How sorry I am": Weaver, *Glad Tidings*, 200.

197   "From where I sit": Vidal, *Myra Breckinridge*, 8.

198   "Three in the morning": Ibid., 178.

198   "For me," Myra writes: Ibid., 77.

198   "much too much": Ibid., 10.

198   "resembles an upside-down two-leaf clover": Ibid., 8.

199   "a tired, smirking elephant": Howard Thompson, " 'Myra Breckinridge' Unveiled on Screen," *New York Times*, June 25, 1970.

199   "both dirtier and more aberrant": Charles Champlin, " 'Myra Breckinridge' Plays on Decadence," *Los Angeles Times*, June 25, 1970.

199   "about as funny as a child molester": "Some Sort of Nadir," *Time*, July 6, 1970.

199   "I believe he is working": Peabody and Ebersole, *Conversations with Gore Vidal*, 71.

203   "It was very kind of exotic": Homes, *Los Angeles*, 28.

203   "would invite one and all": Matt Mullen, "Intimate Images of Joan Didion Through the Years," www.interviewmagazine.com, Oct. 20, 2017.

204   "I was so aware of people": Sam Kashner, "The Making of 'The Graduate,' " *Vanity Fair*, March 2008.

206   "Sharon loved its rundown appearance": Polanski, *Roman*, 268.

206   "It was a congenially seedy": Richard Sylbert, "Sunset Roost," *Interview*, Oct. 1988.

208   "It was a pretty cushy deal": Unterberger, *Eight Miles High*, 107.

209   "I think I've done everything": Busby, "Tales of the Chateau Marmont," 10.

210   "The only roles being offered": Roderick Mann, "Cort Gets the Keys to 'Bates Motel,' " *Los Angeles Times*, June 29, 1987.

210   "I tried to talk to them": Dana Shapiro, "Deconstructing Harold," *New York Times*, Dec. 17, 2211.

210   "We both at the same time gasped": Ibid.

211   "The band were like a little family": Michael Bonner, " 'We Were Like a Little Family': An Interview with Doug Yule and Moe Tucker About the Velvet Underground," www.uncut.co.uk, Dec. 5, 2014.

211   "I was up at four in the morning": Ibid.

211   "I went there for a night": Hodenfield, "Tales of the Chateau."

212   "It was late at night": McDonough, *Shakey*, 430.

213   "OH SHIT," she remembered: Simon, *Boys in the Trees*, 251–52.

215   "You had to know what he was saying": Shales, author interview.

215   "Dracula answering the phone": Hodenfield, "Tales of the Chateau."

215   "the rustle of bats' wings": Ibid.

215   "It was like performance art": Homes, *Los Angeles*, 136.

216   "Alice Cooper look-alike": Busby, "Tales of the Chateau Marmont," 15.

216   "I would never dream of using": Haden-Guest, "Castle Kitsch."

PART FIVE. RESCUE AND RESTORATION (1975–1990)

220   "twin . . . right next door": Grace Glueck, "Peep Shows and Put-Ons," *New York Times*, April 6, 1969.

220   "One day I was in the elevator": Nicks, author interview.

220   "run by eccentrics": Marian Christy, "Carol Lynley—a Free Spirit," *Boston Globe*, Jan. 7, 1973.

221   "The shower knob came off": Wasson, "Hotel California."

221   "The only reason anything was off-white": Babitz, *Black Swans*, 60.

221   "the kind of people who *like* to spill things": Eve Babitz, "Better Days," *Esquire*, Jan. 1992.

221   "people would come in": Sarlot and Basten, *Life at the Marmont*, 283.

221   "started to chain the furniture": Carol Lynley, "Me and My Chateau," *L.A. Weekly*, Aug. 29, 1986.

222   "You start at the Montecito": Victor Navasky, "It's Shabby-Genteel but the Stars Love It," *New York Times*, May 5, 1974.

222   "Folklore is folklore": "Letters: Pursuing New Travel Records," *New York Times*, May 26, 1974.

223   "The bank was ready to foreclose": Sarlot and Basten, *Life at the Marmont*, 286.

223   "Occupancy had never been a problem": Ibid., 288.

223   "He fell in love with the place": Elaine Woo, "Raymond Sarlot, 1924–2014; Investor Restored Chateau Marmont," *Los Angeles Times*, May 11, 2014.

223   "When I came in here": Art Seidenbaum, "Renaissance of the Marmont," *Los Angeles Times*, May 27, 1977.

224   "Well, they repainted": Tom Burke, "Can Tuesday Be a '70s Star?," *Chicago Tribune*, Jan. 22, 1978.

224   "Probably the only reason": Hodenfield, "Tales of the Chateau."

225   "forever popping a button": Woo, "Raymond Sarlot, 1924–2014."

229   "a more enduring urban monument": Aaron Betsky, "Marlboro Man Billboard Stands as Image of Our Episodic Culture," *Los Angeles Times*, Dec. 26, 1991.

229   "My world was in ruins": Polanski, *Roman*, 377.

230   "listen[ing] to some doleful jazz": Sanford, *Polanski*, 231.

230   "I'd crossed the fine line": Polanski, *Roman*, 379.

231   "The judge seemed determined": Ibid., 400.

232   "I moved into a bungalow": James, *Glow*, 235.

233   "He stiffed us": Gaye, *Marvin Gaye, My Brother*, 105.

233   "I stayed at the Chateau Marmont": Roderick Mann, "Bianca's Living Down Her 'Frivolous Image,'" *Los Angeles Times*, Sept. 4, 1977.

234   "We don't want to go out": Hodenfield, "Tales of the Chateau."

234   "They don't walk out here": Jack Smith, "L.A. Walker Treads Water," *Los Angeles Times*, Nov. 4, 1970.

235   "I lived all around": Sarlot and Basten, *Life at the Marmont*, 281.

235   "Are you sure you want": Woodward, *Wired*, 303.

236   "He would pace around": Al Reinert, "Lost in Space," *Texas Monthly*, Feb. 1990.

237   "*Sunset Boulevard*," she repeated: Woodward, *Wired*, 371.

240   "There has been a slight disturbance": Sarlot and Basten, *Life at the Marmont*, 294.

241   "I'm having trouble": Brillstein, *Where Did I Go Right?*, 206.

242   "like a little stuttered giggle": Ibid., 207.

242   "It was bedlam": Sarlot and Basten, *Life at the Marmont*, 294.

242   "Where's John?" he asked her: Woodward, *Wired*, 405.

243   "It was the first time": Sarlot and Basten, *Life at the Marmont*, 294.

243   "as though he had gone to bed": Ron Harris and Michael Seiler, "Actor John Belushi Found Dead in Hollywood Hotel," *Los Angeles Times*, March 6, 1982.

243   "New York people": Levy, *De Niro*, 348.

244   "What people don't realize": Hodenfield, "Tales of the Chateau."

244   "We need somebody like you": Busby, "Tales of the Chateau Marmont."

245   "The scene was not only depressing": Brillstein, *Where Did I Go Right?*, 209.

245   "It was no longer the same unit": Sarlot and Basten, *Life at the Marmont*, 297.

246   "came to town and looked": Brillstein, *Where Did I Go Right?*, 211.

247   "He painted a portrait": Shales and Miller, *Live from New York*, 275.

247   "Woodward—that cocksucker": Ibid.

247   "He made it sound": Mary A. Fischer, "Author Bob Woodward Trashed a Famous Hollywood Hostelry, Then Had to List It as a Coming Retraction," *People*, July 23, 1984.

247   "Ray had spent so much time": Woo, "Raymond Sarlot, 1924–2014."

247   "It was the author's opinion": Fischer, "Author Bob Woodward Trashed a Famous Hollywood Hostelry."

248   "The Chateau has a charming": Ibid.

248   "tell Feldman who did this": Feldman, *Tell Me How You Love the Picture*, 163.

248   "exceptional. . . . It deals with the themes": Jack Matthews, "Crowd Jeers, Walks Out on 'Wired,'" *Los Angeles Times*, May 19, 1989.

249   "They told me they were putting me up": George F. Will, "A 'Catcher' for the '80s," *Washington Post*, Feb. 27, 1986.

249   "a small, elderly man": Busby, "Tales of the Chateau Marmont," 11.

249   "It is a place apart": Quentin Crisp, "Visiting Lotusland," *New York Times*, May 16, 1982.

250   "a back room": Roderick Mann, "Frank Perry Comes in from Critics' Cold," *Los Angeles Times*, Sept. 8, 1985.

251   "funky—not quite dumpy": Shales, author interview.

252   "I remember arriving": Steven Zeitchik, "A 'Bizarre' Music Duet: Cusack, Giamatti Take a Deep Dive into Brian Wilson's Life," *Los Angeles Times*, April 26, 2015.

252   "I was living by myself": Kristine McKenna, "On the Rebound with Anthony Michael Hall," *Los Angeles Times*, April 3, 1988.

252   "My wife and I were sitting": Wasson, "Hotel California."

253   "Happy holidays from everyone": Rupert Everett, "Unmasked," *Vogue*, March 2013.

253   "If someone spun you": Jean Nathan, "What's Up in the Old Hotel?," *New York Times*, Aug. 1, 1993.

254   "I hope you enjoy reading": Homes, *Los Angeles*, 38.

254   "my dorm for 15 years": Joanne Kaufman, "If the Marmont's So 'Seedy,' Why Is It a Retreat for the Elite?," *Chicago Tribune*, Aug. 5, 1984.

254   "Oh, don't mention the hotel!": Gordon, *Ultimate Hollywood*, 120.

255   "This ain't rock 'n' roll": Overend, "When the Sun Set on the Strip."

PART SIX. A GOLDEN AGE (1990–2019)

258   "They wanted to mind-fuck": Carlos Greer and Ian Mohr, "Jay-Z and Beyoncé Wanted to 'Mind-Fuck' VIPs at Secret Oscars Party," *New York Post*, March 5, 2018.

264   "It's surprisingly closed-minded": Vanessa Grigoriadis, "Prince Street Prince," *New York*, Oct. 31, 2005.

265   "For my thesis": Ibid.

265   "I couldn't write fast enough": Julie V. Iovine, "Granting Entry to the Land of the Hip," *New York Times*, Dec. 12, 2004.

265   "how much control one had": Lucie Young, "He Makes Princely Hotels out of Frogs," *New York Times*, July 10, 1997.

265   "There was a big dichotomy": Grigoriadis, "Prince Street Prince."

266   "The fact he is Hungarian": Charlotte Edwardes, "Hotelier André Balazs'
       Deliciously Naughty Life," *Tatler,* June 14, 2017.

266   "master of taking credit": Young, "He Makes Princely Hotels out of
       Frogs."

267   "We never really wanted": Ron Russell, "Hip or Not So Hip," *Los Angeles
       Times,* April 10, 1989.

268   "It felt like a very neglected": Janelle Brown, "The Chateau Marmont Is
       Ready for Its Close-Up," *New York Times,* Dec. 3, 2010.

268   "A lot of people hated": Haden-Guest, "Heartbreak Hotel."

268   "The full weight": Nathan, "What's Up in the Old Hotel?"

268   "It was not initially clear": Michael Kaplan, "Resurrecting the Mar-
       mont," *Graphis,* Jan./Feb. 1996.

269   "Things from different eras": Ibid.

269   "We scoured archives": Haden-Guest, "Heartbreak Hotel."

269   "It was important not to be": Helaine Olen, "Battle of the Hollywood Hide-
       aways Pits a Legend Against Luxury," *New York Times,* Nov. 10, 1996.

270   "I don't think he has": Young, "He Makes Princely Hotels out of Frogs."

270   "We put ourselves into the minds": Glynis Costin, "Hollywood Love
       Nest," *Elle Decor,* April/May 1995.

270   "It's not a real past": Young, "He Makes Princely Hotels out of Frogs."

270   "To me, the greatest sign": Kaplan, "Resurrecting the Marmont."

270   "So little has been changed": Babitz, "Better Days."

271   "I can't tell you": Nathan, "What's Up in the Old Hotel?"

271   "If the romantic depressiveness": Babitz, "Better Days."

271   "Oh no! I've lost": Nathan, "What's Up in the Old Hotel?"

271   " 'Nobody's going to believe' ": Babitz, *Black Swans,* 82.

272   "When they first ran": Kaplan, "Resurrecting the Marmont."

272   "He admires artists": Edwardes, "Hotelier André Balazs' Deliciously
       Naughty Life."

273   "I think a lot of people": David Wharton, "Poetry Books a Room at the
       Chateau," *Los Angeles Times,* Sept. 29, 1991.

273   "Ridiculous! People come here": Anthony Haden-Guest, "Castle Babylon,
       Hollywood," *Independent Magazine,* July 16, 1994.

274   "I lived, worked, and conceived": Busby, "Tales of the Chateau Marmont."

274   "The grand, mysterious house": Wagner, author interview.

276   "Harvey was in bed": Wasson, "Hotel California."

277   "as if a wonderful party": Balazs, *Chateau Marmont Hollywood Hand-
       book,* 227.

278   "One of my earliest memories": Wasson, "Hotel California."

278   "Norma Desmond's living room": Tony Castro, "Celebrity Crime Reporter
       Inspired by Own Tragedy," *New York Daily News,* Sept. 27, 2007.

279 "I was spirited into a back office": Balazs, *Chateau Marmont Hollywood Handbook,* 227.

279 "I did not do that smart thing": Steve Proffitt, "John Gregory Dunne and Dominick Dunne: Experiencing L.A. Through the Eyes of the Writer," *Los Angeles Times,* Jan. 30, 1994.

280 "Judith Krantz in pants": Bob Pool, "The O. J. Simpson Trial: Back-Seat Treatment Rankles Many Journalists," *Los Angeles Times,* Jan. 25, 1995.

280 "the toast of the town": Balazs, *Chateau Marmont Hollywood Handbook,* 228.

280 "I was walking out of my room": Irene Lacher, "Inn Hollywood," *Los Angeles Times,* Dec. 29, 1996.

281 "Dominick was very appalled": Wasson, "Hotel California."

281 "Something terribly embarrassing": Balazs, *Chateau Marmont Hollywood Handbook,* 229.

283 "If you made a reservation": Homes, *Los Angeles,* 144.

283 "agents were the worst": Ibid., 143.

283 "It's only sixty-three rooms": Ibid., 145.

283 "Oh, we don't tell anybody": Navasky, "It's Shabby-Genteel but the Stars Love It."

283 "As a child," he recalled: Ali Trachta, "Phil Pavel: The Ringmaster of the Chateau Marmont," *L.A. Weekly,* May 18, 2012.

284 "I work hard to keep up": Maer Roshan, "You: 'Do You Know Who I Am?' Him: 'I Do, and I Don't Care': Hosts to the A-List Spill All," *Hollywood Reporter,* Feb. 20, 2015.

284 "Working here was a blast": Ari Karpel, "On His Terms, Unbranded," *New York Times,* July 4, 2010.

284 "Let's just say": Wasson, "Hotel California."

284 "People do things here": Brown, "Chateau Marmont Is Ready for Its Close-Up."

285 "was like winning": Trachta, "Phil Pavel."

285 "three different psychics": Wasson, "Hotel California."

285 "The first manager": Homes, *Los Angeles,* 150.

286 "The old Marlboro Man": Steve Garbarino, "Party Pooper?," *New York Times,* May 30, 1999.

287 "When I bought the Chateau": Michael Kaplan, "Showdown on Sunset," *Los Angeles,* March 1998.

288 "the night even movie stars": Heidi Siegmund Cuda, "CLUBS: She'll See You in Her Dreams," *Los Angeles Times,* March 29, 2001.

289 "I would be embarrassed": Kaplan, "Showdown on Sunset."

289 "this organic chaos": Dave Gardetta, "The Strip," *Los Angeles Times Magazine,* Dec. 15, 1996.

290 "I don't want to have people": Rodney Tyler, "Hotel D'Amour," *Sunday Mirror Magazine*, Feb. 12, 1989.

290 "one of the little rooms": S. Irene Virbila, "Hideaway up on a Hill," *Los Angeles Times*, July 3, 2003.

290 "at a rather grand country house": S. Irene Virbila, "Romancing the Castle on the Hill," *Los Angeles Times*, Feb. 4, 2004.

292 "Apparently there was somebody": John Colapinto, "Girl with a Career on Fire," *Elle*, June 2004.

292 "Did I ever have sex": Mike Sager, "Benny the Troublemaker," *Esquire*, April 2005.

293 "I went home alone": William Keck, "Scarlett Johansson: Big Dreams but No Puffed-Up Ego," *USA Today*, Dec. 31, 2004.

295 "I used to stay for months": Luke Leitch, "Hedi Slimane's 'Secret Society,'" www.businessoffashion.com, Aug. 3, 2017.

295 "I was meeting with my DP": Van Sant, author interview.

296 "I stay on campus at the Chateau a lot": Jeff Miller, "Anthony Bourdain's L.A.: A Q-&-A with the Legend," *Thrillist Los Angeles*, October 5, 2016.

297 "There was this very recalcitrant": Wasson, "Hotel California."

298 "I have this fascination": Newton, *Autobiography*, 270.

299 "His photographs had more": Mimi Avins, "Helmut Newton, 83: Provocative Master of Fashion Photography," *Los Angeles Times*, Jan. 24, 2004.

299 "Helmut would say": Ibid.

299 "One afternoon," he recalled: Everett, "Unmasked."

300 "a gigolo and a gigolette": Avins, "Helmut Newton, 83."

300 "It was very sad": Sarah Mower, "The 'King of Kink' Made Naughty Fashionable," *New York Times*, Sept. 21, 2003.

301 "It was like having": Ibid.

301 "I'm a frustrated paparazzi": Elizabeth Venant, "Checking Out Odd Couple of Photography," *Los Angeles Times*, Jan. 4, 1987.

302 "He was used to much darker": Judy Graeme, "Helmut Newton and Los Angeles," www.laobserved.com, July 1, 2013.

302 "taught everyone how to live": Avins, "Helmut Newton, 83."

302 "Every year [they] would come": Wasson, "Hotel California."

302 "I don't want to own anything": Venant, "Checking Out Odd Couple of Photography."

303 "I have the feeling": Wagner, author interview.

303 "He was coming home": Wasson, "Hotel California."

304 "It's another fancy L.A. hotel": Jane Gayduk, "A Rare Interview with Eve Babitz, the Long Sober, Cool Again Author," www.interviewmagazine.com, April 6, 2018.

306 "I was living in Paris": Karina Longworth, "Sofia Coppola's Journey to 'Somewhere,'" *L.A. City Pages,* Dec. 29, 2010.

306 "That's where that kind of guy": Mark Olsen, "Sofia Coppola Takes a Floor at the Chateau Marmont," *Los Angeles Times,* Oct. 31, 2010.

307 "Me and my friends": Sheryl Garratt, "L.A. Confidential," *Telegraph* (London), Dec. 6, 2010.

307 "There was a year I did nothing": Longworth, "Sofia Coppola's Journey to 'Somewhere.'"

308 "The Chateau doesn't allow": *Somewhere* press notes.

308 "People ask all the time": Olsen, "Sofia Coppola Takes a Floor at the Chateau Marmont."

309 "The goal," she explained: *Somewhere* press notes.

309 "It's amazingly quiet": Ibid.

310 "I had some money": Mark Rozzo, "Somewhere Man," *New York Times,* Sept. 12, 2010.

310 "It was kind of a trip": *Somewhere* press notes.

311 "I was able to give some gossip": Olsen, "Sofia Coppola Takes a Floor at the Chateau Marmont."

311 "I got my own Johnny Marco": *Somewhere* press notes.

311 "The vibe of Sofia's movie": Longworth, "Sofia Coppola's Journey to 'Somewhere.'"

314 "I regret to inform you": "Lindsay Lohan BANNED from Sunset Strip Hotel," www.tmz.com, Aug. 29, 2012.

314 "discourteous, irresponsible, and unprofessional": "Lindsay Lohan Blasted for 'Heavy Partying,'" *People,* July 28, 2006.

315 "Chateau Marmont places guest privacy": "LA Hotel 'Horrified' over LiLo's Leaked $46K Bill," *New York Post,* Aug. 30, 2012.

315 "We are not commenting": Don Dicker, "Lindsay Lohan Banned from Chateau Marmont Hotel After $46,316 Unpaid Bill," www.thehuffington post.com, Aug. 29, 2012.

316 "We've brought criminal charges": Wasson, "Hotel California."

317 "The Chateau Marmont has built": Lauren Dugan, "Former 'Apprentice' Contestant Kicked Out of Chateau Marmont for Tweeting," *Adweek,* April 21, 2011.

317 "Our hotel's success": A. J. Daulerio, "How to Get Kicked Out of Chateau Marmont Without Drugs: A Liveblog," www.defamer.com, June 28, 2013.

317 "André tends to know": Lacher, "Inn Hollywood."

319 "slipped a hand": Laura M. Holson, "André Balazs, Celebrity Hotelier, Is Accused of Groping," *New York Times,* Nov. 9, 2017.

319 "I witnessed behavior": Ibid.

319   "the account of André Balazs's outrageous": Ibid.

319   "he grabbed her arm": Ibid.

319   "felt a presence": Ibid.

320   "He needs that hotel": Edwardes, "Hotelier André Balazs' Deliciously Naughty Life."

321   "If you wanted to work": Jacob Bernstein, Matthew Schneier, and Vanessa Friedman, "'I Felt Helpless': Male Models Accuse Photographers of Sexual Exploitation," *New York Times*, Jan. 14, 2018.

BIBLIOGRAPHY

THE PEOPLE

Anger, Kenneth. *Hollywood Babylon*. New York: Dell, 1975.

———. *Hollywood Babylon II*. New York: E. P. Dutton, 1984.

Benjamin, Peter. *Super Freak: The Life of Rick James*. Chicago: Chicago Review Press, 2017.

Bernstein, Samuel. *Mr. Confidential: The Man, His Magazine, and the Movieland Massacre That Changed Hollywood Forever*. New York: Walford Press, 2006.

Biskind, Peter. *Easy Riders, Raging Bulls: How the Sex-Drugs-and-Rock 'n' Roll Generation Saved Hollywood*. New York: Simon & Schuster, 1998.

Bosworth, Patricia. *Montgomery Clift: A Biography*. New York: Harcourt Brace Jovanovich, 1978.

Bowers, Scotty. *Full Service: My Adventures in Hollywood and the Secret Sex Lives of the Stars*. With Lionel Friedberg. New York: Grove Press, 2012.

Bowman, Manoah. *Natalie Wood: Reflections on a Legendary Life*. Philadelphia: Running Press, 2016.

Bream, Jon. *Whole Lotta Led Zeppelin: The Illustrated History of the Heaviest Band of All Time*. 2nd ed. New York: Voyageur Press, 2015.

Brillstein, Bernie. *Where Did I Go Right? (You're No One in Hollywood Unless Someone Wants You Dead)*. With David Rensin. New York: Little, Brown, 1999.

Bugliosi, Vincent, and Curt Gentry. *Helter Skelter: The True Story of the Manson Murders*. New York: W. W. Norton, 1974.

Capua, Michelangelo. *Montgomery Clift: A Biography*. Jefferson, N.C.: McFarland, 2002.

Cohen, Mickey. *In My Own Words*. With John Peer Nugent. Englewood Cliffs, N.J.: Prentice-Hall, 1975.

Crowe, Cameron. *Conversations with Wilder*. New York: Alfred A. Knopf, 2001.

Dalton, David. *James Dean: The Mutant King*. Chicago: A Cappella, 2001.

Davis, Stephen. *Hammer of the Gods: The Led Zeppelin Saga.* New York: William Morrow, 1985.

Densmore, John. *Riders on the Storm: My Life with Jim Morrison and the Doors.* New York: Delta, 1991.

Dougan, Andy. *Untouchable: A Biography of Robert De Niro.* New York: Thunder's Mouth Press, 1996.

Dunne, Dominick. *The Way We Lived Then: Recollections of a Well-Known Name Dropper.* New York: Crown, 1999.

Eisenschitz, Bernard. *Nicholas Ray: An American Journey.* London: Faber and Faber, 1996.

Feldman, Edward S. *Tell Me How You Love the Picture: A Hollywood Life.* With Tom Barton. New York: St. Martin's Press, 2005.

Folsom, Tom. *Hopper: A Journey into the American Dream.* New York: It Books, 2013.

Frascella, Lawrence, and Al Weisel. *Live Fast, Die Young: The Wild Ride of Making "Rebel Without a Cause."* New York: Touchstone, 2005.

Gaye, Frankie. *Marvin Gaye, My Brother.* With Fred E. Basten. San Francisco: Backbeat Books, 2003.

Gilmore, John. *Laid Bare: A Memoir of Wrecked Lives and the Hollywood Death Trip.* Los Angeles: Amok, 1997.

Golden, Eve. *Platinum Girl: The Life and Legends of Jean Harlow.* New York: Abbeville Press, 1991.

Gottlieb, Robert, ed. *Reading Jazz: A Gathering of Autobiography, Reportage, and Criticism from 1919 to Now.* New York: Vintage Books, 1999.

Holley, Val. *Mike Connelly and the Manly Art of Hollywood Gossip.* Jefferson, N.C.: McFarland, 2003.

Hopkins, Jerry. *The Lizard King: The Essential Jim Morrison.* London: Plexus, 2010.

Hopkins, Jerry, and Danny Sugerman. *No One Here Gets Out Alive.* New York: Grand Central, 1980.

Horton, Robert, ed. *Billy Wilder Interviews.* Jackson: University of Mississippi Press, 2001.

Hunter, Tab. *Tab Hunter Confidential: The Making of a Movie Star.* With Eddie Muller. New York: Algonquin Books, 2005.

Idol, Billy. *Dancing with Myself.* New York: Touchstone, 2014.

Jacobs, Diane. *Christmas in July: The Life and Art of Preston Sturges.* Berkeley: University of California Press, 1992.

James, Rick. *Glow: The Autobiography of Rick James.* With David Ritz. New York: Atria, 2015.

Jeffers, H. Paul. *Sal Mineo: His Life, Murder, and Mystery.* New York: Carroll & Graf, 2000.

Kaplan, Fred. *Gore Vidal: A Biography.* New York: Doubleday, 1999.

Lally, Kevin. *Wilder Times: The Life of Billy Wilder.* New York: Henry Holt, 1996.

Lambert, Gavin. *Natalie Wood: A Life.* New York: Alfred A. Knopf, 2004.

———. *Nazimova: A Biography.* New York: Alfred A. Knopf, 1997.

Levy, Shawn. *De Niro: A Life.* New York: Crown-Archetype, 2014.

———. *King of Comedy: The Life and Art of Jerry Lewis.* New York: St. Martin's, 1996.

———. *Paul Newman: A Life.* New York: Harmony, 2009.

Matthew, Christopher. *A Different World: Stories of Great Hotels.* New York: Paddington Press, 1976.

McDonough, Jimmy. *Shakey: Neil Young's Biography.* New York: Jonathan Cape, 2002.

McGilligan, Patrick. *Nicholas Ray: The Glorious Failure of an American Director.* New York: HarperCollins, 2011.

Medina Cotten, Patricia. *Laid Back in Hollywood: Remembering.* Los Angeles: Belle, 1998.

Michaud, Michael Gregg. *Sal Mineo: A Biography.* New York: Crown Archetype, 2010.

Miller, Gabriel, ed. *Martin Ritt: Interviews.* Jackson: University of Mississippi Press, 2002.

Newton, Helmut. *Autobiography.* New York: Doubleday, 2003.

Otash, Fred. *Investigation Hollywood!* Chicago: Henry Regnery, 1976.

Parini, Jay. *Empire of Self: A Life of Gore Vidal.* New York: Doubleday, 2015.

Peabody, Richard, and Lucinda Ebersole, eds. *Conversations with Gore Vidal.* Jackson: University of Mississippi Press, 2005.

Petersen, Anne Helen. *Scandals of Classic Hollywood: Sex, Deviance, and Drama from the Golden Age of American Cinema.* New York: Plume, 2014.

Poitier, Sidney. *This Life.* New York: Alfred A. Knopf, 1980.

Polanski, Roman. *Roman.* New York: Ballantine, 1985.

Randall, Stephen, and the Editors of *Playboy* Magazine. *The "Playboy" Interviews: The Directors.* Milwaukie, Ore.: M Press, 2006.

Ray, Nicholas. *I Was Interrupted: Nicholas Ray on Making Movies.* Edited by Susan Ray. Berkeley: University of California Press, 1993.

Rees, Paul. *Robert Plant: A Life.* New York: It Books, 2013.

Rooney, Darrell, and Mark A. Vieira. *Harlow in Hollywood: The Blonde Bombshell in the Glamour Capital, 1928–1937.* Santa Monica, Calif.: Angel City Press, 2011.

Sanders, Coyne Steven, and Tom Gilbert. *Desilu: The Story of Lucille Ball and Desi Arnaz.* New York: It Books, 2001.

Sandford, Christopher. *Polanski.* London: Palgrave Macmillan, 2008.

Scott, Henry E. *Shocking True Story: The Rise and Fall of "Confidential," "America's Most Scandalous Scandal Magazine."* New York: Pantheon Books, 2010.

Shales, Tom, and James Andrew Miller. *Live from New York: An Uncensored History of "Saturday Night Live."* New York: Little, Brown, 2002.

Sikov, Ed. *On Sunset Boulevard: The Life and Times of Billy Wilder.* New York: Hyperion, 1998.

Simon, Carly. *Boys in the Trees: A Memoir.* New York: Flatiron Books, 2015.

Skolsky, Sidney. *Don't Get Me Wrong—I Love Hollywood.* New York: G. P. Putnam's Sons, 1975.

Sperber, A. M., and Eric Lax. *Bogart.* New York: William Morrow, 1997.

Stenn, David. *Bombshell: The Life and Death of Jean Harlow.* New York: Doubleday, 1993.

Stine, Whitney. *Mother Goddamn: The Story of the Career of Bette Davis.* With Bette Davis. New York: Berkley Medallion, 1974.

Sturges, Preston. *Preston Sturges by Preston Sturges: His Life in His Words.* New York: Touchstone, 1990.

Szwed, John. *So What: The Life of Miles Davis.* New York: Simon & Schuster, 2002.

Thomas, Bob. *King Cohn: The Life and Times of Harry Cohn.* New York: Bantam Books, 1968.

Tosches, Nick. *Dino: Living High in the Dirty Business of Dreams.* New York: Doubleday, 1992.

Vidal, Gore. *Palimpsest: A Memoir.* New York: Random House, 1995.

———. *Snapshots in History's Glare.* New York: Abrams, 2009.

Weaver, John D., ed. *Glad Tidings: A Friendship in Letters: The Correspondence of John Cheever and John D. Weaver, 1945–1982.* New York: HarperCollins, 1993.

Wilkerson, W. R., III. *The Man Who Invented Las Vegas.* [Beverly Hills, Calif.]: Ciro's Books, 2000.

Winecoff, Charles. *Split Image: The Life of Anthony Perkins.* New York: Dutton, 1996.

Winkler, Peter L. *Dennis Hopper: The Wild Ride of a Hollywood Rebel.* Fort Lee, N.J.: Barricade, 2011.

Winters, Shelley. *Shelley II: The Middle of My Century.* New York: Simon & Schuster, 1989.

Woodward, Bob. *Wired: The Short Life and Fast Times of John Belushi.* New York: Simon & Schuster, 1984.

Zolotow, Maurice. *Billy Wilder in Hollywood.* New York: Limelight, 1996.

THE PLACE

Balazs, André, ed. *Chateau Marmont Hollywood Handbook.* New York: Universe, 1996.

Blumenthal, John. *Hollywood High: The History of America's Most Famous Public School.* New York: Ballantine, 1988.

Dawes, Amy. *Sunset Boulevard: Cruising the Heart of Los Angeles.* Los Angeles: Los Angeles Times Books, 2002.

Friedrich, Otto. *City of Nets: A Portrait of Hollywood in the 1940's.* New York: Harper & Row, 1986.

Gold, Herbert. *Bohemia: Where Art, Angst, Love, and Strong Coffee Meet.* New York: Simon & Schuster, 1993.

Gordon, William A. *The Ultimate Hollywood Tour Book.* El Toro, Calif.: North Ridge Books, 1998.

Graham, Sheila. *The Garden of Allah.* New York: Crown, 1970.

Heiman, Jim. *Hooray for Hollywood: A Postcard Tour of Hollywood's Golden Era.* San Francisco: Chronicle, 1983.

———. *Out with the Stars: Hollywood Nightlife in the Golden Era.* New York: Abbeville Press, 1985.

———. *Sins of the City: The Real Los Angeles Noir.* San Francisco: Chronicle, 1999.

Heiman, Jim, and Rip Georges. *California Crazy: Roadside Vernacular Architecture.* San Francisco: Chronicle, 1980.

Heiman, Jim, and Kevin Starr. *Los Angeles: Portrait of a City.* Los Angeles: Taschen America, 2009.

Homes, A. M. *Los Angeles: People, Places, and the Castle on the Hill.* Washington, D.C.: National Geographic, 2002.

Kennelley, Joe, and Roy Hankey. *Sunset Boulevard: America's Dream Street.* Burbank, Calif.: Darwin, 1981.

Kleinfeld, Sonny. *The Hotel: A Week in the Life of the Plaza.* New York: Simon & Schuster, 1989.

Koestenbaum, Wayne. *Hotel Theory.* Brooklyn: Soft Skull Press, 2007.

Kubernik, Harvey. *Canyon of Dreams: The Magic and the Music of Laurel Canyon.* Edited by Scott Calamar. New York: Sterling, 2009.

Priore, Dominic. *Riot on Sunset Strip: Rock 'n' Roll's Last Stand in Hollywood.* Rev. ed. London: Jawbone, 2015.

Rosten, Leo. *Hollywood: The Movie Colony, the Movie Makers.* New York: Harcourt, Brace, 1941.

Sandoval-Strausz, A. K. *Hotel: An American History.* New Haven, Conn.: Yale University Press, 2007.

Sarlot, Raymond, and Fred E. Basten. *Life at the Marmont: The Inside Story of Hollywood's Legendary Hotel of the Stars—Chateau Marmont.* New York: Roundtable, 1987.

Tereba, Tere. *Mickey Cohen: The Life and Crimes of L.A.'s Notorious Mobster.* Toronto: ECW Press, 2012.

Tippins, Sherill. *Inside the Dream Palace: The Life and Times of New York's Legendary Chelsea Hotel.* New York: Mariner Books, 2014.

Unterberger, Richie. *Eight Miles High: Folk-Rock's Flight from Haight-Ashbury to Woodstock.* San Francisco: Backbeat Books, 2003.

Walker, Michael. *Laurel Canyon: The Inside Story of Rock-and-Roll's Legendary Neighborhood.* New York: Faber and Faber, 2006.

Walsh, Joanna. *Hotel.* New York: Bloomsbury Academic, 2015.

INSTRUCTIVE DIVERSIONS

Babitz, Eve. *Black Swans.* New York: Alfred A. Knopf, 1993.

————. *Eve's Hollywood.* New York: New York Review Books, 2015.

————. *Slow Days, Fast Company: The World, the Flesh, and L.A.* New York: New York Review Books, 2016.

Bachardy, Don. *Stars in My Eyes.* Madison: University of Wisconsin Press, 2000.

Carpenter, Don. *The Class of '49.* San Francisco: North Point Press, 1985.

Cheever, John. *The Stories of John Cheever.* New York: Ballantine Books, 1978.

Connelly, Michael. *The Drop.* New York: Little, Brown, 2011.

Dunne, Dominick. *Another City, Not My Own: A Novel in the Form of a Memoir.* New York: Crown, 1997.

Franco, James. *Directing Herbert White: Poems.* Minneapolis: Graywolf Press, 2014.

Janigian, Aris. *Waiting for Lipchitz at Chateau Marmont.* Los Angeles: Rare Bird Books, 2016.

Moody, Rick. *Hotels of North America.* New York: Little, Brown, 2015.

Stone, Robert. *Children of Light.* New York: Alfred A. Knopf, 1986.

Vaughan, Brian K., Marcos Martín, and Muntsa Vicente. *The Private Eye.* Berkeley, Calif.: Image Comics, 2015.

Weisberger, Lauren. *Last Night at Chateau Marmont.* New York: Atria Books, 2010.

FILMOGRAPHY

Barfly—Barbet Schroeder, 1987*

Blume in Love—Paul Mazursky, 1973

Dangerous Game—Abel Ferrara, 1993

Danny Collins—Dan Fogelman, 2015*

The Doors—Oliver Stone, 1991**

Four Rooms—Allison Anders, Alexandre Rockwell, Robert Rodriguez, Quentin Tarantino, 1995*

Hangmen Also Die!—Fritz Lang, 1943

Hitler's Madman—Douglas Sirk, 1943

Maps to the Stars—David Cronenberg, 2014**

The Mayor of Sunset Strip—George Hickenlooper, 2003***
Mondo Mod—Peter Perry Jr., 1967*
Myra Breckinridge—Michael Sarne, 1970
The Night Walker—William Castle, 1964
Rebel Without a Cause—Nicholas Ray, 1955***
Riot on Sunset Strip—Arthur Dreifuss, 1967*
Somewhere—Sofia Coppola, 2010
The Strip—László Kardos, 1951*
Summer Storm—Douglas Sirk, 1944
Wired—Larry Peerce, 1989

* = just a glimpse
** = one scene only
*** = background research

INDEX

Page numbers in *italics* refer to illustrations.

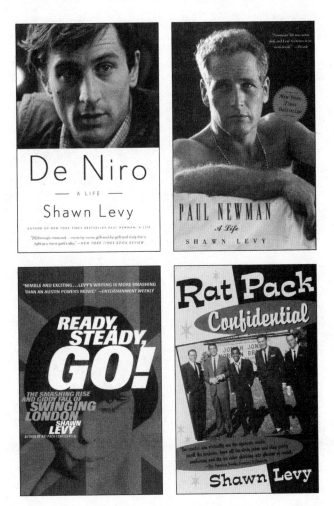

MY LIFE WITH CLEOPATRA
The Making of a Hollywood Classic
by Walter Wanger and Joe Hyams

Cleopatra faced countless problems during its filming and production: passionate casting disputes, broken contracts, a costly relocation from London to Rome, an emergency tracheotomy for its star, Elizabeth Taylor, scandal-ridden gossip surrounding relationships on set, and a budget of $2 million that ballooned to final costs of $44 million. Legendary producer Walter Wanger recalls the drama that occurred both on and off the set, including the incredible obstacles he had to overcome and the exhilaration of producing a cinematic triumph. A revealing story about Elizabeth Taylor and Richard Burton's tempestuous romance and an insightful filmmaker's journal, *My Life with Cleopatra* shares the true story of the relationship and film that enthralled the world.

Film/Memoir

TOUGH WITHOUT A GUN
The Life and Extraordinary Afterlife of Humphrey Bogart
by Stefan Kanfer

In this comprehensive biography of one of the great movie icons of our time, Stefan Kanfer illuminates the life and career of Humphrey Bogart. Along the way, Kanfer gives us a wide-reaching cultural appraisal of the movies many of us know and love as masterpieces of American cinema. He evaluates each of the films with an unfailing critical eye, weaving in lively accounts of behind-the-scenes fun and friendships, including, of course, the great love story of Bogart and Lauren Bacall. What emerges in these pages is a portrait of a great Hollywood life.

Biography/Film

KAZAN ON DIRECTING
by Elia Kazan

Elia Kazan was the twentieth century's most celebrated director of both stage and screen, and this monumental, revelatory book shows us the master at work. Kazan's list of Broadway and Hollywood successes—*A Streetcar Named Desire*, *Death of a Salesman*, *On the Waterfront*, to name a few—is a testament to his profound impact on the art of directing. This remarkable book, drawn from his notebooks, letters, interviews, and autobiography, reveals Kazan's method: how he uncovered the "spine," or core, of each script; how he analyzed each piece in terms of his own experience; and how he determined the specifics of his production. In the final section, "The Pleasures of Directing"—written during Kazan's final years—he becomes a wise old pro offering advice and insight for budding artists, writers, actors, and directors.

Performing Arts/Directing

JOSEPH P. KENNEDY PRESENTS
His Hollywood Years
by Cari Beauchamp

Joseph P. Kennedy's reputation as a savvy businessman, diplomat, and sly political patriarch is well-documented. But his years as a Hollywood mogul have never been fully explored until now. In *Joseph P. Kennedy Presents*, Cari Beauchamp brilliantly explores this unknown chapter in Kennedy's biography. Between 1926 and 1930, Kennedy positioned himself as a major Hollywood player. In two short years, he was running three studios simultaneously and then, in a bold move, he merged his studios with David Sarnoff to form the legendary RKO Pictures. Beauchamp also tells the story of Kennedy's affair with Gloria Swanson; his masterful mergers that created the blueprint for contemporary Hollywood; and the ventures that made the fortune that became the foundation of his empire.

Biography

WHICH LIE DID I TELL?
More Adventures in the Screen Trade
by William Goldman

If you want to know why a no-name like Kathy Bates was cast in *Misery*, it's in here. Or why Linda Hunt's brilliant work in *Maverick* didn't make the final cut, William Goldman gives you the straight truth. On why Clint Eastwood loves working with Gene Hackman and how MTV has changed movies for the worse, William Goldman, one of the most successful screenwriters in Hollywood, tells all he knows. Devastatingly eye-opening and endlessly entertaining, *Which Lie Did I Tell?* is indispensable reading for anyone even slightly intrigued by the process of how a movie gets made.

Film

MONSTER
Living Off the Big Screen
by John Gregory Dunne

In Hollywood, screenwriters are a curse to be borne, and beating up on them is an industry blood sport. But in this ferociously funny and accurate account of life on the Hollywood food chain, it's a screenwriter who gets the last murderous laugh. That may be because the writer is John Gregory Dunne, who has written screenplays, along with novels and nonfiction, for thirty years. In 1988, Dunne and his wife, Joan Didion, were asked to write a screenplay about the dark and complicated life of the late TV anchorwoman Jessica Savitch. Eight years and twenty-seven drafts later, this script was made into the fairy tale "Up Close and Personal," starring Robert Redford and Michelle Pfeiffer. Detailing the meetings, rewrites, fights, firings, and distractions attendant to the making of a single picture, *Monster* illuminates the process with sagacity and raucous wit.

Film/Biography

MAKING MOVIES
by Sidney Lumet

Why does a director choose a particular script? What must they do in order to keep actors fresh and truthful through take after take of a single scene? What does it take to keep the studio honchos happy? From the first rehearsal to the final screening, *Making Movies* is a master's take, delivered with clarity, candor, and a wealth of anecdote. For in this book, Sidney Lumet, one of our most consistently acclaimed directors, gives us both a professional memoir and a definitive guide to the art, craft, and business of the motion picture. Drawing on forty years of experience on movies that range from *Long Day's Journey into Night* to *Network* and *The Verdict*—and with such stars as Katharine Hepburn, Paul Newman, Marlon Brando, and Al Pacino—Lumet explains how painstaking labor and inspired split-second decisions can result in two hours of screen magic.

Film

HAYWIRE
by Brooke Hayward

Brooke Hayward was born into the most enviable of circumstances. The daughter of a famous actress and a successful Hollywood agent, she was beautiful, wealthy, and living at the very center of the most privileged life America had to offer. Yet at twenty-three her family was ripped apart. Who could have imagined that this magical life could shatter so conclusively, so destructively? Brooke Hayward tells the riveting story of how her family went haywire.

Memoir